RESURRECTING RETAIL

Resurrecting

Retail

The Future of Business in a Post-Pandemic World

Doug Stephens

Foreword by Imran Amed, Founder
and CEO, The Business of Fashion

Figure 1
Vancouver / Berkeley

21 22 23 24 25   5 4 3 2 1

Cataloguing data is available from Library and Archives Canada
ISBN 978-1-77327-143-9 (hbk.)
ISBN 978-1-77327-144-6 (ebook)
ISBN 978-1-77327-145-3 (pdf)
ISBN 978-1-77327-146-0 (audio)

Jacket design by Jessica Sullivan and Ingrid Paulson
Interior design by Ingrid Paulson
Author photograph by David Leyes

Editing by Tyee Bridge
Copy editing by Marnie Lamb
Proofreading by Renate Preuss
Indexing by Stephen Ullstrom

Front cover image by Inna Bigun/shutterstock.com

Efforts have been made to determine copyright holders and to obtain
permission for the use of copyrighted material. The publisher apologizes for
any errors or omissions and would be grateful if notified for future printings.

Printed and bound in Canada by Friesens
Distributed internationally by Publishers Group West

Figure 1 Publishing Inc.
Vancouver BC Canada
www.figure1publishing.com

For all those who rose
to confront the threat,
to seize the moment,
to embrace the future.

TABLE OF
CONTENTS

FOREWORD

Growing up in the southern suburbs of Calgary, Canada, in the 1980s, I spent a lot of time at Southcentre Mall. When I wanted to hang out with my friends, we went to the mall. When my family wanted to have a quick bite and catch a movie, we went to the mall. And of course, when I wanted to go shopping, it was the best place to go, especially during August and December when anchor tenants Eaton's and The Bay would conduct competing back-to-school and Boxing Day sales that were thronged with people.

My regular destinations were HMV, where I could go listen to the latest records and check out the Billboard charts to see how my favorite artists were doing on the Hot 100 chart, even if I couldn't afford to buy the music; the Gap, where I worked summers on the shop floor, selling jeans and t-shirts; and the movie theatre, where Tuesday nights were always packed because tickets were less than five bucks. Looking back now, I realize that going to the mall wasn't just about shopping. It was about everything. It was the center of our community, offering entertainment, inspiration, and escape all in one place.

Long before COVID-19 rocked the world around us and altered the lives we live every day, the slow, inexorable decline of the North American shopping mall had already begun. First came the big box stores, which made shopping feel like going to a formulaic emporium with an endless choice of generic products. Then came Amazon and online retailers, which made shopping from home efficient and convenient without all the frustration and hassle of shopping in-store.

Now, the pandemic has turbocharged the shift to digital, as years of online sales growth happened in a matter of months, resulting in the permanent closure of thousands of underperforming retail stores around the world.

Indeed, there were times during 2020 when it seemed like the final death knell for physical stores had sounded. But as Doug Stephens vividly illustrates in his new book, *Resurrecting Retail*, the global pandemic and ensuing economic crisis is not simply accelerating a long-term trend, it is catalyzing a once-in-a-generation transformation in human behavior that will change everything: how we live, how we work, how we learn—and of course, how and why we shop.

In his inimitably frank and straightforward way, Doug outlines ten key archetypes for retail executives and marketers to consider as they grapple with how to reimagine retail for a post-pandemic world. If Doug's new reality comes true, the last-standing shopping centers will become more like community hubs and town squares—complete with residential developments, fitness studios, libraries, restaurants, and concept stores—just like Southcentre Mall was for me. But the shopping center of the future will also embrace new technologies and mindsets about retail and shopping that will help build brand loyalty and awareness, no matter where the customer chooses to conduct the final transaction. It's no longer about sales per square foot and cost per click, but rather about experiences per square foot and sales per click.

Nobody knows for sure what the world will be like when this is all over, but one thing's for sure: nothing will ever be the same, underscoring that old adage that with every crisis comes an opportunity. *Resurrecting Retail* will help you figure out how to seize it.

Imran Amed
Founder and CEO of The Business of Fashion
London, November 2020

HANDSHAKES AND HUGS

By the pricking of my thumbs,
something wicked this way comes.
William Shakespeare

F rom above, it's difficult at first to comprehend the sheer scale of what you're looking at. You see only an ocean of white and gray curtains, aluminum framing, and acoustic tile stretched out across the cavernous space. Together, the materials form row upon row of cubicles, spanning almost 2 million square feet. Below, there is a flurry of activity as supplies, furniture, and equipment are hurriedly shuttled to their final destinations on forklifts and pallet trucks.

"We worked 24 hours a day, seven days a week with our vertical team to spec out the sites [and] award contracts, and then began work immediately after the contracts were awarded," said Michael Embrich, a spokesperson for the U.S. Army Corps of Engineers, in an article for the U.S. Department of Defense. In the spring of 2020, the Corps of Engineers helped New York City assemble this facility to provide beds for over two thousand people affected by the COVID-19 virus.[1] It immediately became one of the largest medical facilities in America, substantially greater in capacity than any other neighboring hospital. According to health experts, the facility was ideal given the ready access to electricity and water, waste management, and adequate ventilation. While it may not have been luxurious relative to some modern medical facilities, the patients brought here would likely welcome their new surroundings.

What was perhaps most impressive is the speed with which the facility was completed. "It was much quicker than we usually design, engineer and construct a project," Embrich said.[2] In fact, the entire facility was outfitted in roughly two weeks—a Herculean task by any measure.

It's challenging to conceive of a project of this scale being completed so quickly and equally hard to believe that less than three months earlier, the makeshift field hospital was a convention center, home to one of retail's largest annual global pilgrimages: the National Retail Federation's Big Show, held each January in New York City. I had been there in January, along with colleagues from all corners of the globe—thirty-seven thousand of us gathered in its halls, atriums, and auditoriums to discuss the fate and future of the retail industry.

Amidst the countless collegial handshakes and hugs, shoulder-to-shoulder lineups, and close conversations held in noisy session halls, few of us could have imagined that only weeks later such basic human behaviors would be widely discouraged, even forbidden. Even fewer could have appreciated the degree to which 2020 would impact the retail industry and nearly every other livelihood on the planet, marking a milestone unlike any other in our personal or professional lives.

It would be hard to find a better symbol of the global transformation wrought by the pandemic. The massive Jacob K. Javits Convention Center—the teeming hub of retail industry optimism and anticipation only three months before—had now been transformed into a U.S. Army field hospital, ready to treat thousands of overflow patients in the worst global pandemic in more than one hundred years. None of the Big Show's attendees could have envisioned that the themes, concepts, and conversations being exchanged there would, in hindsight, seem so trivial relative to what was coming. Like reveling

Home to the National Retail Federation Conference, the Jacob Javits Center in New York City was converted to an Army Corps of Engineers field hospital as case counts in New York City spiked

passengers on the *Titanic*, we saw no omens or warnings that the global retail industry was about to collide with an obstacle so large and immovable that it would rip the industry from stem to stern.

RETAIL CIRCA 2019

Even as I write this, in the thick of the pandemic, 2019 seems a remarkably distant and, dare I say, nostalgic memory for the global retail industry. That's not because things in 2019 were great. They weren't. But rather, it's because things in 2020 became so horrible by comparison.

In fact, the primary industry storyline in 2019 was one of slowing global growth. Trade wars, tariffs, geopolitical tensions, brands struggling under mountains of debt, rumblings of an impending global recession—all of these took their toll on the industry, resulting in weakening business expectations and outlooks for the coming year. In turn, this softened global demand for durable goods and resulted in lower domestic outputs across almost all markets, including China.

In the United Kingdom, for example, 2019 marked the worst year on record for the nation's retail industry. A combination of anxiety surrounding Brexit and a continual drum beat of High Street closures both served to shake consumer confidence.

Even the U.S. economy, with what at the time was historically low unemployment, bargain basement borrowing rates, and a recent round of income tax cuts, could muster only a 0.3 percent year-on-year increase in retail sales in all of October, November, and December. "The Golden Quarter," as it's often hailed in retail, had lost its luster. Many brands clung to life, eking out just enough to get by but not nearly enough to rekindle relevance with shoppers. Ailing channels, such as department stores, struggled against what seemed an eternal battle to redefine their value in a world that had clearly moved on.

By October of 2019, according to a Credit Suisse report, U.S. domestic store closures numbered seventy-six hundred—the most ever recorded in the first nine months of a given year since the company began tracking closures twenty-five years earlier. The report called out particularly anemic performance in the U.S. apparel sector as being one of the primary underlying drags on the sector as a whole.[3] But suffice to say, U.S. retail, in general, wasn't breaking any records. Far from it.

One of the few bright lights in the economy, for those with the capital to benefit from it, was the stock markets, with every major index riding high. The S&P 500 gained 28 percent in twelve months. The Nasdaq Composite Index posted an even loftier 35 percent year-on-year lift, and the Dow Jones Industrial Average crossed the finish line 22 percent better than it did in 2018.

The disparity between the nosebleed-inducing gains in stocks and the stubborn stagnation in retail highlighted a growing and potentially fatal disconnect between Wall Street and Main Street.

Roughly 10 percent of the U.S. population, for example, owns over 80 percent of all stocks.[4] While those with the means to play the markets were doing just fine, the average shopper on the ground was feeling less optimistic.

Nonetheless, I was hopeful. While not without some obvious weak spots, the retail industry overall finally seemed to be making slow but meaningful progress on perennial issues like digital commerce, data science, and experiential retail design. The annual National Retail Federation tour of New York City's store scene included visits to new and progressive experiential concepts like Neighborhood Goods, a start-up out of Texas; Camp, a new-era toy store experience; and Showfields, a unique alchemy of gallery, retail, and event space. All of this was promising, and as someone who has felt for many years like one of only a handful of voices of change in the retail wilderness, I was hugely gratified to see the roots of the retail revolution finally taking hold. The industry seemed to be awakening.

I had also decided, by late 2019, to write a new book. The intention at the time was to focus on what I saw as a growing intersection between art and retail. In fact, by December 31, I was in the process of writing the introduction—oblivious to the fact that over seven thousand miles away, Chinese government officials had, more than two weeks prior, alerted the World Health Organization to several cases of an unusual pneumonia in Wuhan, a port city of roughly 11 million people in the central province of Hubei. We would learn sometime later from leaked Chinese government memos that the first indications of the virus may actually have surfaced in mid-November.[5]

Like most, I paid little attention to the news, assuming the virus was something that would be relatively well-managed and effectively contained by Chinese health officials. It wasn't their first rodeo, and I, like many, thought that if we all just used common sense and washed our hands frequently, we'd be back to normal in no time. After all, we in the West had, over the past two decades, grown increasingly accustomed to hearing about viral outbreaks in other parts of the world, but none of these occurrences had disrupted everyday life or commercial activity to any great extent. So there was some sense that we'd seen this movie before and we had little to be nervous about.

The markets, however, belied any such carefree sentiment. In fact, on that very same day, December 31, 2019, the Dow fell 183.12 points or 0.6 percent, to close at 28,462.14. The S&P slipped 18.73 points or 0.6 percent to close at 3,221.29 while the Nasdaq closed at 8,945.99, sliding 60.62 points or 0.7 percent. In hindsight, this seemingly inconsequential downtick in the markets would later be understood as the first and faintest of seismic indications of a gathering tsunami of human and economic disaster.

Not long after, we would learn that in the world of epidemiology, there are two kinds of viruses: viruses the scientific community knows of and novel viruses. In layperson's terms, a novel virus is one that has not been previously presented or studied. Thus, no known therapies, antibodies, or vaccines exist. It's a new and entirely unknown beast.

A few short months later, almost the entire global retail industry would enter a state of lockdown.

On March 3, 2020, amid the gathering chaos, I contacted my publisher to recommend a pivot away from my earlier book premise. Only one story was worth writing about in the retail industry: COVID-19.

THE TWO-HEADED MONSTER

Part of the challenge in assessing any crisis is that of calibrating the threat and its dimensions.

What makes a pandemic particularly difficult to quantify is that the danger it poses runs along two completely different axes. On one axis lies the health threat. Here, we can compare COVID-19 to previous pandemics such as Severe Acute Respiratory Syndrome (SARS), Middle East Respiratory Syndrome (MERS), Swine Flu (H1N1), Ebola, and of course the Spanish flu of 1918. To put it simply, from a health perspective, COVID-19 is the most widespread and deadliest health emergency since the 1918 pandemic claimed 50 million lives

Outbreak	Duration	Mortality	Treatments
Spanish flu	1918–19	50,000,000	None
SARS	2003	774	Vaccine
H1N1	2009–10	151,700–575,400	Vaccine
MERS	2012–present	881	None
Ebola	2014–16	11,323	None
COVID-19	2019–present	2 million plus	Therapies and multiple vaccines in progress

Comparing COVID-19 to Other Pandemics

worldwide. As I write this, over two million people have lost their lives due to COVID-19. By the time you're reading this, I suspect that the mortality number will be much greater, possibly multiples more.

The second axis of a pandemic pertains to the economic threat it represents. Here again, a historical means of comparison is available. If you're over the age of thirty, you may still bear some scarring from the financial crisis of 2008–9, a crisis that by all accounts was the worst

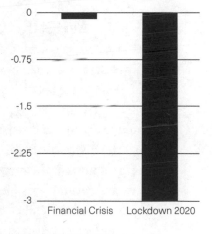

Impact of COVID-19 Lockdown on Global GDP

economic downturn many of us had ever experienced. The pandemic, however, almost immediately made that crisis look like a walk in the park.

In fact, the World Economic Forum estimates that the change in global GDP during the Great Lockdown of Q1 2020 was –3 percent or, in other words, thirty times greater than that experienced during the financial crisis of 2008–9. In the G20 states, which include the European Union, the United Kingdom, and the United States, the figure was somewhat worse at –3.4 percent.[6]

United Kingdom	-20.4
Euro Zone	-12.1
Canada	-12.0 *
United States	-9.5
Mexico	-17.3
China	+3.2
Japan	-7.8

*Estimate

Change in GDP by Country
Q2 2020

Few could have imagined this would prove rosy by comparison to what would follow in the second quarter.

And while the Chinese economy managed to remain above water, most economists agree that the true test for China lies ahead and will be linked inseparably to customer demand from the West—demand that may take years to fully return.

WHERE TO FROM HERE?

So how long does recovering economically from a global pandemic take? Little data is available without reaching back more than one hundred years to the Spanish flu outbreak of 1918.

Surprisingly, the Spanish flu (which by the way may not have originated in Spain)—a disease carrying a far higher IFR (Infection Fatality Rate) than COVID-19—did *not* ruin the global economy. That may seem totally out of sync with where we currently find ourselves, but there are several possible reasons. First, during most of 1918, governments like the United States' were still spending heavily on supporting the war effort and in doing so, bolstering factory production and their national economies. Second, when the war ended, consumers who had been scrimping and saving throughout it resumed normal levels of spending, furthering economic growth. But as *Bloomberg Opinion* columnist Noah Smith points out, several other important structural and societal considerations may account for the difference between the economic impact of the two pandemics.[7] First, a far greater percentage of workers in 1918 were engaged in agriculture and manufacturing, industries less prone to viral spread. Today, almost three-quarters of Americans, for example, work in service industries,[8] industries that frequently involve coming in close contact with others. Second, communication systems in 1918 were virtually non-existent beyond newsprint. Many governments at the time pressured newspaper publishers to refrain from stoking fears about the virus. Newspapers in many cases complied. Hence, fewer people even understood the danger and simply kept working and carrying on with their lives.

It's worth noting, however, that by 1920 a deep global recession did take hold, lasting until 1921. Neither economists nor historians have reached a clear consensus as to the cause of the delayed downturn. Some blame falling commodity prices due to the end of the war. Others maintain that because the Spanish flu primarily attacked young working-age people, most of whom were employed in manufacturing, it caused a slowdown of manufacturing output that wasn't realized until sometime after their deaths.

Once the recession lifted in the summer of 1921, however, continued and robust economic growth paved the way for the Roaring Twenties—a time of tremendous productivity, innovation, and growth (which, at the risk of being a total buzzkill, I would point out gave way to the Great Depression). But that's another story entirely.

Whether history will repeat itself is difficult to say. Not only are medical systems and knowledge significantly more advanced today, so too are our use and understanding of economic interventions and stimulus tools, factors that could assuage the severity of the economic fallout.

Let's hope so.

"UNTIL THERE'S A VACCINE"

Through the pandemic, it has seemed like almost any discussion about the retail industry during the early stages of the pandemic concluded with someone saying, "until there's a vaccine..." or the somewhat more emphatic, "Holy shit! Let's hope there's a vaccine!"

The good news is that there are now several vaccines being approved, distributed, and administered. The challenge comes in transporting, storing, and ultimately administering billions of vaccinations, some of which may require two doses to be effective. And while vaccination has begun in parts of the world, beginning with frontline healthcare workers and the most medically vulnerable, many more months may pass before the vaccine has reached enough of the general population to achieve a level of herd immunity.

Therefore, it's reasonable to assume that while we will surely return to something, the chances that "something" will be the pristine pre-pandemic business world as we knew it are remote at best. We may have to live with a lingering risk of flare-ups for some time.

So how should business leaders prepare for an uncertain and largely unprecedented future? Some maintain we can't predict the future at all. I wholeheartedly agree, nor should we try to predict the future. But that doesn't mean we can't prepare for it.

To that end, before we go any further, it's worth understanding the common pitfalls that business leaders fall victim to when tasked with building strategy for the future.

WHY WE GET THE FUTURE WRONG

SHORT-TERMISM

When we attempt to envision the future, the first reason we get it wrong is that we are often drawn into a state of short-termism, focusing on a myriad of seemingly critical questions that, in the end, are likely to have limited long-term relevance or business impact. Here are a few that have come up frequently about the pandemic:

➤ *Will customers remain germophobes when this is over?* It's quite likely. And yes, it will mean new standards and protocols for retailers, at least in the short term (but could be considered a best practice in the long term).

➤ *Will customers retreat to frugality in the face of depressed economies and job loss?* Yup. We usually do, at least for a while. And yes, it may mean that retailers adapt their value propositions somewhat.

➤ *Will certain emerging categories, like apparel, resale, and rental, suffer in the short term?* While apparel retail has generally suffered, resale apparel has, in fact, endured surprisingly well. Some attribute this to the fact that many resellers already offered well-established online shopping sites that consumers could turn to while stores were closed. Others pointed to the treasure-hunt nature of resale as a form of entertainment that shoppers could enjoy from their sofa. Still others suggest that it's economically driven by consumers concerned for their financial futures. Regardless of which theory you subscribe to, a fuller return to pre-pandemic apparel sales will depend heavily on shoppers feeling confident and comfortable shopping in physical stores and the degree to which the work-from-home trend continues.

➤ *Will we be inclined to visit stores less and buy more online?* It's already happening and seems certain to continue. According to a study by McKinsey & Company—in the United States, United Kingdom, France, Germany, Spain, Italy, India, Japan, South Korea, and China, across twenty different categories of goods—in almost every country and in every category, more spending is expected to shift online, post-pandemic. The only truly notable exceptions are found in China, where customers actually index negatively in ten of the twenty categories, suggesting that they anticipate using online options less when shopping in specific categories.[9] It's my belief that this is due, at least in part, to the fact that this isn't China's first viral crisis. During the SARS epidemic of 2003, China underwent a transformation that would see meteoric growth of online commerce. We, in other parts of the world, should expect a similar level of transformation now.

All these things are relatively foreseeable. I'm not trying to dismiss them, but I also can't help minimizing them, because in the long term these are not the things that will blindside most businesses. These short-term concerns, while relevant, are not what ultimately consume an industry. It's the really big change that happens while you're minding the little stuff that wipes out a business and even whole industries.

Therefore, wise business leaders will be casting their gaze much further ahead to identify the deeper and more endemic changes to the retail landscape and customer behavior. This book is aimed at providing such a vantage point.

TUNNEL VISION

The second risk is myopia, the inclination to look to a narrow view of your own industry or category for all the answers with respect to emerging customer behavior. Retailers will tend to focus solely on retail, hoteliers on hospitality, bankers on the financial sector. Even worse, within categories, shoe sellers will look at other shoe sellers, electronics retailers at other electronics retailers. Before you know it, executives are looking at the universe through a pinhole. It's a natural response to look for the danger on your own doorstep, but looking inside only your own category or industry tells you little about the more momentous changes in the customer, society, or broader retail market.

PRESENTISM VERSUS FUTURISM

Next, there's a tendency when attempting to divine the future to quite crudely extrapolate the present, as journalist Rob Walker put it recently on Marker: "Anything is possible, but take a closer look at how often definitive predictions about permanent change are simply extrapolations of recently observable trends taken to some maximum extreme. In other words, the future will be like this new present—only much more so."[10]

He's absolutely right, and we do this because the present is infinitely more comfortable for most of us than the future. The present is familiar and quantifiable, just the way most business managers like it. It's far less daunting to simply extrapolate what we already know and understand than to have to cross into the realm of abstraction and projection. Managers tend to gravitate to the statistical, verifiable, and provable. The future provides none of these empirical guardrails— but we have to prepare for it nonetheless.

To sum up, the future doesn't really care if we're comfortable with it or not. As business leaders, we must look beyond what's present and apparent and dig deeper for the less obvious societal and behavioral shifts taking shape.

ALL VERSUS NOTHING

Will people abandon cities or not? Will we educate our children online, or will they remain on campuses and in classrooms? Will customers still shop in physical stores or not? The media loves questions like this because they make great headlines. The problem with these sorts of questions is that they treat the future as a binary argument. But change, as I have discovered, is rarely absolute, nor does it have to be in order to have significance in our lives. A business need not lose all its customers before it goes out of business. Likewise, a company doesn't have to sell to everyone in order to become wildly successful.

In other words, when tracking the impact of various trends, we must remember that even fractional change, as it pertains to meaningful aspects of our lives, can change everything.

INSTANCES VERSUS PATTERNS

Every day, we are being deluged with data on a wide variety of subjects and issues. It's important to recognize that there are two distinct kinds of data. If you're a data scientist reading this, I apologize in advance for generalizing. I know data encompasses far more than two kinds, but in my world, only two matter: instances and patterns.

Instances can involve anything: developing medical facts, economic reports, or industry news. If they're significant enough, instances can also alter the course of events, sometimes dramatically. The incident involving the assassination of Franz Ferdinand, for example, set the wheels of World War I in motion. The incidents that took place on 9/11 brought decades of instability and war in the Middle East, a barrage of terrorist attacks, and ever stricter air travel protocols.

But while such isolated instances can lead to broader change, they are inherently unpredictable and unreliable as a means of forecasting the future. Predicting the next instance of something happening is close to impossible—that is, unless it becomes an identifiable trend.

Trends are, by definition, simply patterns across a range of instances. Patterns within medical data, economic reports, or industry performance form a trend. And trends ultimately change things. Case in point: the death of George Floyd at the hands of Minneapolis police on May 25, 2020, was a tragic incident. But the reason it sparked global protests was that it was viewed as part of a long and obvious pattern. The incident caused outrage, but the pattern is what sparked the change in public perception and reception to calls for racial justice.

For retailers, patterns found in completely different industries and categories can be even more important than those in the retail industry. Could a pattern of technological advancement in the live entertainment industry inform the future of retail? Could a pattern of innovations in healthcare? In education? All such influences are entirely possible. So rather than looking for the future under a microscope, it's better to use a radio telescope that listens intently to the entire universe of change taking place as we speak. We can do this only by raising our heads and peering out farther onto the horizon.

THE MYTH OF BLACK SWANS

The theory of black swan events was developed by the essayist and scholar Nassim Nicholas Taleb to describe events that are unpredictable yet highly disruptive, events for which there is no historic precedent that would allow us to anticipate them. By Taleb's definition, COVID-19 was not a black swan.

We know this because while most companies were scrambling to react to the pandemic, other companies were following plans that had been engineered, years in advance, for just such a crisis. Intel Corporation, for example, has had a standing committee on pandemics for almost twenty years, formed during the 2003 SARS outbreak.[11] When COVID-19 emerged, the committee was activated into a task force, empowered with learnings from previous pandemics, vastly speeding Intel's response.

Your organization has the same capability, but harnessing that capability means formalizing and internalizing responsibility for organizational intelligence. This is precisely why every business should have a person or persons whose role should be to do nothing but staff the organizational crow's nest, monitoring the horizon for anything and everything that could impact the course of the company. When the potential for any threat is identified—particularly one with the magnitude of a pandemic—it's up to the organization to monitor that threat and build contingency plans to deal with it, should it transpire.

WE'VE NEVER BEEN HERE BEFORE

As an industry, we're already beginning to stumble into some of these pitfalls. For example, some people are already engaging in extreme presentism, framing the changes taking place in the retail industry as a mere "acceleration" of trends that were already underway. "Nothing to see here folks! All just stuff that would have happened already!" I couldn't agree with this statement less. I feel it's intellectually lazy, not to mention perilous, to adopt such a position. In fact, as long as we regard the pandemic under this sort of fatalistic lens, it blinds us to the deeper, unique, and unprecedented societal and industry changes taking place. Changes that could have happened only as a result of this pandemic. Changes that will not simply speed the arc of retail history but alter it entirely. A retail butterfly effect, if you will, on a massive scale.

What I discovered in this crisis was not merely an acceleration but a once-in-a-century wrinkle in time, a wormhole leading to an entirely different era of retail, an era that will bring new societal norms, consumer behaviors, and competitive threats—not just for retail businesses but for all businesses. When we look back, we'll see that the pandemic was an evolutionary turning point, allowing some retailers to scale to new and, in some cases, disturbing proportions. Others, sadly, will succumb to corporate Darwinism.

However, what I also found was a narrow but crucial window of opportunity for brands with courage. The courage to forge new customer value, purpose, and relevance. The courage to see COVID-19 as not only a cataclysm but also a catalyst for positive change.

Such courage will require leaders with the temerity to, in kinship with the Spanish explorer Hernán Cortés, burn the ships that brought them to this new place. There is no going back.

1

PRE-EXISTING CONDITIONS

There are three deaths: the first is when the body ceases
to function. The second is when the body is consigned to
tho grave. The third Is that moment, sometime in the future,
when your name is spoken for the last time.
David Eagleman

Threathe world of retail that will emerge from COVID-19 will be a
very different place. The scattered bones of small to medium-
sized businesses, troubled legacy brands, ailing distribution
formats, and cash-strapped retailers and shopping mall owners will
be strewn across the landscape. In 2020 alone, analysts at Coresight
Research estimated that the United States would shutter twenty-five
thousand stores[1] and that 25 percent to as many as 50 percent of all
enclosed malls[2] will cease operations in the next three to five years.
While the U.S. market can afford to shed a few pounds of retail square
footage from its oversized waistline, it's hardly the only country
losing large swaths of retail.

By mid-June of 2020, the United Kingdom had also lost thirty-one
retail companies to bankruptcy, putting an end to over sixteen hundred stores.[3] Canada, whose retail-per-capital footprint was already
about half of that found in the United States, saw brands like Aldo, a

shoes and accessories company that had steered its way through half a century of previous downturns and crises, tap out under the stress of COVID-19. Germany went so far as to forestall corporate bankruptcy filings until as late as March of 2021 provided businesses could validate that COVID-19 was the key source of their insolvency—all in order to avert a debilitating spate of closures. France and Spain adopted similar measures.

By September of 2020, thirty-one North American retail chains had declared bankruptcy or filed for creditor protection:

- Century 21 Department Stores
- Stein Mart
- Tailored Brands
- Lord & Taylor
- ascena
- The Paper Store
- RTW Retailwinds (New York & Co. parent)
- MUJI U.S.A.
- Sur La Table
- Brooks Brothers
- G-Star RAW
- Lucky Brand
- GNC
- Tuesday Morning
- Centric Brands (owner or licensor of brands such as Hudson, Robert Graham, Swims, Zac Posen, Calvin Klein, Tommy Hilfiger, and Kate Spade)
- JCPenney
- Stage Stores
- Aldo
- Neiman Marcus
- J.Crew
- Roots USA
- True Religion
- Modell's Sporting Goods
- Art Van Furniture
- Bluestem Brands (Appleseed's, Blair, Draper's & Damon's, Fingerhut, Gettington, Haband, and Old Pueblo Traders)
- Pier 1
- SFP Franchise Corp. (Papyrus parent)
- Sail
- Reitmans
- Groupe Dynamite
- Le Château

But as you review the list of early victims, something becomes apparent. Just as COVID-19 exploited the vulnerabilities of human

Seattle's Westlake Center during the city's lockdown resembles a ghost town

beings with pre-existing medical conditions, such as diabetes, heart disease, or asthma, it assumed an identical modus operandi in its attack on the retail industry. Companies that came into the crisis with weakened immune systems or already ailing health never stood a chance.

Brands like J.Crew, JCPenney, and GNC, burdened by mountains of debt, succumbed early. Fabled high-end department store Neiman Marcus entered bankruptcy in May of 2020, primarily in an effort to restructure much of its more than $5 billion in debt.

Others were simply victims of dying channels. Department store retailers like Lord & Taylor, which had struggled for years to find relevance, also rapidly fell in the face of the pandemic. Brands that depended on department stores for the majority of their volume quickly followed suit. Flagging trademarks like True Religion, Pier 1, and Lucky Brand also collapsed under the strain. Many had never regained currency with customers going into the crisis—a truth that would prove fatal, as any remaining drip lines of revenue dried up completely during lockdowns.

By the fall, just as daily updates of the mounting human toll of COVID-19 resulted in little reaction by many of us, news of new bankruptcies in the retail market came and went with little shock.

In a 2020 *Business of Fashion* article, Andrew Rosen, founder of the apparel brand Theory, put it this way:

> There will be a cleansing of our whole industry, where those that were struggling before are going to go away…and the ones that make it will have a bigger share of market. It will also open up room for new players to come in and new opportunities to arise.[4]

And while I agree with Rosen's assessment in the long run, the short run is more worrisome.

While the volume of bankruptcies in the very earliest stages of the pandemic was unsettling, the unfortunate truth is that most of these brands were already in intensive care; some were on life support. And if we're being honest, beyond the human tragedy of employment losses, how many of these brands will be missed? How many will have a tear shed for their demise? The truth is most had already become invisible to us in a pre-pandemic world. While their downfall is tragic, it wasn't unexpected.

The problem is the pandemic is not over. Sure, the first wave of bankruptcies in the retail sector took the weak and vulnerable. It was predictable. But soon, perhaps by the time you're reading this book, another and more profound wave of failures will likely have arrived. And this one will come for the otherwise healthy.

THE FRACTIONAL FUTURE

In June of 2020, the United States reported that 4.8 million jobs had been added back into the economy. The Trump administration looked to use the news as a signal that all was returning to normal. At a time when good news was hard to come by, many accepted the announcement at face value.

On closer inspection, however, the numbers told a different story. First, the 4.8 million jobs being announced were not "created," so to speak, but had simply returned to an economy in the process of reopening. What's more, the number represented only a small fraction of the jobs lost during the initial stages of the pandemic. Second, buried deep in the jobs report was another line item that didn't make it to the presidential podium: almost 600,000 Americans reported that they had been permanently terminated from their jobs, bringing the total number of those permanent pandemic layoffs to almost 3 million.

The unemployment condition was by no means limited to the United States. By July of the same year, the United Kingdom had seen a similar reality emerge, as 5 million workers, furloughed at the outset of the lockdown, remained on the unemployment rolls.

One month later, Canada, a country that had done better than the United States at controlling the virus, saw nearly a quarter of a million jobs come back to the economy. The reality, however, was that even these positive numbers left a net 10.2 percent level of joblessness. By contrast, during the depths of the 2008–9 recession, unemployment in Canada stood at a comparatively rosy 8.4 percent.[5]

Globally, according to the United Nations, the equivalent of 400 million jobs were lost in the second quarter of 2020[6]—a number equivalent to the combined populations of the United States and Canada.

Political leaders seeking to game the lockdowns had to pay a steep price, too. Some countries reopened much earlier than others, only to be forced, almost immediately, to institute even more Draconian states of lockdown. Even countries like South Korea and New Zealand, both of which represented the gold standard in pandemic management, experienced flare-ups. It's rational to assume that until we achieve a reasonable level of global immunity to this virus, countries, corporations, and their global supply chain partners will have to deal with ongoing flare-ups and business interruption.

This matters tremendously because until effective vaccines can be distributed and we can once again feel safe, the entire global economy, not just the retail economy, will be forced to operate in a fractional state. Will employment numbers improve? Sure, but a return to full employment is unlikely. Will shoppers come back to retail stores?

Of course, but those who feel vulnerable will not, at least not unless it's essential. In addition, occupancy caps and social distancing measures will further reduce sales volumes. Will customer spending loosen up? To an extent, yes. But a percentage of us, out of concern for our financial stability, will keep our money under lock and key, saved for essentials. The result is a state of commercial purgatory where businesses, although reopened, simply cannot return to pre-pandemic sales levels, due to customer reluctance and virus mitigation measures, thus kneecapping sales and profits over a protracted period of time.

As it becomes clear that sales and profits are likely to remain fractional, businesses across categories will quite naturally look to slash expenses—a process already underway in many companies. Purchase orders will be suspended, staff will be permanently discharged, conferences will be cancelled, and offices permanently closed. The trickle-down impact of this retraction will create a broadening wave of unemployment, not just among lower-paid frontline retail and service workers as was the case in the initial lockdown but also reaching into the ranks of white-collar workers. The contagion doesn't stop there. Soon, fallout in the commercial real estate sector will rise to crisis levels, as retail and office space becomes dark. Down the food chain, janitorial services, security companies, and even institutional investors will feel the pain of this fractional future.

SIDELINED

What makes the COVID-19 pandemic particularly daunting is its multifaceted nature. It represents both a prolonged and a profound medical threat followed closely by lagging economic destruction. The medical threat is most daunting for older people and those with underlying medical issues but doesn't exclude the young entirely. The economic threat, on the other hand, is most real for younger people and the financially vulnerable but certainly doesn't exclude the elderly. The result is that almost every economic stratum of every generational cohort has a struggle ahead—medical, financial, or both.

MILLENNIALS

Going into the pandemic, Millennials, or those born between 1981 and 1996, had fallen behind every preceding generation with respect to income, wealth, and assets. A recent study by the U.S. Federal Reserve Board, for example, found "millennial households had an average net worth of about $92,000 in 2016, nearly 40 percent less than Gen X households in 2001, adjusted for inflation, and about 20 percent less than baby boomer households in 1989."[7] Additionally, the report suggests, these deficits are likely to have a lifelong impact on the fortunes of Millennials, affecting both livelihood and lifestyle.

In fact, copious studies have confirmed that generations entering the workforce during economic downturns almost invariably suffer deficits in both income and wealth, compared with demographic cohorts that begin their careers during times of stability or growth. Add to that the levels of student debt that many Millennials (particularly in North America) were burdened with, and continue to shoulder, and it amounted to a recipe for a lost generation.

That all proved true. Indeed, ten years after the financial crisis of 2008–9, Millennials were just beginning to see their incomes catch up with those of their older demographic cohorts—only to be slammed once again by COVID-19.

Moreover, as Pew Research points out, Millennials also tend to be disproportionately impacted by layoffs in many of the hardest-hit industries, such as travel and leisure, because these industries tend to employ younger workers.[8] With older Millennials well into entering what should be their prime spending years, the double hit of economic hardship doesn't bode well for their financial health going forward.

GENERATION Z OR CENTENNIALS

Those born after 1996 find themselves today precisely where Millennials did a decade earlier. They face high student debt levels and spiraling costs for staples like housing and insurance. Now, the job market is being ripped out from under them. According to a 2020 study by Data for Progress,

While over half of voters under 45 (52 percent) have lost their job, been placed on leave, or had hours cut, only 26 percent of those over 45 fall into this category. While the burden of the coronavirus has fallen heaviest on the elderly, it is younger voters who are paying a higher economic toll.[9]

GENERATION X

Generation X, or those born between 1965 and 1980, while somewhat less vulnerable medically—and arguably more stable financially—have their own set of problems. Many are currently caring for both their children and their aging parents while preoccupation with retirement grows among the oldest in the cohort. The problem with pinning hopes on Generation X to shoulder any economic recovery is that they're simply too small as a percentage of total population to carry the day. In the United States, for example, the Gen X cohort is 18 percent smaller than the Baby Boomer cohort and 28 percent smaller than the Millennial cohort.

Even if every Gen X consumer spent disproportionately through this crisis, it's mathematically impossible for them to pick up the slack in the economy.

BABY BOOMERS

While the Baby Boomer generation in most developed countries remains the wealthiest demographic cohort, this does not mean that those born between 1946 and 1964 are out of the woods. In fact, they face a dual threat. Not only are those over fifty-five more at risk for the worst medical outcomes of contracting the virus, they are also in the position of being retired or planning to retire. Coming into the crisis, we knew that an alarming percentage of Baby Boomers were financially unprepared for retirement. One recent report from the U.S. Government Accountability Office found that 48 percent of those fifty-five and over had absolutely no savings in a 401K or any formal retirement fund.[10] Many countries in Europe face similar savings shortfalls among retirement-aged workers.

With 58 percent of Boomers saying their jobs have been adversely impacted by COVID-19, many will have new cause to review their financial situations entirely. For some Baby Boomers, the pandemic has meant digging into their retirement nest eggs. Those who planned to retire early may now be rethinking that plan and choosing to work longer. This in turn has a cascading effect, making fewer jobs available for younger workers.

SILENT AND GI GENERATIONS

For the oldest among us, the virus carries roughly a twenty-fold greater infection fatality rate. Thus, most will be shut in, waiting for a vaccine to be distributed and keeping their financial resources close as the pandemic drags on.

Against this backdrop, there has perhaps never, in recent history, been another time where understanding the consumer's mindset has been so vital. This brings us to some of the most critical and frequently asked questions: What's going on in the minds of customers through this crisis? What are their innermost fears and concerns? And above all, what will it take to get them shopping again?

DECODING THE CUSTOMER IN CRISIS

Marketing is many things, but at its core, it is the art of persuasion. It's the science of delivering just the right message to a specific customer at the perfect moment to awaken a need or desire that causes a predictable action or response, most often measured as a purchase. At the best of times, getting all this right is like hang gliding through a hurricane. And, in the midst of a global pandemic, these are clearly not the best of times. In fact, it's no overstatement to say that the COVID-19 pandemic may indeed be the most traumatic and prolonged event that any of us will experience in our personal and professional lives. Add to this the levels of social unrest and conflict we've witnessed throughout much of the pandemic, and it results in significant psychological turmoil for most of the audience we, as marketers and retailers, hope to reach and connect with.

So what is the customer mindset during times of crisis? How does fear influence our behavior? And what messages are customers receptive to or repelled by? All these questions led me to a man named Ernest Becker.

Becker was a professor of anthropology at Simon Fraser University. During his tenure at Simon Fraser, Becker wrote his 1974 Pulitzer Prize-winning work, *The Denial of Death*. The central premise of Becker's work is that humans are unique relative to other animals, in that we are conscious that we are alive. We can consciously wake up in the morning, see the sun rising, and think, "It's great to be alive!" But according to Becker, that singularly unique evolutionary trait is a double-edged sword, in that we are also cognizant of death. We know what death is, we know it's inevitable, and we sense its permanence.

It is Becker's underlying premise that this unique feature of human consciousness—the cognizance and fear of death—drives an outsized share of our day-to-day behavior. Becker also surmises that in order to cope with the prospect of our own mortality, human beings construct elaborate world views that serve to give our lives meaning and purpose, as well as distract us from the inevitability of death. Work, school, family, teams, and places of worship all form a psychological buffer of activity that diverts us from consciously dwelling on our inevitable demise. We further evade thoughts of death by planning for the future and in doing so, build in the assumption that we'll be around in the future to enjoy those plans. Finally, within this world view, we seek to assign value and meaning to our lives and assure ourselves that we somehow matter in the grand scheme of things. We convince ourselves that our employer depends on us, that our families need us, and for some, that observance of various religious beliefs and practices may assure us of a life after death. Once established, this world view allows us to carry on with our daily lives, diverted, for the most part, from conscious thoughts of death. Periodically, Becker asserts, events occur that pierce the safety and security of our world views, bringing the concept of mortality to our doorstep and with it, a significant series of psychological changes—changes that include modified consumer behaviors.

Becker's seminal work has been expanded upon by a team of American social psychologists: Sheldon Solomon, Jeff Greenberg, and Tom Pyszczynski. According to Solomon, "What Becker hypothesized is that if that's all we thought about, 'I'm going to die someday, I can walk outside and get hit by a comet or smoked by a virus,' you just wouldn't be able to stand up in the morning. You'd be a twitching blob of biological protoplasm, cowering under your bed, groping for a large sedative."[11]

Professor Sheldon Solomon, PhD, is a pioneer in studying the impact of crisis on human behavior

That, he says, is where Becker's theory of the cultural world views comes in, to distract and insulate us from death's inevitability.

Although compelling, Becker's theory had never been proven out in the real world. So Solomon and his team set about doing just that. Through a series of controlled tests, they consciously and subconsciously reminded people of their death and then took them through a series of tests to measure any behavioral and cognitive changes.

What they found was remarkable.

Reminders of death, or what Solomon and team called "mortality salience," did indeed abruptly change attitudes and behaviors in research subjects. Reminders of death increased people's desire to be with people who looked and sounded more like them and who were of the same nationality, religion, or political belief system. Death reminders also affected attitudes toward politics and community; after being reminded of their death, people gravitated toward more populist and charismatic leaders. The salience of mortality also tended to make people value the natural and animal worlds less, prompting a greater willingness to exploit natural resources for their own financial gain.

While the findings were an impressive extension of Becker's thesis, little did Solomon know that in 2001 an event would take place that would become a profound real-world test of the mortality salience theory.

At 8:45 AM on Tuesday, September 11, 2001, the first plane slammed into the North Tower of the World Trade Center. Eighteen minutes later, as the world watched in collective horror, a second aircraft pierced the sixtieth floor of the South Tower. The deep, unnerving feeling that so many of us felt that day was that it could have been any of us in those towers. To varying extents, we all felt the salience of our own mortality.

"After September 11 of 2001, we were asked to write a book about terrorism," Solomon says. "And in that book, we argued that the events of September 11th were like a giant mortality salience induction."[12] And just as Solomon and his team had seen behaviors change in the lab, they saw the same sorts of changes playing out in the real world after 9/11.

Specifically, the team observed conspicuous levels of consumption. Money, for example, figured more prominently in people's minds. Material possessions became more important. Activities like movie rentals, gambling, and alcohol consumption rose dramatically, as did rates of psychological disorders.

What became apparent to Solomon was that there is indeed a defined and surprisingly predictable response to the salience of mortality in which customers aggressively work to reassemble their world views.

SAFETY AND DISTRACTION

First, in times of existential crisis, we seek to regain safety and security. Money, Solomon points out, is a resource to help us do just that. In fact, he's quick to add that in many cultures, money has become a proxy for immortality. "When folks in the U.S. doubt that," he says, "I tell them to look at the back of a $1 bill where there says, 'In God, we trust,' and then on the left side of the back of an American dollar is

Grocery store shelves in Orlando, Florida, show the effects of panic buying, as consumers hoarded key food and household items at the pandemic's outset

a pyramid and on the top of the pyramid, there is a little floating eyeball, and that's an ancient Egyptian symbol of immortality."[13] For some, he says, money has become a death-defying fetish and a religion unto itself.

This need to reassert control over chaos results in an immediate impulse to spend on those resources we believe will help us to do just that. This explains many of the behaviors we witnessed periodically throughout the pandemic. The panic buying of hand sanitizer and disinfectant, the heavy shift to spending on home repairs and improvements, and the explosion in home cooking and baking—all these are means of establishing a sense of security, safety, and comfort.

Solomon points out, though, that safety is only one part of the equation. There were also unprecedented levels of spending on things like board games, Netflix subscriptions, bicycles, and gardening supplies—all things that offer distraction from the threat.

Perhaps unsurprisingly, a recent study across multiple countries found that consumers generally intended to pull back on spending, with notable exceptions in categories such as household supplies, personal care products, groceries, and home entertainment.[14]

It makes sense, then, that in times of crisis, marketing messages that offer customers safety, a sense of security, and a regained level of control over their financial resources will be most immediately received, understood, and acted upon.

With a potentially long wait for widely available vaccines and with looming economic worry, customers, generally speaking, may be stuck in varying degrees of this *safety and distraction state* for a prolonged period. Unlike 9/11, a highly traumatic yet short event, it's logical to assume that COVID-19 will present a persistent medical and economic threat through 2021 and possibly even well into 2022.

Until such time, marketers attempting to aggressively move customers beyond the control state are likely to find minimal traction for their messaging. If you're a marketer in any category, read the room, as they say, and tailor your messaging appropriately.

VALUE AND BELONGING

It might have been surprising to some that at the height of the pandemic, amidst rising case counts and mortality rates, a sizable and vocal segment of society seemed more preoccupied with one thing: when their favorite sports teams would once again resume play. Whether it was European football or American football, baseball or cricket, fans around the world were clamoring to see their local squads and sports idols back in uniform.

Some might look at this high prioritization of sports in the midst of a pandemic as wholly irrational. Yet when viewed through the lens of mortality salience, it makes perfect sense. For many of us, the teams we cheer for are an integral psychological component of who we are. It's an affiliation that feeds our intrinsic sense of personal value and belonging. Sports not only provide a healthy form of distraction from the stresses of life, but they often constitute a bridge to our social circle.

According to Daniel Wann, a professor at Murray State University, following and supporting sports teams is a "very psychologically healthy activity." "Fandom," he says, "connects us to other like-minded people, which satisfies our human need for belonging." Further, Wann says, those who self-identify as sports fans "have higher levels of self-esteem, lower levels of loneliness and tend to be more satisfied with their lives compared to those who aren't interested in sports."[15]

The desire to resume sporting events is just one example of how, once we perceive that the immediate threat has passed or at least been greatly diminished, we, as customers, aggressively seek to reconstruct our lives and work to reestablish our sense of self-esteem and value.

How we do this varies greatly by individual. Former Estée Lauder Chairman Leonard Lauder coined the term "the lipstick effect" when he realized that during times of crisis or economic downturn, the company's lipstick sales grew. He surmised that women purchased small indulgences such as lipstick during such times as a replacement for other, perhaps pricier, luxury goods. The point is that one person might satisfy the need for self-esteem by buying a new car. For someone else, it may be by taking a trip. For another, it may be getting a manicure, a haircut, or even a simple tube of lipstick. And in an alarming percentage of cases, people also resort to negative behaviors such as using drugs and alcohol and gambling.

Ultimately, customers will seek to acquire products, services, and experiences that uniquely support their individual sense of self-worth and value—whatever that may be.

It's during this phase that messages around responsible levels of indulgence and pampering will be well-received. As marketers, you may find that promoting your product or service as a small, safe, and responsible reward can be highly effective as customers enter this phase of world-view reconstruction.

LEGACY AND AFTERLIFE

Finally, brushes with our own mortality lead us to consider what lasting imprint our lives will leave on the world and how we will be remembered—our afterlife, if you will. For some, this need will be fulfilled through spiritual means, with every dominant religion promising some iteration of the hereafter.

For others, their sense of legacy is gained through earthly achievements like fame, wealth, power, prestige, and the acquisition of material goods, a phenomenon that psychology professor Elizabeth Hirschman calls "secular immortality."[16] In this state, customers may be more receptive to messages about self-improvement, personal transformation, bucket-list experiences, philanthropic ventures, and more major purchases like homes, cars, and larger investments.

So as marketers, we need to be even more sensitive to the psychological state of our customers now and for the foreseeable future, as they work through the trauma of the pandemic. In an effort to remove some of the complexity regarding the unfolding of human behavior during COVID-19, I've attempted to provide some shorthand in the chart on the following page.

The point is that we humans are not binary in our behavior. We don't simply exist in states of saving or splurging. Today's demand for a particular product or experience does not necessarily remain pent-up indefinitely until some future date that suits retailers and marketers. This is especially true in times of crisis, as we all move through a complex but essential psychological process where we may be highly receptive to some marketing messages and ignore others as if they were invisible—or worse yet, avoid or scorn them as tone deaf and out of sync with our need-state.

It is also very likely, according to Solomon, that the pandemic may bring in its wake a period of significant prosperity, productivity, and spending. But one thing is certain: we cannot endure such a prolonged assault on our thoughts and feelings without a sustained change in our shopping behaviors.

WHAT'S GONNA STICK?
Another question that has dominated headlines, analyses, and live streams through the pandemic revolves around which customer

Customer Orientation	Need State	Observable Behaviors		Responsive to Products and Services That...
		Positive	Negative	
Safety	Desires control over and security against the threat	Seeks products and services that mitigate the immediate threat	Focuses intensely on money, hoarding resources, and panic buying	Emphasize safety, security, and control
Distraction	Needs psychological diversion from the threat	Pursues new hobbies, recreation, and entertainment	Is preoccupied with the trivial and shows potential for drug and alcohol abuse	Provide relief from preoccupation with the threat
Self-esteem	Wants to regain a sense of personal value and purpose	Buys small material indulgences, products and services that promote personal care and appearance	Shows conspicuous levels of consumption, and riskier, even addictive and anti-social, behaviors	Promise responsible and healthy means of shoring up a sense of self-worth
Belonging	Wishes for reconnection with family, community, and social, political, and spiritual institutions	Desires to reconvene with friends and family, and reconnect to teams and community, work, and religious groups	Is at risk of demonstrating more extreme political views and xenophobia	Promote safe and responsible means of reconnecting with a social circle or provide a bridge to branded communities of interest
Legacy	Seeks the promise of secular or spiritual afterlife	Indulges in major purchases, personal transformations, bucket-list experiences, philanthropy, and enhanced spiritual affiliation	Overspends and displays religious or political extremism	Promise position, status, or achievement; suggest opportunities for transformation; prompt an appreciation of life's finitude and the need to create positive and enduring family memories; and engage in efforts to create positive change in the broader world

Consumer Mindset in Crisis

behaviors observed during the COVID-19 outbreak are likely to remain after the pandemic. Which habits will form and become sustained?

You've probably heard at some point that it takes twenty-one days to form or to break a habit. What you might not know is that statement is not true—well, not exactly. The twenty-one-day idea was first propagated by Dr. Maxwell Maltz, an American plastic surgeon. Maltz observed that twenty-one days seemed to be an average length of time for his patients to adapt to their surgery. Nose job patients took twenty-one days to get used to their new look. Amputees took about three weeks to lose their sense of having a phantom limb. Although never clinically tested, these professional observations, as well as reflections on his own personal behavior, led Maltz to publish his thoughts in a 1960 book called *Psycho-Cybernetics*, where he said: "These, and many other commonly observed phenomena tend to show that it requires a minimum of about 21 days for an old mental image to dissolve and a new one to jell."[17]

Ironically, the medical community and organizational behaviorists began making a habit of quoting Maltz's habit theory. The truth is Maltz was wrong—at least partially.

While it may take a minimum of twenty-one days to loosen or strengthen our attachment to a given behavior or routine, it actually takes much longer to truly form new habits. According to the *British Journal of General Practice*, it takes sixty-six days, to be precise.[18]

But here's the thing: by the time we finally emerge from this pandemic, it's possible that your customers will have had something in the range of six hundred days to forge new habits and behaviors. Six hundred days to explore new channels, brands, and shopping technologies.

But to divine precisely how those habits and behaviors will shift, we can't simply look to the retail industry for answers. Life is not a reflection of retail. Retail is a reflection of life. A reflection of where and how we live, work, educate, communicate, travel, and entertain ourselves. In other words, before we can even attempt to understand how the pandemic will reshape retail, it's essential that we first understand how it will reshape life.

2

THE WORMHOLE

I put instant coffee in a microwave oven
and almost went back in time.
Steven Wright

My wife and I were recently out for a drive near our home
when we noticed a new school under construction. Neither
of us thought much of it at the time, but later, I realized that
simply by glancing at the skeletal framework of the construction project, both of us were able to determine with relative certainty that it
was a public elementary school, a fact that we later confirmed.

That led me to wonder why it is that most public schools are so
predictable in their design. Turns out there's a reason for it that dates
back about two hundred years. Public education as we know it today
is a product of the industrial revolution.

In fact, prior to industrialization, formal education was something reserved almost exclusively for royalty or the wealthy elite. But
the changing nature of work and the new skills that factory workers
required led the owners of those same factories to create an education system with the sole intent of transferring basic skills and
knowledge to legions of future workers. "Factory schools," as they
are now referred to, first originated in Prussia but quickly proliferated
in other major centers around the world. For the first time, students

were segregated by age group and tracked through a standardized education curriculum. But the aim was not to develop deep or creative thinkers. It was a system specifically designed to produce individuals with just enough knowledge, skill, and behavioral modification to work compliantly, productively, and without issue in factories. A system aimed solely at bolstering industrial productivity, prosperity, and wealth. Like the occupations it was preparing its students for, education itself became a manufacturing system, with the product being a sufficiently competent and compliant labor force. This became our modern public school system. It's no coincidence that many of today's public schools resemble factory buildings built not to inspire great thinking but rather to push adequate students along an academic assembly line.

Schools, though, are hardly the only artifacts of the industrial age. In fact, the next time you find yourself in a major city, stand on any street corner and take a good look around you. Almost everything within your field of vision—the buildings, businesses, universities, commuters, students, subways, taxis, buses, trains, even the media you see—almost all of them are products of the industrial era. They are a consequence of events that began more than two hundred years ago when productivity, prosperity, and wealth became increasingly concentrated in cities.

In fact, before the 1800s, life in most of the world was rural and the work agrarian. Most goods were made and sold locally. The village shoemaker, potter, and weaver were not only the manufacturers of their products but also the sellers, most often crafting their wares to individual customer specifications. I always find this interesting because while today we observe a shift among brands to direct-to-consumer models for sales, the truth is, the direct-to-consumer format is as old as commerce itself.

However, by the mid- to late 1800s, as industrialization grew and centralized, populations in major cities began to explode. In 1870, only two U.S. cities had populations of over 1 million inhabitants. By 1900, that number had increased to six, and 40 percent of Americans had migrated to urban environments.[1] With population came power, and cities became the epicenters of politics, culture, and economic activity.

It was around this time that retail too began to reflect the visage of the industrialized world and the first department stores were born: Le Bon Marché, Selfridges, Macy's, Marshall Field's, and many more. These all arose from a historic explosion in demand. Where once the maker and seller of a product were often likely to be the same business, labor was now increasingly divided in the name of efficiency and productivity. Makers made. Sellers sold. Customization, typical of manufacturing prior to the 1800s, rapidly gave way to the mass production of standardized commodity goods, often coming at lower prices, through economies of scale.

Growing demand meant an even greater need for robust supply, and by the mid- to late 1800s, the earliest incarnations of today's modern supply chains evolved. Thanks to new transportation technologies like steam engines, automobiles, trains, and trams, it was now not only possible but also economical to source raw materials in one market for the manufacture of goods in another market, and the ultimate sale of those goods in yet another market. The European garment industry, for example, which had relied on raw materials like cotton coming from India, could now source American cotton at competitive prices and sell the finished goods back to America. By the mid-1900s, further innovations such as containerization made the movement of goods even easier.

As cities grew in population, the imaginations of architects gazed upward, and the first skyscrapers were born, housing retail on the ground level and offices and manufacturing sites above. Armies of workers poured in each day to earn their wages. Cities began to solidify their position as the engines of the global economy.

In the aftermath of World War II, economies like that of the United States rebuilt themselves powered by what Harvard professor Lizabeth Cohen refers to as "a consumer's republic."[2] Prior to 1945, the United States was primarily a nation of renters. In the post-war era, however, with the support of subsidies contained in programs like the GI bill, the opportunity to own your own home and land drew millions to suburban communities. Thanks to unprecedented levels of automobile ownership and newly created highway networks, the modern daily commute was born.

Retailers followed the scent trail, and in the 1950s, the first suburban shopping malls were born. They became the centerpiece of consumer life for more than thirty years. As suburban customers clamored for the trappings of an emerging, modern middle class, the shopping center industry could barely keep pace. By the late 1950s, the majority of the most populous generation in history, the Baby Boomers, was between four and fourteen years old with needs that drove an unprecedented boom in consumption. The sheer demographic scale of this generation reverberates through the economies of the developed world to this day.

As the newly minted middle class defected from cities to the suburbs, urban cores began to diverge into upper- and lower-class neighborhoods. By the 1960s, income inequality in cities led to a sharp increase in crime, something experienced on both sides of the Atlantic. As Harvard professor Steven Pinker puts it, "For all the lags and mismatches between the historical trajectories of the United States and Europe, they did undergo one trend in synchrony: their rates of violence in major cities did a U-turn in the 1960s."[3] The United States led the way to a crime rate not seen in more than a century, with rates doubling over the course of the decade.

As cities fell into decay, so too did the commercial hubs inside them. High unemployment and crime would plague many major Western cities for almost three more decades.

However, beginning in the late 1980s and continuing through to today, a new revolution began. Along with other factors leading to increased urbanization, technology companies—from the early pioneers like IBM, Microsoft, and Apple to the second wave of newcomers including Facebook, Amazon, Uber, and Twitter—promised cities heaps of tax dollars, shiny new infrastructure, and thousands upon thousands of young employees eager to spend their programming salaries within the city's bounds. Cities not only offered these companies centralized, high-profile locations; they also gave proximity to some of the most illustrious engineering schools in the world. Just as the industrial barons before them, these new tech barons had a growing market for their products and a constant flow of solidly trained workers to power their growth.

Today, half the world's population resides in metropolitan areas, which account for an outsized share of economic productivity. According to a 2016 report from the World Economic Forum, "From now until 2025, one-third of world growth will come from the key Western capitals and emerging market megacities, one-third from the heavily populous middle-weight cities of emerging markets, and one-third from small cities and rural areas in developing countries."[4]

It's a trend that has also caused a significant imbalance in wealth, growth, and mobility. According to The Brookings Institute, for example, 90 percent of all the growth in "innovation sector" jobs since 2005 has taken place in only five metropolitan areas in the United States.[5]

But all of this could be about to change. The urbanization, centralization, commercialization, and ultimate globalization of cities, forged in the industrial age, may be about to undergo a historic reversal. COVID-19 will be the catalyst. Where we live, work, educate, and entertain ourselves, and perhaps most particularly how we shop, are all set to change fundamentally and permanently.

This is the point where some readers might be tempted to call bullshit and put this book down.

I get it. We've all heard similar sorts of sweeping predictions at different times that haven't panned out. One of the most obvious comparisons drawn against the COVID-19 pandemic is the Spanish flu pandemic of 1918—and it's fair to note that, despite a degree of de-densification, the 1918 pandemic did not put an end to cities, large gatherings, restaurants, shops, or the use of public transportation.

The key difference, though, and one that is often overlooked, is that unlike any other time in history, today we have a choice. Never before in the history of humanity have we had the spatial and temporal freedom that technology now affords us. We can do almost anything from anywhere at any time we wish. It's a life that would have seemed like science fiction to our 1980s counterparts, let alone our 1918 ancestors.

The concentration of industry and labor, the centralization of work, the systematization of education, and the distribution systems for products are all set to come undone. The problem is that the retail that we see around us today was woven into the fabric of that industrial era. Store locations, designs, formats, operating hours, and even revenue models have all been built on an industrial foundation that is now crumbling in the digital era.

In the end, the companies that survive will be those with not only the fortitude to withstand the pandemic but also the prescience to understand the world that sits beyond it. Retailers able to shed their industrial skins will survive the transition. Those that cannot will indeed be history. Let me explain why.

THE FUTURE OF WORK

In 2017, I was engaged on a strategy project for a large Japanese multinational with offices in New York. Over the course of several meetings with their teams, I had an opportunity to experience firsthand Japanese office culture, albeit outside of Japan.

The work ethic, dedication, and loyalty to their employers demonstrated by Japanese employees is a thing of legend. In fact, the Japanese even have a specific word, *karoshi*, which means dying from being overworked. Central to this cultural ethos is the sacred concept of the office.

In my work with this particular client, what surprised me most was the degree to which such a technologically sophisticated culture was also so seemingly entrenched and reliant on a centralized and in-person office culture. Despite plenty of opportunities to advance conversations, milestones, and project objectives via email, conference call, or Skype—precluding any need for an in-person meeting—meetings (lots of them) were nonetheless held in person. In fact, in one such meeting, almost an hour was spent trying to figure out how to livestream a remote audience in Tokyo into the meeting for a presentation I was slated to give.

The following year, I would visit Tokyo and develop an even keener insight into the intense Japanese in-person work ethos. According to Hiroshi Ono, a professor specializing in Japanese work culture at Tokyo's Hitotsubashi University, "There's only one way to do things here. Work has to be done at the company and during certain hours, learning has to take place at school, doctor visits at the hospital."[6]

Nonetheless, COVID-19 forced even this most fiercely dedicated of office cultures to rethink its approach. Digital contracts, Zoom meetings, and even after-work online sake parties have become de rigueur. Even the days of the *hanko*, a stamp used to imprint a signature on paper documents in order to approve them—until now a fixture in Japanese business life—may be limited. It's an odd but interesting cultural tidbit I learned about prior to visiting Japan for the first time. Surprisingly, some Japanese executives have pointed to the *hanko* as one of the primary roadblocks to working from home, given the need to go to the office to review and approve documents using a *hanko*. This is one of the many long-standing traditions coming under scrutiny since COVID-19 swept across the Land of the Rising Sun, proving that anything can change, including our reliance on offices.

THE DEATH OF THE OFFICE

On May 21, 2020, Facebook announced that it would allow tens of thousands of its employees to not only work from home on a permanent basis but also have the freedom to spin a globe and point to wherever they'd like "home" to be. Mark Zuckerberg told The Verge,

> We're going to be the most forward-leaning company on remote work at our scale [...] I think that it's possible that over the next five to 10 years—maybe closer to 10 than five, but somewhere in that range—I think we could get to about half of the company working remotely permanently.[7]

That same day, Canadian retail tech giant Shopify and social media platform Twitter both made similar announcements. Shopify founder and CEO Tobias Lütke said that he expects most of the company's employees to choose the work-from-home option, adding, "the choice is really, are we passengers on this tidal wave of change? Or do we jump in the driver's seat and try to figure out how to build a global world-class company by not getting together that often."[8]

By late July, Google had announced that it was allowing its employees to stay home until summer 2021—a move that affects almost 200,000 employees worldwide.[9] Tech companies are hardly alone in their position. Banks too are contemplating an officeless future, including Canada's Bank of Montreal and the United Kingdom's Barclays. Snack food manufacturer Mondelez, Nationwide Insurance, and Morgan Stanley also joined the chorus of businesses completely rethinking the value and utility of the twentieth-century office. In Nationwide's case, the action was decisive, closing five offices completely and allowing their 4,000 affected employees to work from home permanently.

Barclays CEO Jes Staley recently remarked that "there will be a long-term adjustment in how we think about our location strategy... the notion of putting 7,000 people in a building may be a thing of the past."[10]

Clearly, the work-from-home trend will not apply evenly across all types of work. As you might expect, the potential to work from home is significantly higher for developed versus developing nations and also considerably concentrated among jobs categorized as white collar.

So on balance, what percentage of jobs could be performed from home? A series of recent studies have attempted, using various methods of analysis, to quantify just that.

While hardly the majority, the percentage of work that can be done from home is, nonetheless, significant. And that's assuming use of only the work-from-home tools and technologies we have today— tools that are already being reimagined and improved. In September of 2020, for example, Facebook announced a new work-from-home platform called Infinite Office: a multi-screen, augmented reality platform, activated through a headset device. With Infinite Office, Facebook said, users would be able to toggle back and forth between fully immersive, collaborative virtual environments, like a team meeting, and augmented reality functionality, in which digital information is overlaid onto real-world surroundings.

It's a reasonable assumption that as the pandemic drags on, more dynamic and productive tools like this will be launched for remote workers. Tools that will make Zoom look like a payphone.

Country	Percentage
Argentina	26–29
France	28
Germany	29
Italy	24
Spain	25
Sweden	31
United Kingdom	31
United States	34
Uruguay	20–34

Percentage of Jobs That Can Be Performed from Home by Country

DOES WORKING FROM HOME WORK?

The simple answer appears to be yes.

While the pandemic and its associated closures of schools put additional demands on home-bound workers with children, studies conducted before the COVID-19 outbreak indicate clear upsides in terms of productivity and employee satisfaction among those working from home.

One study out of Stanford University examined a Chinese company called Ctrip, an online vacation-booking site. The company, which was attempting to cut expenses in its Shanghai office, recruited five hundred call center employees, half selected randomly, to engage in a work-from-home experiment. The thesis going into the experiment was that any savings in real estate expense would be eaten up by lower productivity among the group working from home. In fact, the opposite occurred. Productivity improved by 13 percent, with 9 percent coming from working more minutes per shift (fewer breaks and sick days) and 4 percent from more calls per minute.[11] Workers in the same study also reported a greater degree of satisfaction at work, resulting in an overall drop in attrition.

Another survey of over one thousand work-from-home employees found that part of the productivity increase came from the fact that they actually work an additional 16.8 days per year—likely a result of eliminating daily commuting time, which coincidentally amounted to an average of 17 days per year among respondents![12]

There are other potential benefits. First, lower office density may contribute to better employee health overall. Stay-at-home orders that took effect in cities like New York and Hong Kong not only served to quell the rampant spread of COVID-19 but also caused a dramatic shortening of flu season. In Hong Kong, for example, the 2019–20 influenza season was shorter—63 percent shorter, in fact, than those experienced in the previous five years. A similar decline was seen in Hong Kong during the 2003 SARS epidemic.[13]

Second, by lifting the constraints of geographic proximity to an office, employers will dramatically expand their potential talent pool.

Finally, as researcher and author Matt Clancy points out, studies have shown that social relationships can indeed form between remote workers, and the evidence of this reality has manifested in other areas. It is estimated, writes Clancy, that "41% of American adults play video games with other people online, averaging nearly five hours per week, and studies have shown gamers exhibit forms of social capital not dissimilar to the kind formed offline."[14]

So if this all sounds like a momentary kneejerk reaction by a few white-collar companies, consider that a recent survey by PwC found that a full 26 percent of U.S. companies are now actively seeking to reduce their real estate investments.

And let's face it, for most companies, offices have never been paragons of efficiency or productivity. Consider the trillions of person-hours annually spent gossiping at the water cooler or the endless memos about cleaning out the lunchroom refrigerator. No, offices in many cases are two things: a corporate vanity plate and a centralized mechanism for monitoring and exerting control over populations of workers. In the industrial world, this may have made some sense. In a digital world, it's increasingly absurd.

So what does any of this have to do with retail? Lots, as *New York Times* reporter Matthew Haag quite rightly points out: "Entire economies were molded around the vast flow of people to and from offices, from the rush-hour schedules of subways, buses and commuter rails to the construction of new buildings to the survival of corner bodegas. Restaurants, bars, grocery stores and shops depend on workers for their survival."[15]

He's absolutely right. Consider that each day, more than a million and a half people pour into Manhattan. If only 25 percent of those commuters began working from home, it would cause a reverberation that almost every business on the island would feel. Think of how many stores, bodegas, restaurants, coffee shops, nail salons, and other businesses have positioned themselves specifically to capitalize on these daily human migrations. What fate awaits such businesses in a work-from-home future?

Cities like San Francisco, New York, London, Paris, and Hong Kong could be completely reshaped by a work-from-home revolution and the retailscapes in these cities completely transformed with it. Given that over 70 percent of all job creation since the financial crisis has taken place in a handful of American metropolises, the economic impact of such a reversal in urbanization would be staggering.[16]

Consider that San Francisco's Bay Area alone is estimated to have more than 830,000 technology workers;[17] then, add the fact that the average Bay Area technology worker makes 56 percent more annually on average than the same worker in the finance sector in New York City. It's safe to say that technology workers are the engine of San Francisco's economy.

The question then is: What percentage of these workers would consider leaving the Bay Area if their employers allowed them to work anywhere they wish? One recent survey of 4,400 Bay Area tech workers pegged the number at 66 percent,[18] or close to 550,000 of the 830,000 resident tech employees.

But for the sake of argument, let's assume that a more conservative number, say only a little less than a quarter (200,000), of those workers left the Bay Area for more affordable cities and counties across the United States. It would be like the entire population of Salt Lake City simply disappearing from Utah. Imagine the economic impact. And that doesn't even account for the trickle-down damage to the economy: According to a 2010 study, each technology job in the Bay Area supports five jobs in the services sector.[19] This means the impact would not be simply the loss of almost a quarter of a million technology workers; it would also mean losing over a million service sector jobs that are dependent on them.

San Francisco specifically and the United States more generally are hardly the only places contemplating the long-term effects of an office-less or significantly office-reduced society. Cities like Paris, London, Sydney, and Tokyo are bracing for similar outbound migrations.

An April of 2020 study of over two thousand American adults by The Harris Poll suggested that close to 30 percent of those surveyed are either "somewhat" or "very likely" to move out of densely populated areas and toward more rural locales.[20]

CITIES

This certainly does not imply the end of cities, but it may lessen the degree to which we rely on them. As journalist Simon Kuper put it, "In a Zoom economy, many could abandon Paris, exchanging their two-bedroom in the 10th arrondissement for a similarly priced rural château. Popping into town once a week by TGV may be enough. Expect a Depression-era fire sale of Parisian flats, shop spaces and offices."[21]

So no—cities like Paris aren't going away anytime soon, but it's reasonable to assume that beyond the financial toll of a white-collar exodus, these cities will, in the process, lose much of the authentic energy and dynamism that drew people to them in the first place.

Long after the pandemic is over, small, unique shops, restaurants, and service companies will wither in the face of what will almost certainly be a dramatic economic migration of people out of their trading areas. University cities that thrive on student populations, such as Boston, Los Angeles, and Berlin, will see a markedly diminished swell in occupants each September as increasing numbers of students elect to study online at lower cost with perhaps just occasional trips into the city for in-person projects or social events.

Thus, cities as we know them are likely to change, if not forever, for a very long time. *Atlantic* columnist Derek Thompson sums it up this way:

> Cities will still be convenient, but their conveniences will be homogenous: a dependable array of CVS locations, bank branches, fast-casual franchises, and coffee shops. [...] Everything that urban residents typically despise about chains—their cold efficiency, sterility, and predictability— may come to feel like mixed blessings during a period when people feel stalked by murderous pathogens.[22]

That said, it has also been those same homogeneous national and international retail players that have been able to sustain their customers during the pandemic through combinations of delivery, click and collect, and socially distanced shopping. The winners will take the spoils, and these winners will use the victory to further dominate in cities.

Even immigration, once the lifeblood of almost every megacity, is likely to be severely curtailed for medical reasons during COVID-19 and even after the pandemic as countries grapple with staggering unemployment and economic losses.

If there's a silver lining in any of this, it may be an almost certain decline in lease rates for both residential and commercial space. A

longer-term softening of real estate values may bring new, digitally savvy entrepreneurs with grassroots businesses to these cities and over time will rebuild their authenticity, uniqueness, and appeal. By the same token, a dispersion of high-income earners could bring new levels of prosperity and growth to places that have until now not benefited from the spoils of the tech sector. It may be that every new business or start-up need no longer prove itself in a London, New York, or San Francisco, as has been the case for the past decade.

This outbound migration will not only reshape the cities being vacated but will also transform the suburbs surrounding them.

Usually a bustling sea of people, New York's Thirty-Fourth Street is deserted as the city's lockdown is put into effect

SUBURBIA 2.0

Throughout the 1990s and early 2000s, young people in particular flocked from their suburban family homes to cities on the promise of high-paying jobs and the excitement of big city life. They eagerly took tiny apartments at exorbitant rental rates in the belief that they didn't need space. The city was their backyard. The rich tapestries of busy streets, shops, cafés, restaurants, and clubs were an ever-present reminder that they'd made it.

COVID-19, however, changed that.

In Manhattan, for example, residential vacancies soared. In July of 2020, according to reports, there were "21.6% more apartments on the market from only a month prior in June—and 121% more compared to July 2019."[23] In real numbers, according to *The New York Times*, that amounted to 67,300 units available—the highest vacancy number in more than a decade and one that has caused a resulting 10 percent decline in rental rates.[24]

While it's true that some may ditch the coastal megacities like New York and San Francisco for smaller, attractive towns and cities like Jackson, Wyoming; Provo, Utah; or Columbus, Ohio, more may retreat to locations far closer to the cities their companies reside in. After all, many companies, even those willing to allow their employees to work remotely, may still insist on periodic in-person team meetings, making it necessary to be nearby. So like their parents and grandparents before them, young people may too embark on a suburban pilgrimage.

The front end of that migration already appears to be in motion. In fact, as early as August of 2020, *Bloomberg* published a piece titled "Urban Exiles Are Fueling a Suburban Housing Boom across the U.S.":

> The exodus to sparser landscapes is happening across the U.S., but it's most dramatic outside pricey, crowded New York, Los Angeles, and San Francisco. In Manhattan, signed sales contracts for condos and co-ops fell 60% in July, from a year earlier. Meanwhile, in the northern bedroom communities of Westchester County and Fairfield County, Conn., deals for single-family homes doubled.[25]

When taken together, the new level of portability of white-collar work and the promise of more space at a lower cost will drive an exodus not seen in more than seventy years and perhaps the greatest dispersion of income and wealth in modern history.

Moreover, when the concept of work evolves to become vastly more portable and less reliant on centralized physical offices, education won't be far behind.

EDUCATION

In many ways, the education market today mirrors the retail industry over the last twenty to thirty years. Like retailers, many in the education industry have spent decades all but dismissing the digital revolution, eschewing investment in technologies that would make its product—an education—more efficient, productive, and economically accessible. It's an industry that has put revenues, profits, and brand prestige ahead of student outcomes. It's forgotten that its mission is to make education more inclusive and available, not less. Higher education in many countries has become a pedagogical Ponzi scheme of ever-increasing costs and financial burden for both students and their parents. It's an industry that has clearly fractured between luxury schools at one end of the spectrum and low-end community colleges at the other, with any school in the middle finding itself absent of clear positioning and value. Finally, it's a system that has taken a commodified approach to learning, with the goal being units shipped as opposed to customization and quality.

COVID-19 made the vulnerabilities of such a system readily apparent. Vulnerabilities that leave the door open to disruption on a scale not seen since the first factory schools were established centuries ago.

A recent U.S.-based study on the financial health of universities and colleges found the following:

➤ Across the United States, more than 500 colleges and universities were deemed to be financially vulnerable.
➤ Approximately 1,360 colleges and universities had experienced year-on-year drops in first-year fall enrollment since 2009.
➤ Nearly 30 percent received less tuition revenue per student in 2017–18 than they had in 2009–10.[26]

This is not exactly a rock-solid foundation to play from. According to another study in the journal *Nature*,

All institutions are facing major financial problems, however. Wealthy private US universities, such as Johns Hopkins University in Baltimore, Maryland, expect to lose hundreds of millions of dollars in the next fiscal year. UK universities collectively face a shortfall of at least £2.5 billion (US$3 billion) in the next year because of projected drops in student enrolment.[27]

The result is a system of ever-increasing tuitions and rapidly diminishing returns. Gone are the days when an average kid coming from an average background can get a remarkable education without wealthy parents or burdensome loans. Student debt in America, for example, reached $1.5 trillion in 2019,[28] a figure slightly less than the annual GDP of South Korea.

Where do these rapidly escalating fees go? One recent study out of the United Kingdom found that, on average, less than half of tuition fees and other income is even applied to the costs of teaching. The majority is spent on building maintenance, libraries, IT, administration, and marketing.

Meanwhile, education is also an industry that's done a good job of painting online learning as being the poor cousin to in-person lectures, something author and advisor Scott Galloway, for one, predicts will change. As a May of 2020 article in *New York Magazine* featuring Galloway put it,

> The post-pandemic future [...] will entail partnerships between the largest tech companies in the world and elite universities. MIT@Google. iStanford. HarvardxFacebook. According to Galloway, these partnerships will allow universities to expand enrollment dramatically by offering hybrid online-offline degrees, the affordability and value of which will seismically alter the landscape of higher education.[29]

Despite what currently amount to pretty substandard alternatives, the fact is, as in retail, online learning already continues to capture a greater share of an otherwise flat market. In the United States, for example, "while overall postsecondary enrollments dropped by almost 90,000 students, nearly half a percentage point, from fall 2016 to fall 2017—confirming data previously published by the National Student Clearinghouse—the number of all students who took at least some of their courses online grew by more than 350,000, a healthy 5.7 percent."[30]

To Galloway's point, though, it's an opportunity that isn't escaping the purview of big tech. In August of 2020, Google announced that it would be launching a curriculum of certificate programs across an array of in-demand professions. The program, which Google is calling Google Career Certificates, can be completed in six months as opposed to what is often years in traditional college programs. While details on the cost of the program were scant, the company said in its announcement that the courses would cost a fraction of typical tuition fees and focus on the precise aspects of each profession that employers are looking for, ostensibly resulting in higher job placement rates than traditional college programs offer.

What Google's program points to is a big, fat, lucrative, underserved market just waiting to be ripped from the bony clutches of an outdated education system. A system that has been treating digital learning as the coach-class alternative to a proper business-class education, putting generations of students in a state of financial servitude in the process.

With all this said, it's also true that school is not simply about the transfer of knowledge. It's also an important time of self-discovery, friendships, and life experiences.

One recent Canadian poll of over six hundred students aged ten to seventeen years old—taken during the early stages of the pandemic—indicated that while 75 percent said they were keeping up with their studies, 60 percent also claimed to be unmotivated and bored. When probed about what it was that they missed most about actually being at school, more than 50 percent pointed to missing their friends. Sports and extracurricular activities were a distant second at 16 percent. But only 36 percent said they'd like to return to their classes.[31]

In the end, the transformation of education for the digital age will require all levels of education to rethink both their product and how it's delivered. Clearly, we can transfer information digitally with results that rival those of in-person teaching. What we haven't accounted for is a way of also providing a meaningful social structure for distant learners.

These shifts in both work and education will not only restructure our dependency on cities, but they will also have a dramatic impact on how we travel to and from them.

TRANSPORTATION

Among the many things Tokyo has to offer, its public transportation systems are among the best and most efficient in the world. Trains and subways are clean and efficient and generally run according to schedule. Yet as the pandemic hardened its grip on Tokyo, something interesting began to happen. People enrolled for driving lessons. But that's not the strange part. Many of these people already had driver's licenses.

A growing number of urban Japanese who possess a driver's license but don't own a car—dubbed "paper drivers"—began returning for refresher courses prior to purchasing an automobile. No one knows exactly how many drivers this represents, but some believe it could apply to tens of thousands of people in Tokyo, not to mention residents of other Japanese cities.

The same phenomenon is playing out around the world as urbanites, fearful of using public transportation, are resorting to driving. How fearful? According to a Google Mobility Report in March and April of 2020, use of public transportation declined by a staggering 97 percent in cities like Chicago and San Francisco.[32] An interesting finding within the report stated that the heaviest hit form of transportation was commuter rail, which also happens to skew toward wealthier commuters whose white-collar work is more portable. Bus ridership, on the other hand, held more stable in cities like Washington and Los Angeles, remaining at about two-thirds capacity. The difference is a result of the fact that those commuting by bus tend to come from lower-income households. In other words, those with the means to afford a choice of transportation clearly exercised it.

It seems logical to assume, therefore, that a combination of working from home and individual forms of transportation may rewrite the ritual of the morning commute. This would reverse a decades-long trend in the United States that has seen steady declines in the number of drivers. The same phenomenon has played out in the United Kingdom, where the number of drivers began falling precipitously beginning in the 1990s.

Again, though, the transit systems we see today are, like most other things around us, systems of the industrial age, networks built on the assumption of an industrialized society where millions of people make a daily trek from their homes to work or school along defined routes. But as populations disperse, work and education become increasingly portable and digital, and people function without commuting as far or as frequently, opportunities to rethink transportation will open up as well. Could the days of packing into bacteria-laden subway cars, taxis, and trains be something we soon look back on with a sense of horror? Joel Kotkin, for one, believes so.

Kotkin is a fellow at Chapman University and executive director of the Urban Reform Institute, a national think tank based in Houston. He points out:

> When cities were afflicted with pandemics in the early 20th century, society responded with de-densification. Manhattan went from a population of nearly 2.5 million in 1920 to 1.5 million in 1970. A similar process occurred in central London and Paris. As more people moved to the periphery, cities got safer and more sanitary.[33]

Riders adapt to a socially distanced commute on a Paris subway train during COVID 19

Kotkin too sees a suburban renaissance as a means of better distributing jobs, wealth, and affordable housing opportunities. He's quick, however, to point out that any rethink of the suburbs would also have to "be designed for lower emissions, more home-based work, and shorter commutes." Such a reimagining would almost certainly require new forms of low-cost, personal transportation that could include the advent of autonomous vehicles traveling on specially designed roadways.

In the interim, however, it's more likely that we'll see an emphasis placed on what urban planners call "active transportation" such as walking, riding bicycles, or using scooters. During the COVID-19 pandemic, as cities locked down around the world, air quality experienced a dramatic improvement—an improvement that many major cities are seeking to retain at least somewhat in a post-pandemic return to operation. Already, cities like Milan, as just one example, are undergoing a significant overhaul as city officials seek to maintain the lower levels of automobile usage seen during the pandemic. Part of this involves converting approximately twenty-two miles of city streets to walkable or rideable spaces.[34] Similar rethinks are occurring in other major cities like New York.

What does this mean for retail? Consider the degree to which retail, as we know it today, has conformed to and built itself around transit and commuter routes. Restaurants, fuel stations, convenience stores, and more have all been positioned at great cost to intercept the daily flow of commuters on their way from A to B.

Entire advertising and media ecosystems have been built around the strategy of reaching customers on their commute. Case in point: from the second quarter of 2019 to the same period in 2020, National Public Radio lost a full quarter of its listeners due to the drop in those who listened while commuting to and from work.[35] Now, pan out and extrapolate that across all the other forms of media that have been tied to that same daily migration: the billboards, transit ads, and sea of digital screens, all aiming to capitalize on a ritual trek to work and capture our attention.

Already, we're seeing the front end of a commuter rethink. A study by KPMG suggests that teleworking will reduce commuting by car in the United States by 10 to 20 percent.[36] Another recent Canadian survey found similar evidence, with 25 percent fewer Canadians expecting to commute to work, by any means, post-pandemic.[37] If you're a business that depends on that daily surge of traffic, a quarter of your potential market is now staying home each day and may continue to do so.

But the impact on transportation is hardly restricted to terrestrial modes. Just look up.

AIR TRAVEL

In 2019, I took over 150 flights to various places around the world. In the past four years alone, I've flown almost 1 million miles and have the gray hair to prove it. The work I do and the associated travel necessary to do it seemed an inseparable hand-in-glove relationship. Travel was so primary to who I was and what I did that in 2019, I couldn't have imagined performing my work without sitting on planes.

As I write this in the midst of the pandemic, I find it difficult to imagine sitting comfortably on any flight, regardless of seating class or flight duration. The things I used to force myself to look past—the crowding, the lineups, the lack of cleanliness on aircraft—all now seem somehow more sinister and potentially deadly. And I'm not alone.

"This crisis could have a very long shadow. Passengers are telling us that it will take time before they return to their old travel habits. Many airlines are not planning for demand to return to 2019 levels until 2023 or 2024."[38]

That was the lead-in to the presentation of an industry survey delivered by Alexandre de Juniac, director-general of the International Air Transport Association. The June of 2020 study of forty-seven hundred recent travelers found that 83 percent of them were "somewhat" or "very concerned" about contracting the virus, and 65 percent were concerned about sitting next to someone who was infected. But here's the kicker: of those surveyed, 54 percent said they had no intention of resuming travel for at least six months. Almost 20 percent suggested at least a year, up from 11 percent only two months earlier.

It all raises the important question about the future of air travel and the retail that depends on it.

AIR TRAVEL IS BUSINESS TRAVEL

According to Certify, a business report software company, approximately 445 million business trips take place on airlines each year. The Global Business Travel Association estimates the total cost of travel and meetings to be approximately $345 billion.[39]

While business travelers account for only 12 percent of all travel, they also happen to drive 75 percent of profitability for the airline industry. In the face of the pandemic, business travel all but ceased. The question on the minds of many, including both travelers and airlines, is: Will it come back, when, and to what level?

Chip Rogers, president and CEO of the American Hotel & Lodging Association, believes that by May of 2021 business travel could rebound by as much as 70 percent of pre-pandemic levels.[40] Even if this is true, the first problem is that the airline industry, like many other industries, cannot profitably function at 70 percent of normal volume without major cost cutting. The second, more pressing issue is that Rogers's view doesn't square with business traveler sentiment.

COVID-19 meant new protocols, protections, and anxiety for airline passengers

In a recent survey, the International Air Transport Association found that a full 66 percent of respondents said that they will, in fact, travel less for business. The same percentage believed they would also travel less for leisure.

While the promise of vaccines on the horizon will undoubtedly provide some relief to the industry, I wouldn't be putting my money on robust levels (much less pre-pandemic levels) of air travel anytime soon.

The other unknown is prices. Will we pay more for a seat on a plane in a post-pandemic world? It seems so.

According to Airbus's airline data subsidiary Skytra, by May of 2020 the average fare for a flight between Europe and Asia-Pacific (APAC) had risen by an astounding 34 percent.[41]

As a consequence, the longer the crisis goes on, the more likely business travelers, and the companies they work for, are to seek out safe alternatives to travel. One of which, of course, is videoconferencing.

Not only has videoconferencing proven to be a viable alternative to in-person meetings, but many executives have begun to view the technology as a superior means of communicating. Some point to the fact that unlike in-person meetings—often filled with distractions, like people checking their phones—videoconferencing demands a more focused level of attention and efficiency. Others point to the obvious and substantial savings on business travel. The CEO of International Flavors and Fragrances, for example, told *The Wall Street Journal* last year that the company was "planning for a permanent 30 percent to 50 percent reduction in business travel for his company because he says remote work has proven effective."[42]

Others, meanwhile, point to the limitations of videoconferencing. As someone whose stock-in-trade involves presenting to business audiences, I can say from firsthand experience that Zoom, although perfect in the midst of a pandemic, is hardly perfect. It has limitations, not the least of which is the inability to share dynamic media formats and the impossibility of reading the room, as you might when physically present.

That said, we also have to appreciate that most of these videoconferencing technologies are only in their infancy and are bound to experience massive improvements as we move forward. Think back to the embarrassingly large mobile phones of the 1980s. Today, we carry supercomputers in our pockets. Where there's a market, there's investment in it and technological progress. So to assume that videoconferencing even two years from now will be largely the same as it is today, with the same limitations, is improbable at best if history is any guide.

If the majority of travel is corporate travel and companies engage in a total rethink around travel efficiency and cost, and vacation travelers—still bearing the psychological scars brought by images of ICU patients suffering from COVID-19—become more discerning about where and how often they travel, how will it all impact retail?

In 2018, we at Retail Prophet engaged in a project with a Paris-based company that bought, refurbished, and managed international airports. Our remit was to completely reimagine the retailscape inside Charles de Gaulle and Orly airports. What you learn very quickly on a project like this one is that airport retail lives and dies by two things: luxury brands and duty free.

For many luxury brands, airport retail has been one of the brightest spots in the market over the last decade. According to one recent study performed prior to the pandemic, the global travel retail market was "expected to reach $153.7 billion by 2025, registering a CAGR of 9.6% during the forecast period."[43]

This was a massive year-over-year increase in a world where the broader global retail sector was growing at about 5 percent. Much of that growth was being driven by the golden child of airport retail: duty free. As one report points out, global duty-free sales at airports rose almost 9.5 percent in 2018 to $76 billion.[44]

The sinister mix of higher prices with what are quite likely to be far more arduous air travel conditions, combined with cuts to business and leisure travel, and complemented by innovations in meeting and conference technologies, all means that airport retail may take years to reach the heyday of pre-pandemic conditions. Until that time, luxury brands lose an important jewel in their crown.

EXPERIENCES

"There is nothing like the energy and atmosphere of live music," says Dave Grohl, front man for the Foo Fighters and former Nirvana drummer. "It is the most life-affirming experience, to see your favorite performer onstage, in the flesh, rather than as a one-dimensional image [...] Even our most beloved superheroes become human in person."[45] Who could disagree with this impassioned exaltation of the live concert experience? Who hasn't experienced at least one live event—concert, speech, sports competition—that sent shivers down their spine?

As a speaker, I know firsthand the indescribable feeling of a room of a thousand or more people all sharing a moment, an idea, a laugh. It is electric and unlike anything else.

COVID-19 shut the gate on such experiences. Stadiums, concert halls, movie theaters, hotel ballrooms, and film sets around the world sat empty, relics of a more carefree time.

But then, something else happened. We got wildly fucking creative.

Music events like the One World Together at Home event, produced by Global Citizen in partnership with the World Health Organization and sponsored by Pepsi, brought musicians together to support COVID-19 response and frontline workers. It streamed to an audience of 20 million people and raised close to $130 million. The lineup was a mythic pantheon of stars that included the likes of The Rolling Stones, Billie Eilish, Lizzo, Jennifer Lopez, Keith Urban, Elton John, Stevie Wonder, Shawn Mendes, Camila Cabello, Lady Gaga, Paul McCartney, John Legend, Sam Smith, Celine Dion, and Andrea Bocelli. Getting all these artists into the same stadium for a live event would be next to impossible and astonishingly expensive. The combination of streaming and pre-recorded video allowed artists on opposite sides of the planet to perform together.

Are experiences like live concerts ever likely to be disrupted by live streaming? Some are betting heavily that they will.

Take Canadian company Side Door, for example, which matches up music artists with unique venues for their concerts. Initially in the business of live, in-person concerts, the company quickly pivoted, becoming a platform for artists to easily put together online, ticketed concerts from wherever they may be at the time. "Right away we knew there was something there, so we started to make the formal changes to the platform," said founder Laura Simpson. "What we found in our transition was that we can absolutely stick to our values and our mission to serve artists and create shows anytime, anywhere and move everything online."[46]

Simpson is not alone in her outlook. Mark Lowenstein founded StageIt, a company that has been livestreaming concerts since 2011. "We're [...] going to realize this is not just a form of crisis communication this is absolutely a valid and incredible way to connect with fans on an ongoing basis and something they're going to do more often," Lowenstein remarked.[47]

But concerts weren't the only experiences in our lives to undergo a rethink.

NIGHTCLUBS
Virtual nightclubs sprang up during the pandemic, and yes, people paid to be there. According to *Fortune*, "At a Zoom party called Club

Quarantee, all the usual trappings of a bottle-service club remain—except for the buckets of Champagne. Guests purchase tickets for $10, or can pay $80 for a private room to party alongside Instagram-famous DJs and burlesque dancers."[48]

Club Quarantee is only one of a growing number of nightclubs that are using business tools like Zoom to power online clubbing experiences.

Min-Liang Tan is the co-founder of Razer, a leading gaming hardware manufacturer and e-sports sponsor. Through the pandemic, Tan's company has been working with Singaporean nightclub Zouk Group and a live-streaming partner to host virtual rave parties. The events even allow the audience to chat and interact with DJs. "I believe that after this outbreak, behaviour will change dramatically," said Tan. "So…when clubs [for example] go back to normal, they're not just gonna have the offline clubs, they will continue with streaming."[49]

If Tan is right, the question becomes one of revenue. Are people willing to pay for the virtual version of a live event? If Chinese shoppers are any guide, the answer is a resounding yes. In February of 2020, roughly 2.3 million people tuned into a live stream at Club SIR.TEEN, a Beijing nightclub. Dozens of other clubs in China report raking in millions of yuan hosting what are now being called "cloud raves."[50]

For the nightclub industry, to invoke the immortal words of Prince, it may have taken a pandemic beginning in 2020 for us to finally "party like it's 1999."

ART GALLERIES

In the dining room of my home hangs a wonderful contemporary painting from a talented artist named Brendon McNaughton. Like most artists, McNaughton traditionally relied on presenting his work at live exhibitions.

Today, in addition to creating his own work, McNaughton also founded and manages Art Gate VR, a company that offers art lovers and collectors the ability to experience a variety of full art exhibitions, events, and artist Q&As from the virus-free comfort of your

Using virtual avatars, Art Gate VR allows users to experience and buy from virtual galleries featuring artists from around the globe

own sofa. Using Oculus virtual reality headsets, buyers from around the world can visit, view, and purchase art in an immersive and interactive way. They can speak with artists or gallery owners directly and enjoy curated tours, moving through gallery spaces in a natural and intuitive way. It's an idea that promises to reshape not only the art gallery experience but also the economics of the fine art industry.

In a virtual world, artists can potentially exhibit the same original works in multiple galleries at once. The expense of travel and exhibition setup is spared. And art buyers can now forego the expense of traveling to visit exhibits. Put simply, an artist can expand their audience and lower their cost of exhibition while buyers can expand their exposure to exhibits and save on travel.

The point again is that COVID-19 uncovered a market for new and creative forms of both digital and physical events. While it may be some time before they replace the sounds, smells, and physicality of real-world events, they offer a viable option and potentially new revenue models that enable experiential producers to reach vastly larger audiences.

THE EXPERIENTIAL TRADE-OFF

These kinds of digital alternatives are unlikely to completely supplant their in-person alternatives, at least in the short term. But they do provide experiential options and new business models we've never before enjoyed. And frankly, these sorts of digital trade-offs are not unusual. As customers, we make these sorts of bargains all the time. When streaming music first made its debut, some people were quick to point out its inferior quality relative to either CD or vinyl recording formats. And the naysayers were technically correct. But they neglected to consider a few important things. First, streaming music wasn't just a technological shift; it was an entirely new business model. Now instead of owning entire albums at great cost, music lovers could simply stream unlimited, individual songs for a set monthly fee. Second, the vast trove of music available and the convenience with which it could be enjoyed far outweighed any shortcomings in sound fidelity. Last, the critics discounted the significant and rapid technological improvements that streaming music would undergo. In other words, streaming music didn't need to replicate the fidelity of vinyl or CD to practically wipe out both formats. It was a combination of technology that was good enough for most and a business model that was, for consumers at least, much better.

Similarly, it's logical to expect that the enhanced access, convenience, and potentially lower cost of live-streamed events—from musicians, actors, artists, and even subject-matter people like me—will be an attractive option for many.

This shift in the nature of experiential events is also an opportunity to change the economics of distribution. In 2019, I had to forgo at least a dozen different events due to scheduling conflicts. Most of these conflicts occurred because it would have been impossible for me to get from one place to another in time for the event. During COVID-19, however, multiple events could be livestreamed in completely different time zones in a single day.

The point is not that live streaming, or any other technology, will replace completely the excitement of a live event, but it will definitely have an impact by giving customers a choice. We'll begin to ask ourselves: Do I really need to go to this stadium, store, arena, or nightclub, or should I just catch the live stream? The result will be a world where the effort, cost, and time required to experience *anything* in real life will carry with it higher expectations of value. Was all the time, effort, and expense worth it?

This is particularly important for retailers because, if we're being completely honest, in all but a negligible percentage of cases, retail hasn't made shopping worth our while as consumers. Shopping experiences are often fraught with friction, disappointment, and frustration. In the industrial era of retail, you could get away with it. Consumers had no choice. But those days are gone. Shoppers with new expectations will spend their time and money with retailers that offer clear and distinct value. Retailers that cannot offer this will receive a one-way ticket to obscurity.

EXODUS

All of this—the flight to online, the disassembling of modern life, the portability of work and education, and the reimagining of experiences—is leading us out of the industrial world and firmly across the threshold into the post-digital era. COVID-19 is not merely an acceleration of the future. It's a once-in-a-century wormhole—a wrinkle in time—that will alter the future completely. As we speed across the threshold of this new era, we are leaving behind many of the legacy brands and retailers that paved the way here. They are now footnotes in history as the victims of a Darwinian extinction event. Those brands that survive will have to completely rethink their traditional marketing approaches and selling tactics and adapt to entirely new consumer behavioral patterns. What we find when we do eventually reach the other side of this crisis will not be a retail reality that was merely accelerated by COVID-19. Rather, we'll find an industry and consumers reshaped by it—forever.

3

THE RISE OF
RETAIL'S APEX
PREDATORS

Evolution is the fundamental idea in all of life science.
Bill Nye

Films about the future often present the world that awaits us as a dark dystopia dominated by a handful of malevolent mega-corporations, pervasively controlling much of human life on Earth. *RoboCop*'s Omni Consumer Products, *Alien*'s Weyland-Yutani, or *Bladerunner*'s Tyrell Corporation are only a few examples of such futuristic corporations, operating with the impunity of global super-powers in a world into which they've become inextricably woven. In a post-pandemic retail landscape, as we rocket across the digital divide, such corporations will no longer reside solely in novels or films. They will be a reality.

For retailers, COVID-19 was the commercial equivalent of a meteor impact—a once-in-a-century existential event that has changed the chemical composition of the industry's atmosphere. The result will be a complete eradication of many retail species and frantic efforts at adaptation by others. But from this post-COVID cosmic soup of crisis a new class of predator will emerge, an entirely new and genetically mutated species of retailer that faces no natural enemies or external threats. In nature, they're referred to as "apex predators." In retail, they're called Amazon, Alibaba, JD.com, and Walmart.

As a group, their annual revenues amount to approximately $1 trillion. Their collective active customer counts reach into the billions. They know no geographic, temporal, or categorical boundaries. Minor fluctuations in their share prices on any given day can equal or exceed the market value of major corporations.

While fatal for so many retailers, COVID-19 has been and will continue to be an intravenous drip of metabolic steroids for the apex retailers. As a species, they will all emerge from this crisis bigger, stronger, and with more power than ever before. While some retailers swooned under declines of up to 80 percent in their revenues, these giants posted results deserving of a double take.

Yet as dumbfounding as their growth was, the pandemic will only make them larger. Much larger.

Company	Full-Year 2019 ($billions)	Year-on-Year Growth %
Amazon	280.5	20
Alibaba	72	35
JD.com	83	23.38
Walmart	524	1.9

Full-Year 2019 Revenue Growth for Amazon, Alibaba, JD.com, and Walmart

Company	Percent Year-over-Year Increase
Amazon	26.4
Alibaba	22
JD.com	20.7
Walmart	74*/10†

*Online sales only
†Total sales

Percent Year-on-Year Growth Q1 2020

AMAZON

On February 4, 2020, Amazon joined an elite list of companies: the trillion-dollar club.[1] Amazon, now the largest retail company by market capitalization in the world, having closed that trading day with twelve zeroes in its valuation, stood shoulder to shoulder with a pantheon of other trillion-dollar companies that includes Apple, Microsoft, and Alphabet (the parent company of Google).

Once exclusive to Amazon stores, Amazon's Go technology is now being offered to other retailers, showing the degree to which Amazon is not merely a retailer but also a technology company

In the early stages of the COVID-19 lockdowns around the world, *The Guardian* reported that Amazon customers were spending "$11,000 (£8,845) a second on its products and services."[2] That's just shy of $1 billion per day. In fact, during the first quarter of 2020, Amazon's sales grew by $75 billion.[3] In other words, Amazon's quarterly *increase* in sales fell just short of Target Corporation's full-year revenues for 2019.[4] Let that sink in for a minute.

While most businesses were interrupted by COVID-19, it simply became rocket fuel for Amazon, who had already clocked in a spectacular 2019. In that year, according to *The Economist*, "the company delivered 3.5bn (billion) packages, one for every two human beings on Earth. Amazon Web Services (AWS), its cloud-computing division, enables more than 100m people to make Zoom calls during the day and a similar number to watch Netflix at night. In all, Amazon generated $280bn in revenues."[5]

Heading into the pandemic, Amazon was capturing approximately ¢50 on every dollar spent online in the United States.[6] Almost

70 percent of online searches for products take place on Amazon, and that's when users don't know what they're looking for. When they do know what they want, almost 80 percent of shoppers begin the journey on Amazon. If that weren't enough, more than 150 million of us belong to its Amazon Prime membership program.[7] Prime is not only commercial flypaper for customers, making Amazon's entire platform sticky with benefits and value, including quick shipping, as well as streaming video and music. Prime members also happen to spend 250 percent more than non-Prime shoppers.[8] Prime is also the core of Amazon's data trove, giving it minute-to-minute insight into customer needs and behaviors. "More people start their product search on Amazon in Japan than anywhere else," says James Peters, who heads up the company's fashion business in Japan. "In doing that, they're giving us great data on what they want."[9]

In other words, the Amazon search bar is not simply a means of navigating customers to what Amazon sells. It's a market research tool that informs Amazon in real time of what it should consider selling.

Frankly, once you stop regarding Amazon as a retailer and begin viewing it as a data, technology, and innovation company, many of its seemingly obscure strategic moves begin to make perfect sense. Take its 2017 acquisition of Whole Foods for example. At the time of the purchase, many in the industry wondered what the end game was. Why was Amazon so intent on staking its claim in the grocery sector, a category that historically throws off a 1 percent net profit margin? (You read that right. One percent.)[10]

The answer, in my opinion, resides not in the value of groceries but in the value of the data grocery sales generate. To appreciate what I mean, try this the next time you find yourself in a grocery store. Look at the shopping carts of the people in line with you. See what insights you can glean from the items inside them. Can you tell if they have pets? Children? Are they health conscious? Do they enjoy cooking or prefer pre-prepared items? Are they brand name shoppers or more inclined to store brands? I suspect you'll find all these sorts of insights and more. In fact, perhaps no other category of merchandise reveals so much personal and household data as the grocery sector. The value of such data to a company like Amazon is worth far more than the paltry profit from peddling milk and eggs. And that's precisely what makes Amazon so dangerous to grocery competitors.

How big is Amazon? As author Scott Galloway puts it,

> when their stock goes down 7 percent, that's like losing the value of Boeing. That's where Amazon is right now; it gains or loses the value of Boeing in a single trading day. So when you're talking about a company that's quote-unquote too big, just remember, it can shed or gain Boeing in a trading day.[11]

Similarly, Amazon can merely cast a longing gaze at a category that it doesn't currently play in and in doing so cause a decline in the market values of incumbent players in the category. In 2017, for example, Amazon announced a foray into appliance sales, wiping $12.5 billion from the market capitalizations of Home Depot, Lowe's, Best Buy, and Whirlpool. In a single day!

And if all this weren't significant enough to prove Amazon's dominance, a 2019 study by Feedvisor of two thousand U.S. adults found that 89 percent said they were more likely to buy products from Amazon than other e-commerce sites. Among Prime members that figure rose to 96 percent.[12]

This is not to suggest that Amazon is bulletproof. It isn't. The company has struggled against a reputation for offering a brutal executive working environment and even worse conditions for its warehouse employees. It's also had a sketchy track record for using vendor data to undermine its own marketplace suppliers, in some instances going as far as knocking off competitive products entirely, while undercutting on price and boosting Amazon's own product in Amazon's search results.

Despite these challenges, however, on July 20, 2020, when the vast majority of us worried about illness, job security, and social unrest, Jeff Bezos added $13 billion to his personal net worth, a net worth now equal to the annual GDP of New Zealand. By August of 2020, the company's market capitalization had grown to just shy of $1.7 trillion—a 70 percent growth in value, in only seven months.

While the gale force winds of the pandemic battered the retail industry at large, those same winds filled the sails of Amazon, powering it toward its goal of becoming what journalist and author Brad Stone called The Everything Store.

ALIBABA GROUP

On Singles Day, China's annual shopping event, in 2020 Alibaba processed a gross merchandise sales value of $74 billion. To appreciate the magnitude of that figure, consider that it is roughly equivalent to what the entire nation of Germany spent online in all of 2018.

COVID-19 was a boon for Alibaba, with the company posting a 35 percent sales lift in the year to March 31, 2020, achieving its five-year goal of hitting $1 trillion in gross merchandise volume (the total value of products sold on its marketplaces).[13] For the sake of perspective, that's about 30 percent more than the annual GDP of Saudi Arabia.[14] By the second quarter of 2020, the company's revenue had leapt by 34 percent, its stock price ballooned by 80 percent, and its market valuation stretched to $800 billion. With almost 800 million active customers on its platform, Alibaba's metrics begin to look less like a typical company and more like a sovereign state with its own population and economy.

Alibaba can best be understood as almost a mirror image of Amazon. For example, Amazon currently derives the majority of its income from its cloud computing service (AWS). That is not to suggest that Amazon doesn't make money on retail sales; it does. In fact, over the last two to three years, Amazon's vast product marketplace has been generating a greater share of the company's profit. That said, AWS still represents the lion's share. Alibaba, on the other hand, generates significant profit from its marketplaces, with operating margins stretching into the high teens compared with Amazon's low single digits.[15] This occurs for two reasons. First, unlike Amazon, which owns, stocks, and ships much of its own product assortment, Alibaba has its marketplaces run entirely on a third-party basis. Alibaba doesn't hold inventory or operate its own logistics. Instead, it provides a software platform to its third-party merchant partners to allow them to self-manage logistics through an integrated system.

Second, Alibaba is not a one-size-fits-all marketplace, meaning it doesn't have one platform aimed at satisfying all customers. In fact, the company has five principal platforms:

➤ **Alibaba:** This is a business-to-business platform that connects manufacturers from a variety of countries to global buyers.

➤ **Taobao:** Chinese for "searching for treasures," Taobao is a business-to-consumer and consumer-to-consumer platform, more similar in design to Amazon and eBay. It also happens to be China's largest online shopping destination, with more than 2 billion product and service listings. From consumer goods to food and even travel arrangements, almost everything can be acquired through Taobao. Beyond the products themselves, Taobao is also a discovery engine, enabling brands and key opinion leaders to stream live shoppable content to users. Furthermore, tools such as augmented reality are baked into the platform and available to all merchants. According to Alibaba, Taobao users spend up to thirty minutes per day on the platform. Taobao is a fee-free platform, meaning neither the buyer nor the seller pays a transaction fee. Instead, revenues are generated through advertising from brands seeking to boost their ranking and profile on the site.

➤ **AliExpress:** Recognizing the opportunity to develop a two-lane international highway of e-commerce, Alibaba launched AliExpress in 2010. The site was originally dedicated to making small and medium-sized Chinese domestic merchants accessible to customers outside China. The platform has now been expanded to allow international

On November 11, 2020, Alibaba achieved a record $74.1 billion in sales during its Singles Day shopping event

merchants to connect with customers outside their home markets. A strategy that's clearly working. For example, Ali-Express is now the most popular e-commerce site in Russia.

➤ **Tmall:** Tmall is a business-to-consumer destination for authentic, well-known branded products—a necessity in a market so rife, as China has been, with counterfeit goods. Thus, Tmall has become an essential conduit for Western brands to reach the massive Chinese market, with over 500 million active users.

➤ **Tmall Luxury Pavilion:** This is a by-invitation-only site for both brands and consumers. Alibaba has grown its luxury offering to include more than 150 luxury labels, including haute luxe labels like Louis Vuitton, Chanel, and Gucci. In its first year of operation, Luxury Pavilion customers spent an average of $159,000 each on the site.[16]

Part of Tmall's success is attributable to its disregard for channels and its focus instead on seeing the consumer's journey as a chain of moments across digital and physical formats. Moments that, as Christina Fontana, fashion and luxury director for Europe at Tmall, described to me, can be connected and interwoven.

By illustration, she points to a fashion brand on Alibaba's Tmall platform that was attempting to determine the best location for a new store. "They wanted to test different areas in Beijing, so they built a physical pop-up store. It was beautiful. We made it all 3D and put it online," Fontana says. "They wanted to understand if they had the right traffic in that neighborhood to support a full-fledged flagship store in that location." So using data from both the brand and Alibaba, the brand identified specific key customers who were interacting with the online media surrounding the pop-up. It then used that connection to invite them to the grand opening of the pop-up—an event that was then broadcast out to millions more shoppers online.

In essence, what Fontana describes is an ability to leverage specific customer data to identify high-value shoppers, bring them to a location for a specific event, and then use the same platform to stream that event as a media experience out to millions more customers. Online interactions with that media then once again provide robust data back to Alibaba and its brand partner. It becomes a circular ecosystem of media, entertainment, customer interaction, data, and insights.

STORES AS AN INTERFACE

Perhaps most counterintuitive about Alibaba, one of the world's largest online retailers, is its clear belief that physical stores are an integral aspect of that "digital transformation." The company operates two principal chains of physical retail stores: Freshippo (originally called Hema) grocery stores and Intime Department Stores, the latter of which it acquired in 2017.

Alibaba now operates about two hundred Freshippo stores across multiple formats according to the needs of the local market. Those formats include Freshippo Pick'n Go, a grab-and-go, prepared-food concept, often positioned along subway commuter routes. Orders can be placed using the Freshippo app and then simply retrieved from digital warming lockers by using your mobile device. Freshippo also offers several other formats:

> Freshippo F2 is a food hall concept. Aimed at younger professionals, these concepts are usually located in high-traffic business centers in cities like Shanghai.

> Freshippo Farmers Market is a modernized version of a fresh produce market where customers can buy in bulk, and it offers thirty-minute delivery locally. The concept is aimed more toward price-sensitive shoppers living on the outskirts of top-tier cities like Beijing.

> Freshippo Mini, essentially a smaller, neighborhood-based version of the full-line Freshippo store, is mostly found in lower-tier markets in China.

> Freshippo Station offers online ordering of produce for urban residents with hyper-local delivery services of up to approximately half a mile.

All stores in the Freshippo chain integrate completely with the company's mobile app. Shoppers can gather information in-store, order products for delivery, make restaurant reservations, and pay.

While Western retailers wring their hands and speculate about the death of the shopping mall, Alibaba is redesigning malls for the digital age in what it calls its Freshippo mall concept. The first, located in Shenzhen, includes roughly sixty tenants, with clothing shops, restaurants, drug stores, grocers, beauty parlors, and recreational facilities for children—all connected through the Freshippo app, which offers shoppers digital discovery tools, mobile checkout, and one-hour delivery for shoppers within a radius of approximately two miles.

In 2017, Alibaba upped its ante on physical retail, with its majority position in China's Intime Department Stores, a chain of approximately sixty stores across thirty-three Chinese cities. Intime CEO Xiaodong Chen shared with me that the early stages of Intime's adoption of Alibaba's operating strategy meant ensuring that everything became connected. Products in store had to be scannable. All systems on both the front and back end of the operation had to be integrated and merged.

According to Chen, customers can shop at Intime in a variety of ways. Some may choose to shop at their local Intime store using the Intime app. If they need assistance, they can connect directly in the moment with an Intime sales associate. Others may choose to shop in-store, but rather than be burdened with shopping bags, they can simply add items to an online cart, once again using the app. Their order can then be paid for and all items delivered to the shopper's home in as little as two hours.

"Before in the traditional retail business, we only broadcasted to our customer in a one-way system, from the store to the customer," says Chen. "But, in a New Retail model, we can have the two-way communication, between a store and our customer."

When you speak to Alibaba executives, what is both inspiring and somewhat disarming is the degree to which they see the world through the lens of opportunity. They are largely unhindered by legacy systems or antiquated paradigms. The brand and its platforms, technologies, and ecosystems are as malleable as warm clay, ready to be molded into any shape necessary to delight shoppers. All of these moments, systems, technologies, and selling opportunities fit within the specific framework of what has been dubbed New Retail.

NEW RETAIL

Mentions of the term "New Retail"—a term coined in 2016 by Alibaba Chairman Jack Ma—generally elicit head nodding and knowing expressions from Western retail executives. "New Retail! Gotcha! You bet!"

In truth, however, many don't understand precisely what New Retail is but are reluctant to admit it. Worse perhaps is that they assume that it simply refers to being "omnichannel" in strategy and execution. I'll be the first to admit that the differences between the concepts of omnichannel and New Retail are nuanced, but it's in those nuances that the differences become profound. And conflating the two concepts is a road to disaster, according to author and advisor Michael Zakkour.

I met Zakkour in the spring of 2018 while speaking at a conference in San Diego on the future of retail. He told me that his area of focus was China and its role in e-commerce. In fact, he had written a book on the subject and was working on another about the Chinese "New Retail" model and why what was going on in China was critical for Western brands to understand.

It was abundantly clear from our short interaction that day that he was someone who clearly knew his stuff. Indeed, Zakkour spent almost ten years with Tompkins International heading up its China and APAC digital and customer practice and its digital transformation practice for clients across geographies. He now heads his own company, 5 New Digital, helping companies import and incorporate the principles of New Retail.

We stayed in touch, and when Zakkour's new book, *New Retail: Born in China Going Global*, hit the market in July of 2019, he sent me a copy. Since then, I've interviewed him more than once on the subject.

Prior to the pandemic, says Zakkour, Western brands had less interest in what was happening in the Asian market. Ever since the pandemic hit, however, and Western brands witnessed firsthand the speed with which Chinese retail was able to bounce back, his phone hasn't stopped ringing.

So why were Chinese retailers vastly more capable of serving customers during the pandemic than were their Western counterparts? The reason is simple, according to Zakkour: "Because grocery retail was used as the tip of the spear for everything they were doing in e-commerce." If this sounds oddly similar to Amazon's foray into grocery, it's no accident. More on that shortly.

WHAT IS NEW RETAIL?

"We are moving from a world of channels and e-commerce to a world of ecosystems and habitats," says Zakkour. These ecosystems and habitats are the product of a complete rethink of how retailers and customers interact. The best way to understand the difference, he says, is to appreciate that in an omnichannel world, the company puts *itself* at the center of the equation and offers the customer *channels* through which to engage. Omnichannel simply implies a stitching together of those channels to be more congruent, consistent, and seamless. The problem, however, is that the company is still at the center of the equation.

New Retail, however, puts the *customer* at the center of an *ecosystem* that is completely integrated across formats, experiences, and platforms. The ecosystem itself is essentially a bubble of experiences or habitats that customers can engage in, from shopping and entertainment to social networking and payments. Once customers are in the ecosystem, the emphasis is on providing convenience and customization (informed by data) and allowing for a contribution or interaction from customers; feedback loops allow customers to communicate vital information back to the brand, which can then be plowed back into its value proposition to add even more value for customers.

The Alibaba ecosystem, for example, contains several "habitats," as Zakkour calls them: Taobao, Tmall, Tmall Luxury Pavilion, Ant Group (the company's financial arm), and many others. Customers can act from within any of these habitats and glide easily from one to the next via technology. In fact, he says, New Retail brands don't even think in channels. Instead, according to Zakkour, the ecosystem builders are saying, "We are building a vast array of habitats inside of this single ecosystem that are completely connected through software, promotions, technology, data science, and we don't care where the customer enters that ecosystem on their journey. There's a hundred on-ramps and a hundred off-ramps inside there."

Alibaba is the best example, says Zakkour, because they've built the most robust system in the world. "When you look at Tmall, and

Tmall Global and Taobao, Freshippo, and Intime stores," he says, "all of those are absolutely, 100 percent connected to their data science system." A system, he points out, that gives Alibaba more than fifty listening points, including physical stores, that feed real-time data about its customers back to Alibaba. "It's this completely immersive, almost bubble-like cocoon that their customers rely on as their operating systems for life."

Understanding New Retail begins with understanding its key structural aspects and the "new power sources," as Zakkour puts it, that energize it. Once a brand activates these power sources, New Retail becomes possible, and the brand graduates to a "Unified Commerce" model, he says:

➤ **New Commerce** accounts for the multitude of ways that customers may be engaging both with brands and with other customers online. These could include online to offline and vice versa, business to consumer, consumer to consumer, and business to business.

➤ **New Media and Entertainment** incorporates the many ways that customers can be engaged, including streaming experiences, augmented or virtual reality, real-world events, gaming, or social shopping.

➤ **New Logistics and Supply Chain** leverages advanced technology and logistics systems to deliver goods rapidly through the supply chain and across the last mile of delivery. It uses data to inform all decisions and stakeholders across the value chain.

➤ **New Digital, Finance, and IT** offers systems, platforms, and services to assist both customers and vendors to support, finance, and inform their operations.

So what does this all look like when it's put together? A great example can be found in Alibaba's creation and promotion of a Chinese movie called *Eternal Love*, which began as a series on Alibaba's video-hosting service, Youku. It was a hit, and owing to its success, in 2017 it was made into a movie and renamed *Once Upon A Time*. The production was financed using Alibaba's crowdfunding arm, Yulebao. It was then marketed to moviegoers using the company's Taopiaopiao ticketing app. Finally, it drove sales of more than RMB300 million (about $44 million) of merchandise on Tmall.[17] This use of an entertainment ecosystem to drive commerce is a core aspect of how Alibaba engages its customers, not simply with advertising but with interactive, shareable, and shoppable media experiences.

It's also worth pointing out that if I had written this book less than a decade ago, I would have been telling you that Asian retailers were largely tracking innovations in the West and migrating them East. Well, the winds of change have shifted, and it appears it is now Amazon, Walmart, and other Western retailers that are adopting the New Retail model. Indeed, Amazon's most recent foray into selling luxury products takes a page directly out of Tmall Luxury Pavilion's playbook.

As Zakkour sees it, the strategic options available to all other brands when attempting to compete with brands like Alibaba will be narrow indeed. "They'll have to plug into one or more of these ecosystems," he says. "They'll have to leverage the tools, infrastructure, and access to customers these mega-marketplaces offer." Beyond that, he says, "they'll have to create a mini-ecosystem of their own."

JD.COM

Pandemics kill businesses. They also give birth to them. Jingdong, or JD.com as it's now known, is one such business. Founded in 1998 by Richard Liu, the company began life as a small electronics retailer with a forty-five-square-foot physical store in Beijing's technology district. It wasn't until the SARS outbreak of 2003 that Liu recognized the opportunity to sell his products via the Internet, at which point he closed his physical location and by 2004 had converted the business to become an online pure-play retailer.

The use of robotics, like this autonomous delivery vehicle, has made JD.com one of the world's preeminent delivery companies

Growth was rapid, and by 2007, the company had built a sophisticated and integrated supply chain, allowing it to control each element of product distribution down the last mile of delivery. A year later, the company began to broaden its assortment to include general merchandise. By 2010, JD had launched its online marketplace platform, enabling an exponential increase in the number of products offered in its marketplace.

The game changer came in 2014 when the company formed a partnership with Tencent. Often referred to as China's Facebook, Tencent not only took an 18 percent share in JD but also provided its new partner with exclusive access to its WeChat platform—essentially a digital Swiss Army knife that allows users to do everything from messaging and ride hailing to social networking and commerce, in addition to hosting myriad third-party apps. The deal gave JD access to more than 1 billion WeChat users.

Tencent wasn't JD's only suitor. Walmart had its own designs involving JD.com. In June of 2016, Walmart essentially waved the white flag on its failed e-commerce venture in China and instead sold its online retail business to JD in exchange for a 5.8 percent stake in the company. In October of the same year, that interest was increased to 10.8 percent.

Between 2015 and 2018, JD.com grew at a whopping average rate, on a constant currency basis, of 41.5 percent.[18] Today, the company holds about a 30 percent share of e-commerce in China, second only to Alibaba, which holds around 50 percent.[19]

Unlike Alibaba, which owns no warehouses, JD.com operates what may indeed be China's (and perhaps the world's) most expansive and effective logistics network. In fact, many have questioned how it is that the brand is able to serve almost the entirety of China, an enormous country, with same-day delivery. The answer, as it turns out, is 2.7.

Why 2.7, you ask? Well, the company discovered through research that whenever shopper clicks on a certain item surged above the norm in a given market area, a corresponding echo of orders for that product in that market would follow, like clockwork. Moreover, these orders, on average, tended to occur within 2.7 days of the click surge. The company also noticed that those order volumes usually amounted to about 10 percent of the incremental volume of clicks. In other words, if there was an incremental increase of one thousand clicks over the mean for a certain item, one hundred incremental units of that item would be ordered precisely 2.7 days later. The 2.7-day time frame, JD.com determined, was the average amount of time necessary for the customer to weigh their alternatives or do more research.

In response, the company redesigned its logistics systems to monitor click surges. When surges are recorded, orders are triggered, and during the 2.7 days between click and buy, the goods are moved into the market(s) where the clicks came from, closer to the shoppers who will ultimately buy them. Assuming the math holds, which it seems to, every customer who elects to order that item can then receive it with same-day shipping.

Deep data science and logistics work like this have galvanized JD's reputation as one of the preeminent logistics companies on the planet.

WALMART

In the late spring of 2015, I was invited to Walmart headquarters in Bentonville, Arkansas, to deliver two presentations to the company's global executive teams. It was that same year, in fact, that Amazon surpassed Walmart in market value for the first time. This milestone had clearly sent reverberations of worry through the company's ranks. Sales levels were also setting off alarm bells. Indeed, 2015 would mark the first year since going public that Walmart would post a sales decline. It was an Earth-shattering reality for a company accustomed to nothing but growth.

My message to the teams that day was urgent and, as usual, unvarnished. I told them that Walmart had missed an important and potentially fatal curve in the evolution of its business: while the company could have and should have been investing in its digital capabilities and the creation of an online marketplace, it had instead invested in building out its supercenter format. Had Walmart made such investments in online, I told them, Amazon would have remained a river in South America and not become the company that was now kicking Walmart's ass.

I went on to share my view that if Walmart didn't embark on an immediate and significant course correction to design better in-store experiences augmented by a best-in-class digital commerce platform, it would likely be torn limb from limb by Amazon. Like it or not, I told the executives, their customers were moving on into the digital world, and Walmart could either lead or lose them altogether. Basically, the message that day in Bentonville was change or die.

It was only after my presentations to these groups that I would learn two things from people on the inside. First, a culture war was raging within Walmart between the old and new guard. Some company veterans believed strongly that the ship that got Walmart to where it was would also be the vessel to carry them home, and that ship was massive supercenter stores. In their mind, the answer was not to depart from the format but rather to double down on it. The new contingent of executives, on the other hand, believed just the

Since 2015, Walmart has built out its e-commerce capabilities to become a force in the industry

opposite. Digital sales, they felt, would be their salvation, and they wanted to see massive investments made in an effort to build a new ship that could carry them into the future.

Whether by virtue of my message that day or other influences, a turnaround ensued. Walmart clearly woke up to the reality that it was fast becoming an anachronism in a retail market that was innovating at warp factor ten. And with that, the company went on a tear.

In 2016, Walmart acquired e-commerce retailer Jet.com, in a $3.3-billion transaction that would bring with it Marc Lore, Jet's founder, to help integrate Jet's capabilities into the Walmart framework.

By 2017, the term "turnaround" had begun to appear more frequently in media reports about the company. One news report declared:

> If there were any doubts about the success of Wal-Mart's […] turnaround efforts, the retail giant just laid them to rest. At its investor day conference on Tuesday [October 10, 2017], the company issued its annual guidance for the coming year and called for 5% growth in adjusted earnings per share in fiscal 2019, which would be its first year of earnings growth in four years.[20]

In the three years following the Jet.com acquisition, Walmart's share value increased by 53 percent compared with a 38 percent rise of the S&P 500.[21]

That said, like many other retailers, Walmart has also experienced firsthand the challenges of turning e-commerce revenue gains into black ink on the bottom line. In 2019, the company reportedly lost $1 billion on $21 million in e-commerce sales.[22] That fact might seem shocking, but I would look at it in context. Prior to the pandemic, Walmart represented less than 5 percent of the U.S. e-commerce market. While that represents a huge achievement for a brand that only four years earlier didn't even have an e-commerce game worth talking about, it's still a far cry from the nearly 50 percent of U.S. e-commerce that Amazon takes. And given that, to a large extent, profitability in e-commerce is a matter of spreading the significant fixed costs of e-commerce systems and delivery infrastructure over volume of purchases, it's reasonable to assume that with further growth on its topline, profitability will follow at some point. Indeed, that point may be now.

In the first quarter of 2020, the company saw its digital sales rise an astonishing 74 percent compared with the same period a year earlier.[23] Full-year estimates of the company's e-commerce gains range as high as 44 percent, which would bring Walmart's topline digital sales to $41 billion, overtaking eBay for the number two position behind Amazon.[24]

After the company was declared an "essential" retailer during the entirety of the pandemic, Walmart's in-store sales gains too were quite extraordinary, with Q1 2020 sales showing 10 percent comparative growth.

Walmart, the company that only five years earlier was staring into the abyss, was now entering an entirely new and jaw-dropping phase of its evolution.

4

BIGGER PREY

Confidence is like a dragon where, for every
head cut off, two more heads grow back.
Criss Jami

Evolution, however, is a double-edged sword. While the view from atop the food chain is worth the climb, the effort to remain there will force these apex predators to find new and more nutritious food sources. With investors on one side pushing to keep the gravy train rolling and a retail industry on the other side that is rapidly improving its capabilities, these behemoths will need new means of sustaining their dominance and the gains their investors will surely demand.

While each has room to grow within the confines of its existing business model, as well as through emerging platforms, programs, and market entries, none of these models will offer the sort of caloric intake the behemoths require to further their growth.

What lies ahead for these apex predator brands will make their innovations and growth to this point pale in comparison.

THE DISPOSABLE WORKFORCE

In May of 2020, Amazon founder Jeff Bezos made a stunning declaration. The company would, he said, be investing approximately $4 billion worth of capital to "vaccinate" its supply chain amid the COVID-19 pandemic.[1] Bezos laid out a vision for this that included everything from infrared cameras to detect feverish workers to personal protective equipment and widely available testing. Some hailed this ambition as visionary, game changing, and bold.

But things are not always as clear as they might seem, and I believe this is precisely one such instance. I say that because only a month earlier, Amazon had a problem by the name of Christian Smalls. Smalls was an Amazon warehouse worker in the Staten Island, New York, facility. Upset with what he saw as significant health risks and safety concerns in the facility, Smalls organized a worker walkout to protest the conditions and to appeal for better safety protections, a move that got Smalls terminated from the company. When a short time later it was revealed that executives— including company lawyers and Bezos himself—had strategized to discredit Smalls by questioning his intellect and articulateness, other warehouse and corporate staff began to raise concerns. This led to the dismissal of three more employees, one from a warehouse and two corporate staffers.

I wrote about this story a short time after. That's when a representative of Amazon reached out to note that, in their words, the company terminated Smalls "for endangering others by violating social distancing guidelines."[2]

I'll leave it to you to make up your own mind about the legitimacy of Small's dismissal. But what we do know is that the Christian Smalls incident was by no means the first case of questionable working conditions in Amazon warehouses. In fact, the company has a well-established reputation for maintaining what have been described as grueling work environments. In 2019, for example, during the company's hallowed annual event, Prime Day, warehouse workers in Minneapolis walked off the job to protest what they cited as inhumane work conditions. Meanwhile, Amazon has also developed a decades-long track record for aggressively staving off union activity in its operations.[3]

So when I hear Jeff Bezos talk about vaccinating his supply chain, I can't help assuming that what he really means—beyond providing protective equipment and infrared temperature monitoring—is eliminating the one thing that makes all supply chains vulnerable to inefficiency and disruption: human beings. Humans get sick. Humans make mistakes. Humans have families they wish to spend time with. And above all, humans expect to be treated humanely. These are fragilities and vulnerabilities that will impede these giant companies from maintaining the extraordinary increases in volume they are intent on.

In the 2017 movie *Blade Runner 2049*, the character of scientist Niander Wallace, portrayed by Jared Leto, says, "Every leap of civilization was built off the back of a disposable workforce."

Throughout time immemorial, human progress has been fueled by the blood, sweat, and tears of legions of expendable workers. The great pyramids of Egypt were built by masses of poor peasants. The towering skyscrapers of New York City were built by a steady stream of European immigrants, more than a dozen of whom died during the construction of the Empire State Building alone. Today, garment factory workers (mostly women) in Bangladesh earn as little as ¢33 per hour.[4] The expendable workforce has been a dark cornerstone of capitalism from its inception.

The retail sector is no different. For the past forty years, the world's retail stores have depended on an expendable workforce—many of whom possess high school educations and are woefully underpaid, vulnerable, and often tasked with thankless and even dangerous work. Women in particular are overrepresented in low-paying retail roles and underrepresented in managerial and executive positions.

For most of that time, customers were content to turn a blind eye to the plight of retail workers, but COVID-19 changed attitudes. The uncomfortable reality that society's lowest-paid workers were risking their lives and those of their families to pick our groceries, pack our online orders, and keep *us* safe while shopping—all the while teetering on the poverty line themselves—brought the conditions these workers face into sharp relief.

In response, some retailers hailed their frontline workers as "heroes" and instituted pay increases, acknowledging the degree to which their ability to function depended on these people showing up each day. But as the heat of public and labor union scrutiny subsided, many of these same retailers quietly rescinded additional hourly wages while posting unprecedented revenue and profit gains. Nothing says "Thanks for keeping us from bankruptcy" like a rescinded hazard-pay increase. It led one representative from the United Food & Commercial Workers union to say, "as long as we are wearing gloves, as long as we are wearing masks and social distancing, it seems obvious to me that we are working in hazardous circumstances. [...] It is manifestly unfair to eliminate the hazard pay at this point."[5]

The blowback from consumers and governments alike was immediate and harsh, with offending companies taking a flogging in the court of public opinion. An April of 2020 study by Morning Consult confirmed why. Against the backdrop of the pandemic, 90 percent of consumers said it is important to them that brands treat their employees well, surprisingly ranking it on par in importance with having products in stock. Close to 50 percent said they consider how companies treat their employees as one of their top five purchasing considerations.[6]

So COVID-19 has pushed retailers to a precipice regarding their treatment of people. Either pay their workers a living wage or find a new "disposable workforce."

That new workforce will be composed of robots.

In truth, retailers and robots have had an on-again, off-again love affair. Some of this has purely been a consequence of cost. Until quite recently, the cost-to-benefit ratio of robots in the retail environment has been questionable. Robots have traditionally been expensive pieces of technology with a limited scope of capabilities.

The other, and perhaps more immediate, obstacle has been that of public perception. Robots are a clear threat to human employment. For example, a 2017 Pew Research study found that 73 percent of Americans were either somewhat worried or very worried about the notion that robots and computers could be capable of taking over jobs being done by humans.[7] Additionally, the majority of those surveyed believed negative outcomes such as economic inequality would become worse in a world where robots displace human workers. Thus, retailers have been reluctant to engage in widespread public testing of robots for fear of backlash from their own staff and customers alike.

Despite these challenges, the pre-pandemic market for robots in the retail sector was rapidly growing. Estimates of market size have been rising. Consulting firm Roland Berger, for example, estimates that the global market for retail robots will grow to a value of $52 billion by 2025,[8] representing a compounded annual growth rate of almost 11 percent.

Post-pandemic, it's a market that has been kicked into overdrive. In fact, a 2020 World Economic Forum study found that four out of five executives were "accelerating plans to digitise work and deploy new technologies," undoing employment gains made since the financial crisis of 2008–9. The report went on to suggest that as many as many as 85 million jobs will be vaporized at small to medium-sized companies and replaced with technology by 2025.[9]

Advances in artificial intelligence, gains in computing power, and reductions in cost have all been factors influencing the rise. For example, in 2019 Walmart began testing a robotic grocery order picking system in its Salem, New Hampshire, supercenter. The system, called Alphabot, can pick and pack eight hundred products per hour,[10] ten times the productivity rate of a human being. Moreover, the entire process takes place in the back, in the warehouse area of the store, thereby eliminating any crowding or disruption on the sales floor.

Additionally, Walmart has already deployed more than fifteen hundred robots in its largest stores. Many of the most mundane tasks, from robotic floor cleaners to inventory scanners, are now being offloaded to a workforce that never asks for a raise, never gets sick, and never stops working. Warehouses are equipped with cameras; artificial intelligence and fast unloaders that unpack and sort orders are becoming the norm. For staff working alongside this new workforce, it's difficult at times to know who's working for who. As *The Washington Post* notes,

> That has added a layer of discomfort to a job some workers said already could feel demeaning. Quitting or getting fired, some joked, is like getting "promoted to customer." Now they find themselves in the uneasy position of not only training their possible replacements but also tending to them every time something goes wrong.[11]

It's also no secret that Amazon has operated with two primary challenges: first, pumping merchandise in and out of its distribution centers at ever-escalating rates; and second, delivering merchandise, which is perhaps the single biggest drain on profitability that Amazon faces.

As *Fortune* editor and author Brian Dumaine puts it,

> Bezos sees a future where packages will be delivered by self-driving vans, small bots rolling through neighborhoods and drones buzzing to their destinations. And they will be unstoppable because robots don't catch the flu. When that day comes—and Bezos is betting billions that it will—one could imagine our robotic brethren bringing everything from Beyond Meat to oat milk to millions of quarantined souls. While helping the afflicted is a noble cause, that's not why Bezos is embracing this technology. The challenge for Amazon and all other grocers is that delivering food and other goods is costing the company a fortune.[12]

The term "fortune" is no exaggeration. In 2018, for example, Amazon spent almost $27 billion to ship orders to its customers.[13] About 40 percent of that cost is attributable to the wages of the delivery drivers. That makes drivers a target. In 2020, Amazon made clear its intention to attack the issue, acquiring self-driving transport company Zoox for $1.3 billion[14] and revealing plans for an autonomous taxi company. There can be little doubt that such a venture will also include the advent of autonomous delivery vehicles that will dramatically reduce Amazon's last-mile expense.

If anything, the pandemic provided the perfect rationale for these companies to forge deeper into robotics and other autonomous technologies. For example, in February of 2020, while the virus raged in Wuhan, JD.com began making deliveries to hospitals using what it calls Level 4 autonomous delivery robots. The Level 4 designation denotes a high level of sophistication whereby no human intervention is needed to operate the robot—provided it's being operated within a specific and geofenced area.

This is hardly JD's first signal of its desire to incorporate autonomous vehicles. According to one report, Neelix Technologies, a Chinese self-driving vehicle manufacturer, produced an autonomous delivery vehicle to be used on the practically vacant roads in China during the quarantine. The report went on to say that "leading online retailers Alibaba and JD.com [...] have ordered about 200 of the tiny robotic vehicles."[15] But such innovation in driverless delivery isn't limited to China. Waymo, an Alphabet company, already has a fleet of 13 self-driving transport trucks that it's currently road testing on interstate highway systems in Texas.

Nowhere will the use of robotics be more prevalent than in the grocery sector. In pre-pandemic America, for example, a mere 3 percent of grocery spending was transacted online.[16] During the pandemic, however, that number rose to 15 percent, with pre-pandemic estimates pointing to 20 percent of grocery sales being online by 2025.[17] That estimate now looks light given the exponential acceleration of customers buying groceries online. By June, for example, online grocery shopping in the United States had ascended to six times that of pre-pandemic levels.[18]

Therefore, it's reasonable to assume that maintaining such an exceptional increase in sales and delivery volumes will require Amazon to employ equally exceptional measures and innovations when it comes to logistics and delivery.

To be fair, Amazon isn't the only apex predator that will seek to mitigate the vulnerability and inefficiency brought on by a human workforce. In order to maintain costs and ramp up productivity, all of them will have to find a means of taking humans out of the equation, wherever possible.

The financial upside for the apex predators is worth enduring a little public scorn. A 2018 study by McKinsey & Company suggests, for example, that autonomous deliveries to a customer's door alone will allow retailers to slash shipping costs by between 10 and 40 percent in cities.[19] For Amazon alone, this would produce a potential savings in excess of $10 billion a year.

The robotic workforce is not science fiction; it's science fact. We are embarking on a new era where, for the first time in history, the disposable workforce will no longer be composed of human beings. Whether that's a good thing or not remains to be seen.

THE NEW DIGITAL FRONTIER

This might come as a surprise, but Amazon actually *lost* market share in the e-commerce market during the pandemic. The reason for that is simple. Other retailers finally began putting their online games together. In a remarkably short time, businesses everywhere finally got the memo. If you can't sell fluidly online, you can't sell. Period. And with that, the industry as a whole accelerated its online selling and fulfillment capabilities, closing the gap with Amazon substantially.

The problem is that what many retailers were catching up to is an e-commerce convention already twenty-five years old. Amazon, Alibaba, JD.com, and Walmart—all are operating their business using an e-commerce format that is more than a quarter century old.

So just as each of these brands has, in its own way, reinvented the modern concept of retailing, look for them to do it again by reinventing how we shop online. Within a decade, the systems and interfaces we use to shop online today will seem as outmoded and nostalgic as a Sears catalogue.

GOODBYE TO THE GRID

In 2018, I was contacted by a venture capital fund to see if I had an interest in speaking with the founder of one of their start-ups. These sorts of calls from venture capitalists aren't uncommon and are often just a means of pressure testing the concept by putting the founder in front of industry people to gauge reaction, gather information, and ultimately bridge introductions to potential customers. Often, they go nowhere, but for some reason, this one piqued my interest.

The company was called Obsess and claimed to be pioneering an entirely new online shopping experience. A few days later, I was on the phone with founder Neha Singh. A computer science graduate from MIT, Singh had spent five years working as a software engineer at Google. Despite her tech education and background, she confessed that she had always had a love of fashion design and so began studying in her spare time at the Fashion Institute of Technology in New York City. Singh's interests in technology and fashion converged when she took a role building a luxury e-commerce platform for a start-up in the fashion industry.

In a later interview I had with her, Singh shared that through this job experience, she came to a realization: "The e-commerce front end interface has really not changed. Amazon created this interface originally to sell books twenty-five years ago, and all the e-com platforms today, they have innovated so much on the back end, but the front end has pretty much stayed the same."[20]

The same standard grid interface, says Singh, was the starting point for almost every retail brand. Furthermore, for brands that wanted to break free of that mold, costs of development were usually steep.

These early observations were further confirmed when Singh took a role with Vogue and began working more closely with brands as Vogue launched its digital platforms. She was seeing firsthand how undifferentiated most brands were when it came to the experience on their websites or mobile apps.

Then, something happened that would change Singh's perspective and the course of her work moving forward. "I tried on a VR

An example of Obsess's virtual stores, which allow customers to navigate and discover products in a more natural and intuitive way

headset, at some point," she said, "one of the Oculus DK2s, the early versions and it was just like, 'This is how I would want to shop. Yeah, this is going to be the future.'"[21]

It was then that Singh began building that future with her company, Obsess. Obsess works with brands to build engaging and immersive online shopping experiences. Singh and her team are in the business of creating online environments that can take any imaginable shape or form, unlike conventional brand or marketplace websites, which tend to use a typical grid format. Using Obsess, customers can navigate these virtual spaces with their mobile devices as well as desktop browsers. Experiences may take the form of more conventional store environments or be entirely unconventional. One brand Obsess worked with created shopping experiences that took place in exotic environments: one on a distant planet, one in a desert, another in a futuristic city and even one that's completely underwater. The only limit, says Singh, is the client's imagination. She tells me that before the pandemic, she enjoyed early interest from brands like Tommy Hilfiger, Ulta Beauty, and Christian Dior, to name a few. Once the pandemic hit, however, her phone lit up and inbound inquiries increased by 300 percent over the same period in 2019.[22]

But does it work? According to Singh, early signs are affirmative, with brands seeing sizable increases in those most sacred of digital commerce metrics: session time, conversion rate, and average order value. All, according to Singh, are significantly higher.

Obsess and platforms like it offer several potential benefits. First, they add elements of discovery to online shopping that don't involve search terms and static product pages. Shoppers can literally move, so to speak, through the space, encountering products and media experiences along the way. Second, such platforms open up the possibility of shopping socially, with friends, for example, from within the same experience.

Singh brings up another interesting possibility. What if eventually, many of the actual "products" we buy are, themselves, virtual. If more of our work and social lives are being spent online, is it conceivable that we could begin buying virtual apparel or accessories, for example? Virtual Estée Lauder cosmetics, or virtual Chanel glasses, to go with your virtual Prada jacket? And instead of waiting for the doorbell to signal delivery, you just download your new products and wear them virtually!

So if we're crossing into a world where virtual products could replace real products, could online experiences ever begin to replace the social value and immersive nature of real-life experiences? In fact, could we prefer an online world free from friction, out-of-stock issues, service issues, and crowds? In other words, will virtual stores soon replace the need for real stores? From a distribution standpoint, undoubtedly. From an experiential point of view, nothing is out of the question.

What is perhaps most interesting is that when you review the list of venture funds that have put a stake in Obsess, you find Village Global, a fund that includes the likes of Bill Gates, Mark Zuckerberg, and, you guessed it, Jeff Bezos.

Speaking of Jeff Bezos, it would be naïve at best to assume that Amazon will just sit back and watch the entire global retail industry catch up. It won't. Just as twenty-five years ago, Amazon became the global reference point for the online shopping experience, I'm convinced that Bezos and team will see this moment as time to raise the bar once again.

SHOPPABLE MEDIA

Video and music platforms, as well as advertising media revenue, provide significant opportunities for continued growth and expansion for apex retailers. Media is a category that both Alibaba and Amazon have cultivated with success. In 2019, Alibaba funded the production of twenty-three films, which combined to represent 20 percent of China's total box office receipts that year.[23]

But the real strength of Alibaba's media arm is its skillful integration of media and commerce. In 2017, for example, in the leadup to China's Singles Day shopping holiday, the company launched See Now Buy Now, a live, shoppable fashion show, featuring an A list lineup of celebrities and a range of popular brands. It's this sort of acuity with technology and willingness to forge new experiences that makes Alibaba so appealing to global brands.

For its part, in 2018 Amazon drove $1.7 billion in revenue on its Amazon Prime Video platform. Only a year earlier, that figure was $700 million. Even before the pandemic, it was estimated that Amazon would grow revenue for Prime Video to $3.6 billion in 2020.[24] The lockdowns around the world only swelled that number with Amazon reporting that Q2 viewing had doubled compared with the prior year's quarter.

Amazon isn't just changing how we access entertainment; it's changing how we consume it. In the second quarter of 2020, the company launched what it calls a Watch Parties feature, which allows Amazon Prime members to chat with one another while watching Amazon's movie or TV programming. It also took a page out of Netflix's playbook, debuting Prime Video Profiles, giving Prime members the ability to manage up to six profiles in one account, with recommendations tailored to each individual user.

Finally, Amazon too is embarking on merging its media and commerce efforts. In 2020, for example, the company launched the series *Making the Cut*, hosted by Heidi Klum and Tim Gunn. The weekly reality-TV format follows twelve fashion designers vying for a shot at launching a global apparel brand and a cash prize of $1 million.

Immediately following each new episode, the featured designs are available for purchase on Amazon.

Not to be left out of the media game, in August of 2020 Walmart revealed its designs on acquiring a stake in TikTok, a short-form video app created by Chinese app developer ByteDance. Comprising over 800 million active monthly users, TikTok has proven a sticky platform, with a never-ending stream of shareable, user-generated content, and one that lends itself well to commerce. Moreover, TikTok's audience demographic breakdown shows that almost 90 percent of users are under the age of thirty-four. It's a marketing gold mine.

The deal, should it receive approval, would give Walmart a few things, including 7.5 percent of TikTok Global, as well as commercial agreements to provide e-commerce, fulfillment, payments, and other omnichannel services to TikTok Global.

Whether TikTok proves to be the boon that Walmart is hoping for remains to be seen. Social media platforms can be flashes in the proverbial pan. But the subtext is what really matters: Walmart clearly realizes that if it's going to run with the apex predators, entertainment and media channels will be essential.

GAMING THE SYSTEM

In September of 2020, during the height of the pandemic, luxury brand Burberry held a unique fashion show with forty thousand attendees. No masks, no hand sanitizer, no social distancing. How, you might ask?

The show was broadcast on Twitch, an Amazon-owned social gaming platform and e-sports destination. Burberry, which was the first luxury house to broadcast a virtual fashion show in 2010, also happened to be the first brand to broadcast a fashion show on Twitch. Using Twitch's unique Squad Stream functionality, the brand was able to stream multiple perspectives of the live show out to a global audience.

While that may be surprising, what is perhaps more surprising is that it's taken this long for brands to awaken to gaming platforms as a viable channel for commerce.

In 2017, Amazon began testing the platform as an e-commerce channel when it made video games available for purchase through the platform and incorporated Amazon Prime–like benefits for Twitch users. Today, the platform boasts approximately 140 million unique monthly users across more than 200 countries and territories. In all, it's estimated that there are almost 3 billion video game players worldwide, who as a group watched 2.72 billion hours of live-streamed content through the platform in the second quarter of 2019 alone.[25]

Today, most of what is bought and sold on gaming platforms consists of in-game, virtual goods—a new superpower, weapon, or character adornment of some kind. But the leap to real-world goods seems close. After all, games have all the right ingredients: a highly engaged, global audience using a platform that offers interaction, social discourse, robust processing power, and users with high-speed connections. Moreover, because Twitch allows for commentary between users, when something is happening, word can spread rapidly.

It's a future that companies like Scuti are rapidly helping to shape. The brainchild of veteran marketer Nicholas Longano, founder of Massive Incorporated (an in-game advertising platform sold in 2006 to Microsoft), Scuti allows game makers to add online stores directly to their games, creating a new G-commerce (gaming commerce) revenue stream. Players are incentivized to establish a shopper profile outlining their interests and then are presented with products that meet those parameters.

THE ZERO CLICK ECONOMY

We each have our passions and enjoy shopping for different things. For some people, it may be apparel, jewelry, or electronics. For others, it may be furniture, art, or automobiles. Yet there are also products we need that bring no such joy or interest. In fact, statistically, about 50 percent of the food and household items we purchase are not things we consciously shop for but items we simply and routinely replenish. We're not clamoring to visit our local grocery store to contemplate what kind of diapers, table salt, or garbage bags to buy.

We most often buy exactly what we bought last time, and in many cases, we buy these products at exactly the same time each week or month. Sure, we may enjoy going to the grocery store to personally select some items, but a twenty-pound bag of dog food isn't one of them. This is just one of hundreds, if not thousands, of purchases that represent drudgery in our lives.

It is this half of our routine consumption that apex predators like Amazon are coming for. The means by which they achieve this are already being established.

While the retail industry has been working to wrap its head around omnichannel, Amazon has instead focused on creating *omnipresence* in the lives of its customers. The company has now sold more than 100 million[26] of its Echo in-home assistants which leverage the company's Alexa Voice recognition technology—a platform that according to The Verge now boasts "more than 150 products with Alexa built in, more than 28,000 smart home devices that work with Alexa made by more than 4,500 different manufacturers, and over 70,000 Alexa skills."[27]

This habitual customer tendency is likely what propelled Amazon in 2014 to file a patent for a logistics system it called "anticipatory shipping." In theory, Amazon was proposing that at some future junction, it could begin shipping things to customers before they ordered them—perhaps even before they realized they needed them. This could be possible, according to the patent, through a sophisticated data analytics platform that would anticipate habitual customer purchase behavior and move products that were likely to be ordered closer to the consumer, similar to how JD.com has been anticipating demand on its platform. Such a system would allow Amazon to dramatically reduce shipping times from days to as little as hours, depending on the item and final destination.

Couple this with Amazon's Subscribe and Save program—a program offering auto-replenishment of items its customers use most—and it becomes clear that Amazon wants to lock down the 50 percent of our consumption that requires no consideration.

Meanwhile, Walmart appears to have other designs at getting even further into the lives and the homes of its customers. In 2017, the company filed a patent for the design of a store that is fully automated. What made the filing particularly unusual, however, is that Walmart proposed that these stores would be built directly into the customer's home! According to the patent, the step-in, pantry-like structure would allow customers to simply take what they like, have it billed to their account, and be replenished regularly by Walmart delivery teams. What's more, the system, enabled with artificial intelligence, would actually recommend unique products based on the customer's preferences.

For apex predators, every product ordered via subscription or auto-replenishment does two key things. It reduces logistics and shipping costs and provides one less reason for the customer to shop anywhere else.

BIGGER PREY

None of these opportunities, however, will offer enough nutritional value to sustain the kind of jaw-dropping gains the markets will have come to expect from these behemoths through the course of the pandemic. To fuel their continued growth, these apex predators will need to find entirely new food sources with higher caloric content—much higher than can be achieved by merely peddling more running shoes, electronics, and household items.

This news should be cause for worry among all businesses, but it should be particularly concerning for incumbent companies in sectors that have been ruled largely by gated oligopolies such as the banking, insurance, shipping, healthcare, and education sectors. Not only have these sectors been traditionally reluctant to self-disrupt, but COVID-19 has also now shone a bright light on their respective vulnerabilities. Vulnerabilities that have the apex predators circling them like fresh prey.

Growth Categories for Apex Predators

BANKING AND PAYMENTS

In 2018, I was invited to talk to an audience in the U.S. banking sector. The group was mostly made up of medium-sized, regional banks, although some of the audience members represented larger names in the industry as well. The organizers of the event expressed their desire to "shake the audience up a little." They really wanted to drive home the message of change. It seemed a worthy challenge, and frankly, bankers have scared me most of my life, so this was a shot at payback.

The day of the presentation, I actually started to get a little nervous over what I planned to do, but it was already baked into the presentation. No turning back. This would either work or crash and burn, and I was about to find out which. After getting on stage and doing the usual thank-yous, I started in.

"Fate has a funny way of working," I said. "I'm sure most of you have already seen the news today. A friend of mine in Europe just sent this to me."

With that, I clicked to my first slide. On it, I'd mocked up a fake CNN Breaking News headline. In the chyron, I'd typed the words "APPLE ANNOUNCES MOVE INTO BANKING."

"He also sent me this," I said, clicking to the next slide, which depicted a photoshopped *New York Times* article with a similar headline: APPLE TO OPEN BANKS. The accompanying article went on to say that the company, with cash holdings of over $60 billion, sees an opportunity to reinvent the banking experience.

In that moment, the room went silent. Some in the audience were smiling nervously. Some were madly texting their offices to let them know the purported news. Others were simply silent and somewhat ashen. The collective tension in the room was palpable.

I let it hang out there for a good five seconds before I let them in on the prank. "Of course, this is all fake news."

After a beat, some broke into laughter—the way you do when you just had the shit scared out of you but you're happy you survived to talk about it. Some leaned over to the person next to them with an "I told you so" sort of look. Some remained a little pale in complexion. But everyone was clearly relieved to know it was a ruse.

"How many of you actually thought that was, in fact, happening?" I asked. "How many actually thought Apple was opening a bank?" The majority of the hands in the room went up. Then I asked, "Honestly, how many of you, in that moment, felt your bank immediately becoming vulnerable?"

Again, most of the hands in the room went up. The honest hands, anyway.

The fact is the banking sector has been delivering below-grade customer experiences for decades. From exorbitant fees to reductions in human staffing to predatory lending practices, banks are the institutions customers love to hate. That's like ringing the dinner bell for apex predators. And it's apparent they've heard the call.

Six years ago, Alibaba's Ant Financial didn't exist. Today, its valuation of $150 billion exceeds that of Goldman Sachs. If Ant were stripped out of Alibaba, it would stand as one of the fifteen largest banks in the world. Ant also offers credit cards, credit scoring, loans, and wealth management. If that weren't impressive enough, the Ant Financial fund Yu'ebao is now the world's largest money-market fund at over $250 billion.

Alibaba is not the only apex predator venturing into the sector. By 2019, Amazon had built, bought, or borrowed at least sixteen different fintech products and platforms, stitching them together to fuel growth of its finance ecosystem. It has also been active in providing loans to its merchant partners, with over $1 billion in small-business loans to its third-party merchants processed in 2018 alone.[28] It has also been providing payment terms to customers—all in an effort to feed its own ecosystem. More merchants and more customers with more money to spend with more merchants. Rinse and repeat.

As banking publication *The Financial Brand* recently pointed out,

> What troubles most traditional banking execs is that at any point, Amazon might just decide to help those "merchants and customers around the world" by offering some sort of quasi-checking product. After all, the portion of Americans who belong to Amazon Prime—roughly half the entire adult population—is astounding. That is a huge potential customer base for any kind of financial service, should Amazon decide to offer it.[29]

Walmart too is inching its way closer to the payments sector. The company's MoneyCard program—a prepaid debit card program for unbanked or underbanked customers—is now the largest retailer-exclusive program of its kind in the United States. In addition, Walmart recently announced its controlling stake in a fintech accelerator called TailFin Labs. TailFin Labs will focus on forward-looking technologies in the space between e-commerce and financial services.

INSURANCE

If you live in New York or New Jersey, chances are you've heard of and maybe even shopped in a Century 21 department store. One of the original off-price department stores, the iconic, family-owned retailer was opened for business in 1961 by co-founders, and brothers, Al and Sonny Gindi. The name Century 21 was inspired, at the time, by the upcoming world's fair.

Eventually, leadership transferred to the respective sons of Al and Sonny, and the chain grew to incorporate thirteen stores across the Tri-State area and Florida. The company's flagship store, located at 22 Cortland Street in New York City, directly across from what were the Twin Towers of the World Trade Center, even survived the devastation of the 9/11 terrorist attacks.

It wasn't unusual to meet people from all over the world who had stories of shopping at Century 21. For many, the store was an essential stop on any pilgrimage to New York City. However, in the ensuing years, as the U.S. retail market fractured into luxury and discount offerings, the off-price market saw exponential growth and an array of new entrants. Everyone from Macy's and Nordstrom to Saks opened off-price banners, and TJX flooded the market with stores. Outlet malls grew like weeds, and fast fashion became the hallmark of a new generation of shoppers. Century 21 was now a shrinking presence in a market it once typified. And to top it off, even the name, once emblematic of a bright future, seemed anachronistic—not to mention the company was constantly being mistaken for being a real estate company.

In 2018, I joined a group of advisors who were brought in to help the company rethink, reinvent, and reposition its brand. Every aspect of the brand and its positioning went under the microscope. By 2019, the advisory board was disbanded, but I was asked to remain, working with the team to create a new banner, a new approach to market, and what we all felt could be a bright new beginning for the chain. By late that year, the company had already begun to roll out the new plan with some very encouraging results.

Yet on September 10, 2020, the company, which had survived sixty years of ups and downs, recessions, booms, and cataclysmic terrorist attacks, filed for bankruptcy. In a statement, co-CEO Raymond Gindi said:

> While insurance money helped us to rebuild after suffering the devastating impact of 9/11, we now have no viable alternative but to begin the closure of our beloved family business because our insurers, to whom we have paid significant premiums every year for protection against unforeseen circumstances like we are experiencing today, have turned their backs on us at this most critical time.[30]

Century 21 was closing its doors after almost sixty years because its insurer wouldn't honor the company's $175 million business interruption policy.

Century 21 wasn't alone. Over one thousand other retailers in the United States and the United Kingdom awakened to a similar fate, as insurance companies, en masse, rejected business interruption claims due to the pandemic. For some retailers, it may mean years of litigation. For Century 21, it was the end of the road and a sad finish for such a passionately run family business.

Gaps in coverage like this are made all the worse in the face of ever-escalating insurance premiums. CNBC recently reported that the rising insurance premiums are now outpacing increases in both inflation and incomes. The article goes on to say that over the past five years the average family coverage premium has gone up by 22 percent; over the last ten years, it has gone up by 54 percent.[31]

Incidents and trends like these, especially during times of enormous disruption, are precisely what make industries like the insurance sector vulnerable to disruption and defection by consumers seeking better and more convenient options. With apex predators on the hunt for new prey, the insurance industry is giving off a dangerously powerful scent—one the predators are already closely following.

Through Amazon Protect, the company is already extending insurance on consumer goods ranging from electronics to appliances. There's no reason to believe that as Amazon further expands the realm of its offerings into homes, luxury items, automobiles, and other major purchases that it will not also seek the insurance revenue that comes with them.

Indeed, it's already pursuing a more aggressive entry into insurance markets in places like India. In 2018, Amazon filed with India's Registrar of Companies, expressing the intention of selling its own package of insurance products. According to CB Insights, "In March 2019, Amazon received its corporate agent license from the Insurance Regulatory and Development Authority of India, clearing the way for the company to proceed further."[32]

Amazon isn't the only apex predator eyeing insurance. In 2018, JD.com received approval for a 30 percent investment in Allianz China, making it Allianz's second-largest shareholder. Only a year earlier, JD.com investor Tencent made a similar entry, buying a majority stake in Weimin Insurance Agency and receiving approval to sell insurance products over Tencent's digital network.

Should the industry be worried? Yes, according to Michael Aziz, chief distribution officer at Canada Protection Plan, a Canadian insurer, as he noted in the November 2018 issue of *Insurance Business Canada*:

> Will the Amazons and the Googles come? Yes, I believe at some point they will start looking at our industry a little closer. Can they offer insurance in seconds? I don't think the regulators are quite there yet, but they will get there at some point, which is why it's vitally important for insurance carriers across all sectors to emphasize insurtech and make sure they're ready for the next level of competition.[33]

The overwhelming gap in customer experience means that insurance companies are practically inviting that "next level of competition." What's more, companies like Amazon and Alibaba have shown a tremendous ability to identify, technologize, and solve key problems in verticals they come into as outsiders. This leaves insurers with a choice: fix their own issues or stand by as the apex predators fix them and, in the process, commandeer the industry.

SHIPPING AND DELIVERY

FedEx Chairman Fred Smith said during an interview in March of 2017 with *Fortune*,

> Well, let's make sure we understand the definitions: Amazon is a retailer, we're a transportation company. So what that means is we have a tremendous amount of upstream hubs, sortation facilities, flights, trucking routes, and so forth. Amazon is about you coming to their store [...] Amazon doesn't deliver many of their own packages at all.[34]

Suffice it to say, the interview hasn't aged well.

In the years that followed, as if to vex Smith personally, Amazon expanded its logistics footprint, enlarged its fleet of owned trucks and leased cargo jets, and grew its Amazon Flex delivery program— sort of an Uber for parcel delivery.

Little more than two years later, as it became apparent that Amazon was no longer a customer but a competitor, FedEx announced that it was ending its ground delivery deal with Amazon. What few realized at the time was that Amazon was already delivering 50 percent of its own parcels to customers.[35]

FedEx was already dead. The company just didn't realize it yet.

By late 2020, Amazon had announced its intention to open at least one thousand neighborhood delivery hubs across the United States.[36] The announcement came a month after reports that the company was engaged in talks aimed at a potential buyout of Sears and JCPenney stores with an eye to converting them to locally situated, last-mile logistics hubs. Such a move will put Amazon that much closer to once again raising the stakes in the delivery wars.

The company that made next-day shipping the price to play in retail may up the ante to same-day and even same-hour on some items.

I believe not only that Amazon will set a new benchmark for logistics and delivery but also that this area will become one of the company's next multi-billion-dollar business arms. Much as the company did with AWS, having built a best-in-class cloud storage system for its own purposes, Amazon will eventually offer the shipping service on a third-party basis to other (and even competing) retailers. In doing so, Amazon will not only subsidize its own shipping costs; it will rob incumbent shipping companies like FedEx and UPS of market share. If successful, Amazon will create yet another multi-billion-dollar revenue channel.

And once again, it will be JD.com's lead that Amazon is following. In 2018, JD announced that it was expanding its proprietary logistics and delivery system to offer parcel delivery services to business and residential customers in Beijing, Shanghai, and Guangzhou. It was the first of many steps, the company said, to eventually being capable of servicing all of China, thus putting it in direct competition with Chinese domestic shipping companies.

Meanwhile, Alibaba recently inked a deal with Chinese container shipping company Cosco (not to be confused with retailer Costco) to employ the group's block-chain system to root out inefficiency in the company's shipping activity. Cosco is the world's third-largest container shipping company.

It all points to yet another battle royale, this time between these apex predators and their incumbent transportation competitors. If history is any guide, transportation companies would be well advised to take the threat seriously.

HEALTHCARE

As with so many aspects of our lives during COVID-19, digital healthcare became a new reality for many of us. As *New York Times* writer Benjamin Mueller put it,

In a matter of days, a revolution in telemedicine has arrived at the doorsteps of primary care doctors in Europe and the United States. The virtual visits, at first a matter of safety, are now a centerpiece of family doctors' plans to treat the everyday illnesses and undetected problems that they warn could end up costing additional lives if people do not receive prompt care.[37]

The global healthcare market is estimated to be approximately $10 trillion and, according to Business Wire, is expected to grow at a compounded annual rate of almost of 9 percent.[38] In the United States alone, according to *Bloomberg*, healthcare spending amounts to close to $4 trillion, close to 20 percent of GDP, exceeding that of all other countries.[39]

It's fresh meat for hungry predators, and every one of them is on the scent.

In 2017, Amazon posted a number of internal job openings for a new team it called the "1492 squad"; the reference to 1492 relates to the company's exploratory efforts in finding ways to extract data from medical records. In addition, Amazon has invested in Grail, a start-up that uses technology to detect cancer in the bloodstream at its earliest and treatable stages. Amazon took a stake in the company's $914 million Series B investment round in early 2017. To top it off, Amazon poached healthcare and life sciences director Missy Krasner away from Box, a competing cloud storage company.

In December of 2019, Amazon launched a voice transcription service for medical practitioners that transcribes physician notes and prescriptions directly into patient health records.[40] In one of its most decisive moves, Amazon has also partnered with JPMorgan and Berkshire Hathaway to provide a new healthcare program for their combined 1.2 million employees.[41] The venture, now dubbed Haven, takes direct aim at many of the long-recognized deficiencies in the American health system such as soaring costs, onerous administration processes, and a bias toward treating illness, rather than promoting health.

If that weren't enough, Amazon's $1 billion acquisition of Pill-Pack has given it pharmacy licenses in fifty U.S. states. Amazon's massive and ongoing investment in the grocery sector provides a natural tie-in with health and wellness—and its physical locations like Whole Foods provide on-the-ground destinations for future medical clinics in high-income markets. The company claims to have made adaptations to its Alexa voice technology platform to allow participating healthcare companies to send and receive protected patient healthcare information. It's also deploying its Alexa voice technology for prescription management, reminders, and the like.

On July 14, 2020, Amazon embarked on yet another encroachment into the healthcare market. It announced that it was partnering with Crossover Health—a U.S.-based medical group that helps employers connect employees to care systems—to build a network of healthcare clinics for Amazon employees.[42] According to Amazon, the first of what it is calling its Neighborhood Health Centers will be established in the Dallas–Fort Worth market to accommodate over twenty thousand Amazon employees stationed there.

When Amazon invades a market, it often comes armed with technology. Healthcare is no different. In August of 2020, Amazon announced that it was venturing into the health tech market with a fitness band (think Fitbit but without a screen) and subscription service called Halo. The app not only offers the usual fitness applications found on other apps, but it can also create a 3D body scan showing body fat and monitor your voice to determine your emotional state—presumably as a means of measuring stress levels. That same month, Amazon India announced that it would be piloting an online pharmacy service in Bengaluru. The online pharmacy market in India is expected to nearly quadruple to $4.5 billion in 2021.[43]

And finally, in November of 2020, Amazon sent the stock prices of U.S. pharmacy chains CVS, Walgreens, and Rite Aid tumbling with the announcement that the company was launching a rival online pharmacy—one that would offer discounts and free two-day delivery for Prime members. After three years and nine significant chess moves into the healthcare space, Amazon was ready to put a beating on category incumbents.

Alibaba too has trained its gaze on the healthcare market. The company currently offers health insurance through Ant Financial. Immediately upon its introduction, the plan attracted 65 million users. The goal is to eventually attract 300 million people—just shy of the population of America—on one healthcare plan. This would make Ant Financial the largest insurance entity in the world.

The pandemic provided ideal conditions for a further push by Alibaba into healthcare. In August of 2020, according to news reports, the company announced that it planned to invest the $1.3 billion raised in a recent stock offering to expand its e-commerce pharmaceutical business, now powered by a new wave of growth due to COVID-19.[44] The company stated that most of these funds would be used to build out capabilities in pharmaceutical sales and delivery, with the balance put into building digital tools for healthcare partners participating in the service.

Not to be left out, Walmart is assisting with the kill. In June of 2020, Walmart announced that it was acquiring technology as well as intellectual property from CareZone, a start-up that focuses on helping people manage multiple medications.[45] The company's multipronged approach to both pharmacies and healthcare clinics makes it, in Morgan Stanley's estimation, "a sleeping giant to watch" in the healthcare sector.[46]

And finally, we have JD.com. The company's interest in healthcare stretches back to 2013 when it began selling pharmaceutical products online. In 2016, it launched JD Health, a business-to-consumer platform, using its vast and efficient logistics network to sell and deliver pharmaceuticals. A mere three years later, JD.com became the largest single retailer (online or offline) of pharmaceuticals in China, with a 15 percent market share. The company plans to use its unparalleled logistics network, which reaches 99 percent of all Chinese citizens, to expand its network of healthcare services.

EDUCATION

For reasons noted earlier, the global education market is yet another sitting duck for the apex predators.

The Chinese education market is estimated to be worth RMB453.8 billion ($65 billion) in 2020.[47] Tencent, China's primary social media platform and 18 percent owner of JD.com, is stepping up to take a share with what it calls "smart education," a complete educational platform for K–12, vocational schools, and ongoing education students, one that the company promotes as "a more fair, personalized and intelligent education."[48] With its over 1 billion active users, the sheer penetration of programs like smart education could be staggering.

Similarly, Alibaba has its own stake in the education market. It currently offers Banagbangda, meaning "help me answer," a homework helper app. In addition, Alibaba's Youku recently launched a video home-study platform. This, in combination with the company's DingTalk online collaboration tool, positions it to be a player in China's exploding education market.

If Amazon's playbook of domination in retail is any guide, my hunch is the company will seek to dominate at the commodity end of the education spectrum, and Amazon appears to have some of the working components already in place. It controls the world's largest marketplace of books, replete with its own publishing arm. It has a robust device ecosystem, allowing it to create education packages consisting of course materials, technology, and access to an interactive curriculum. Moreover, Amazon's clear interest in education as a category isn't a secret. There's an Education page on Amazon, listing a wide range of products and services to the education market. From curriculum and course materials to cloud services for educators, Amazon is setting itself up to be a virtual university with everything educators and students could need, including a bookstore.

Indeed, with the apex predators' entries, the education market could come to resemble the retail market, with a handful of luxury brands—the MITs, Stanfords, and Oxfords of the world—at the summit catering to the top 10 percent of society, and the commodity end dominated by massive global companies promising low-cost, frictionless access to basic education. As with retailers, those schools that find themselves caught in the middle—offering neither a prestigious academic brand nor the most convenient and economical education alternative—will be cooked.

In other words, there's a market for the education that Amazon and its fellow apex predators will offer, and it's absolutely astronomical.

BREAK THEM UP? YEAH, SURE

"I can't guarantee you that that policy has never been violated," said Jeff Bezos, beaming into the U.S. capitol building from his office in Seattle. He was referring to the company's purported prohibition of using third-party seller data to knock off merchant products under the Amazon brand. The question had been posed by U.S. Congresswoman Pramila Jayapal, whose district happens, as it turns out, to include Seattle.

Her prodding was part of a marathon congressional hearing in which tech titans Google, Facebook, Apple, and Amazon were peppered with questions from lawmakers surrounding ethical and competitive concerns with each of their companies. In response, Bezos pointed to an internal Amazon policy that, he maintained, prevents employees from looking at anything other than "aggregate data" on product categories before making decisions about which private-label products the company ought to produce.

For those of us who have made a living following Amazon's every move over almost three decades, the response bordered on absurd, and it seemed a clear attempt by Bezos to deflect questions surrounding Amazon's predatory use of its merchant data to calculate which Amazon-branded products to manufacture. The idea that Jeff Bezos didn't know for certain that the "policy" had been violated multiple times over years of practice seemed laughable.

Another congressional member eventually got Bezos to cop to the fact that the same Amazon policy *does* make it entirely permissible to review data from categories with possibly as few as two competitive offerings, even if one of those offerings holds the lion's share of sales in a particular category. For instance, a *Wall Street Journal* investigation found that in one case Amazon had used the data from two different sellers to inform the design of its trunk organizer product. The problem is that an astonishing 99.95 percent of sales in trunk organizer products were being generated by one brand, Fortem. Can you guess which product Amazon's trunk organizer ended up looking exactly like? If you said Fortem's, congratulations, you move on to our bonus round.

In fact, given Amazon's almost singular lock on product search data, you don't even have to be an Amazon merchant to get knocked off. Just ask Joey Zwillinger. Zwillinger is the co-founder of Allbirds, an Australian shoe company that was enjoying significant success with its unique brand of wool runners, selling them direct to its customers. In fact, Allbirds were selling so well that Amazon created an almost stitch-for-stitch knock-off of the shoe. Adding insult to injury, Amazon also undercut Allbirds by $35 a pair. "They know a lot about consumers and they obviously saw that a lot of people were searching for Allbirds," Zwillinger said in an interview. "It feels like they almost algorithmically inspired a shoe that looks very similar so they could capitalize on that demand."[49]

Other accusations during the hearings included reports of Amazon's Echo device being dumped in the market below cost to choke out competitors and the uncanny tendency for Alexa to defer to Amazon products when customers order on the voice platform.

The proceedings never even addressed meaningful questions surrounding reported cases of Amazon's working conditions and union busting. In fact, over the course of the three hours that Bezos took questions, he was often not able to provide definitive answers and frequently promised to follow up. Bezos concluded, "The retail market we participate in is extraordinarily large and competitive," addressing broader concerns about Amazon's power. "There is room in retail for multiple winners."[50]

With that, the session of finger wagging and lukewarm admonishment came to an anticlimactic end. It's unknown what action, if any, will eventually be taken—but I'm inclined to believe that anyone waiting for Amazon, or any other of these apex predators, to be significantly curtailed by government regulation will have to wait a while.

In the pre-pandemic world, public antitrust sentiment and regulatory investigations abounded. But the pandemic has made companies like Amazon into truly indispensable lifelines for their customers, their merchants, and ultimately their respective national economies. Given that political fire is usually a product of voter fuel, it's reasonable to assume that these companies will be treated with kid gloves, at least until the pandemic is well over. They will have become just too indispensable. Governments, many in chaos, as a consequence of the crisis and its fallout, have bigger fish to fry.

Besides, if politicians look at Amazon through squinted eyes, it doesn't look so bad.

In Ireland, the company has unveiled plans to invest in a 170,000-square-foot campus in Dublin to be used by AWS's cloud computing employees, which will number 5,000 over the next two years.[51] In Canada, Amazon will be bringing an additional 5,000 workers on board.[52] In the United Kingdom, the same scenario is playing out to the tune of 15,000 new Amazon jobs.[53] And the list goes on.

In total, according to a July of 2020 piece in *Variety*, Amazon had added 175,000 new jobs since March of that year and was working to make 125,000 of those into full-time positions. This comes as companies from United Airlines to Macy's are decimating their workforces, leaving tens of millions unemployed. So if you're a politician in any Western economy, is now the best time to go after Amazon, one of the most prolific job-creating engines in the marketplace—and that proved during the pandemic to be one of the few supply lines customers could depend on to get the things they need?

And so, again, COVID-19 is not merely an acceleration of things that might have happened eventually but rather a unique portal into an entirely different retail future. One that will pave the way for an inexorable penetration of these companies far deeper into the lives of global customers. Much the same way we forget how much we depend on electricity until there's a power outage, these retailers will become the essential utilities that power customers' lives. This will not only catapult their growth to new heights but also allow these mega-marketplaces to establish a secure foothold in new and far more profitable categories.

It is becoming increasingly easy to imagine a future state where Amazon is supplying not only most of the products you buy but also the insurance on your home and auto, your prescription drugs and physiotherapy, and your child's tutoring. We can easily conceive of a world where Alibaba is not only your online merchant of choice but also your bank and your local shopping center owner. A world where Walmart owns the space inside your refrigerator and also the social media network your teens spend hours on each day.

This possibility presents an existential threat, not just for many retailers but for anyone who sells anything to human beings on Earth. Having lodged themselves in so many aspects of customer life, these massive international marketplaces will construct a barbed wire fence of value and utility around their customers that could become almost impenetrable.

By helping to alter the genetic composition of the apex predators, the pandemic is putting them on a growth path that may seem inconceivable given their already-epic scale and revenues. But they will become larger yet—much larger. As the fallout from the crisis continues, we will find that these companies will not only vaporize almost all mid-tier retailers, chains, and department stores but that they will also have completely redefined selection, convenience, and price competitiveness, rendering many of today's commodity and convenience retail formats scorched earth.

The danger of course is this: once these apex predators move more of their diet over to these more lucrative categories, product margin in their marketplace revenues becomes significantly less important. In fact, taken to the extreme, they will be able to afford to run their

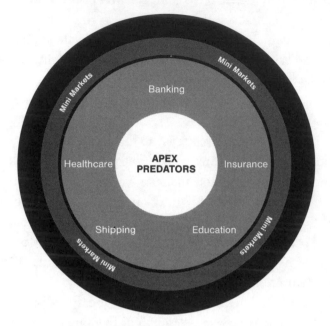

Apex Predators and Mini-Markets

marketplaces at a break-even point, using them purely as a means of acquiring new customers. Products will simply be the breadcrumbs used to attract legions of new customers, who then become entrenched in the life-encompassing ecosystems these companies have constructed. Once you're a bank, an insurance company, a healthcare provider, an educational institution, and a transportation company, you can practically give the products in your marketplace away.

If that weren't enough to lose sleep over, these apex predators pose yet another threat. As they build out their vast life ecosystems, they are giving rise to another species of retailer: the mini-marketplace.

In August of 2020, American grocer Kroger announced plans to launch a third-party marketplace with its e-commerce partner, Mirakl, a company that specializes in business-to-consumer and business-to-business e-marketplaces. According to Kroger, the marketplace will initially offer access to categories beyond grocery, including home, toys, and specialty products.

Eighteen months earlier, in February of 2019, Kroger's competitor Target made a similar announcement. The company intended to begin a small-scale experiment in building a third-party marketplace called Target+. On a by-invitation-only basis, merchants would be offered spots in the marketplace, beginning with 30 merchants selling 60,000 products. By February of 2020, Target+ had grown to include 109 merchants and 165,000 products.[54]

These are only two examples of a rapidly growing breed of retailers racing to open third-party marketplaces. The retailers have no inventory requirement or responsibility for logistics. They simply collect a fee or commission when sales in the marketplace are transacted.

There's good reason for the urgency. Companies like Amazon, Walmart, JD.com, and Alibaba have simply obliterated the traditional notion of selection. For example, Alibaba has millions of merchants selling through its platform. Amazon sells or represents more than 350 million products on its site! This makes these companies the go-to source for anything and everything shoppers might want. That makes other large retailers vulnerable to customer defection.

Thus, as they begin to feel more intense competition, we're likely to see more national big box chains adopting a third-party marketplace strategy to mitigate their vulnerability to the apex predators. This model will allow them to ramp up their offerings without tying up capital in inventory or engaging in laborious buying negotiations. One recent report by *Retail Week* pegs the percentage of retailers operating or exploring the creation of third-party marketplaces at 44 percent.[55]

Adrien Nussenbaum, Mirakl's co-founder and CEO, sees several advantages of operating third-party marketplaces over first-party e-commerce efforts. First, most retailers lack the capabilities to get products to a consumer's door efficiently enough to do so profitably. From a profitability standpoint, click-and-collect systems are superior but don't match the convenience of direct-to-home delivery. That said, retailers still have to offer selection and delivery of the products customers want. These two factors, when put together, support the development of retailer-hosted marketplaces, which Nussenbaum suggests not only fulfill the competitive need for selection but do so at net margins considerably higher than those of first-party e-commerce sales.

An April of 2020 *Forbes* article citing Nussenbaum indicates that the profits available to retailers via third-party marketplaces may even be superior to those attained through their own physical stores. According to Nussenbaum, "the average gross margin of [physical] stores hovers around 45% with net revenue between 2–4%." Most e-commerce channels, he says, have 10–15% lower profit margins than do stores. But third-party marketplaces "can usually sustain a 12–20% take rate (referral fee or commission on 3rd party sales), leaving a retailer with a 6–8% net profit margin." The bottom line, according to Nussenbaum, is that third-party marketplaces can be two to three times more profitable than physical stores.[56]

Beyond the commission fees marketplaces promise to retailers, they also offer retailers the ability to generate ad revenue, transaction fees, and subscription fees. The risk with third-party marketplaces, however, is obvious to anyone who's ever ordered from one. The experience can suck. Service levels can be hit-and-miss across merchants, and shipping speeds can be slow, especially relative to the benchmarks being set by Amazon and others. In other words, marketplaces, if not managed rigorously, can cause reputational damage to a retailer that far exceeds any financial upside.

But it's a risk large national merchants will take—because they have to. With Amazon growing its network of physical stores and formats and with Walmart growing its online offering and logistics capabilities, large U.S. nationals like Kroger and Target have no choice. If they do nothing, they will simply become more prey for the apex predators.

THE ULTIMATE CHOICE

So what does that all add up to? As society has made its way across the Rubicon of the industrial era, the retail industry too has crossed over into an entirely new era of business. It's an era that will be dominated by a small handful of apex predators—massive international marketplaces that control huge swaths of daily customer life and activity. Beyond offering access to hundreds of millions of products, these brands will increasingly push into the realm of unconventional products and services. In order to feed their insatiable appetite for growth, they'll attack vulnerable sectors such as banking, insurance, healthcare, education, and transportation, categories with underserved customers and overabundance of margin. They'll use their vast customer bases to digitize, contemporize, and rethink the customer experience in each of these verticals.

In turn, large brands like Target, Costco, Carrefour, and Tesco will face a constant battle with apex predators. They will differentiate themselves, while they still can, on the basis of convenience and locality and work to build out their own ecosystems to become smaller versions of their larger rivals by incorporating and expanding their third-party marketplace offerings. Some will grow and make the turn to becoming apex predators in their own right. Others will die trying. Either way, the level of market competition in the aftermath of the pandemic will be unlike anything we've seen in modern retail history.

And so, in a market occupied by a handful of apex retailers and a growing class of mini-predators, all other brands and retailers will have a choice: either become part of one, some, or all of these massive ecosystems—or go it alone and attempt to survive, if not thrive, in the shadows of giants. Both paths carry important risks and rewards.

The primary reward of simply appending to Amazon, Walmart, JD.com, or Alibaba is readily apparent: reach, volume, and infrastructure. Amazon's market share is astonishing. Walmart's store network coverage is enviable. Alibaba offers brands a robust technology and data highway that is out of the reach of most other companies, and JD's logistics and delivery prowess, coupled with its strategic partnership with Tencent, makes it a highly desirable host.

The risks of sleeping with these giants are murkier. First and foremost, brands lose complete ownership of their online presence. They are, as Shopify COO (now President) Harley Finkelstein puts it, "renting space on someone else's platform." Sure, some of these ecosystems provide more data and autonomy, but at the end of the day, it's still their house. You're just a tenant and you live by their house rules. Rules, by the way, that can change at any time.

Second, your sales data may be used against you or without your knowledge. Will your products be knocked off? Will customer relationships be misappropriated? And who really owns that customer anyway? All are reasonable concerns.

Even worse, you may be part of a system that is vulnerable to corruption. In September of 2020, for example, a federal indictment in the state of Washington cited six co-defendants in a scheme wherein bribes constituting over $100 million were proffered to Amazon employees in exchange for commercial benefits. Specifically, the indictment reads that the defendants paid $100,000 in bribes to Amazon employees, who in turn

> helped reinstate products and merchant accounts that Amazon had suspended or blocked entirely from doing business on the Amazon Marketplace [...] the fraudulently reinstated products included dietary supplements that had been suspended because of customer-safety complaints, household electronics that had been flagged as flammable, customer goods that had been flagged for intellectual-property violations, and other goods.[57]

Additionally, it alleges that Amazon insiders worked to suspend the accounts of merchants who represented competition to the defendants' business. According to Amazon, the incident was isolated, the company adding that it has systems in place to detect such fraudulent behavior. Whether that's actually the case or not is unknown, but this example highlights the degree to which relying on someone else's channel presents inherent risk.

The other option is to go it alone and create your own powerful brand gravity—to construct your own brand environments that customers can become part of and that keep you a safe distance from the apex predators. That is something much easier said than done.

My friend Joseph Pine, co-author of the groundbreaking book *The Experience Economy*, puts it like this. People want one of two things: time well saved or time well spent.[58] I think it's a great way to sum up consumer needs. But I would add to that a parallel sliding scale on which customers seek either money well saved or money well spent.

It's safe to assume that the apex predators and mini-marketplaces will out-compete in the time and money *well saved* department. All of them have spent the last two decades building value propositions based on having the vastest selections of products, the greatest convenience, and at least the perception of the lowest everyday price. The odds of your brand beating these apex predators on their own strategic battlefields are slim.

That leaves your brand with only one competitive angle: to ensure your consumer's time and money are *well spent*. By offering every customer time and money well spent, you will commandeer the most valuable, viable, and enduring position your brand can occupy.

The question is how.

5

THE ARCHETYPES OF THE NEW ERA

In spite of everything I shall rise again: I will
take up my pencil, which I have forsaken in my great
discouragement, and I will go on with my drawing.
Vincent Van Gogh

T he first and most important step in competing with apex predators is embracing the stone-cold reality that you can't. Nor
should competing be your goal.

The apex predators—not to mention the countless mini-marketplaces they will inspire—have access to deep wells of cheap capital
and armies of staff. Amazon deploys five thousand engineers on
a single technical problem or opportunity. With the stroke of a pen,
Alibaba can form alliances in new markets that drive billions of dollars
in incremental revenue. Walmart's selling, general, and administration costs in 2019 were $107.1 billion,[1] exceeding the entire value of
Costco's annual revenue—and that was pre-pandemic. And the mini-
marketplaces popping up around them will carry tens of millions of
products. You can't compete with that.

But while you may not be able to out-science, out-engineer, or out-
spend any of these companies, you can absolutely thrive in their

lengthening shadows. Doing so, however, will require a total and complete rethinking of your business.

Where Amazon has access to deep wells of capital, you must establish an even deeper well of creativity. Where Alibaba relies on a technology war chest that is unparalleled, you must rely on unique and elegant design. Where Walmart relies on parsing a universe of structured and unstructured data, you must forge deep, organic intimacy with your customers. And where JD.com has established prowess along the supply chain, you must win by building a more beloved and compelling value chain, putting your customer at the center of all that you do.

DEPENDENCE VERSUS ALLEGIANCE

The apex predators will succeed by trading on the notion of dependence, building life ecosystems that consumers rely on for most of their basic needs. Indeed, it's a reality that is already unfolding.

That means for the other 99 percent of retailers on Earth, the only road to salvation will come through building deep customer allegiance. Where the apex predators may become the cognitive default for customers, you must become the emotional default. Where they excel in the science of retail, you instead must lean into the art of it.

Most crucially, with the vast center of the market across categories commandeered by the apex predators, *all* brands, regardless of what they sell, must now rethink and reestablish their market positioning. There will simply be no room for businesses that don't present perfectly clear and compelling value propositions to their customers.

But I don't mean positioning in the traditional sense. Many conventional positioning models are available to brands. Unfortunately, most fail to account for the sort of extreme market dynamics we will find in a post-pandemic world—a market where a small handful of global brands achieve such overwhelming centrality in the lives of global consumers.

Most models assume a marketplace where nuanced differences between competitors can form a sustainable advantage. My belief is that those days are gone. We need a new and perhaps, for some brands, more daunting framework. One that presents a starker and more rigorous litmus test for viability.

PURPOSE IS THE NEW POSITIONING

By "purpose," I do not mean your company's mission, vision, or values. I'm referring to the reason your company exists in the first place. Literally, why does anyone need your brand? What clear value does it add to your customer's life? What purpose does it ultimately serve? And most importantly, is that purpose enough to make you the *emotional default* in the lives of consumers? The answers lie in a brand's ability to respond to an even more pressing query.

IF YOUR BRAND IS THE ANSWER, WHAT'S THE QUESTION?

Brands are, at their essence, a form of shorthand for customers. They provide a means of navigating the sea of options that are available, and they assist customers in narrowing the field of choice. Ideally, they do so by presenting a clear answer to a frequently asked customer question.

Fifty years ago, Sears was an answer to a question for middle-class customers seeking product selection and value. What customer question does the brand answer today and for whom? What would compel someone to put down their tablet, bypass Amazon, and visit a Sears store or website? I don't mean to pick on Sears specifically; this is a condition that applies to the majority of brands. Most of them sell things that I can get somewhere else, and even worse, they do so with no discernible or distinct experience attached. Like Sears, the majority of retailers answer no particular customer question. Consequently, they become invisible to consumers.

Therefore, the first crucial hurdle for every brand that intends on surviving in a post-pandemic era will be to identify the customer question that *that brand* is the clear and unequivocal answer to. Without that, the brand will simply have no leg to stand on.

If this most fundamental of questions can't be answered, no amount of customer segmentation or market analysis will help you. In a post-pandemic landscape, Amazon, Alibaba, JD.com, and Walmart will become ever-expanding answers to the consumer question, "Where can I get anything on Earth fast and affordably?" This will leave precious little space in the market for any brand with ambiguous or obscure value.

So again, I ask you, if your brand is the answer, what's the question?

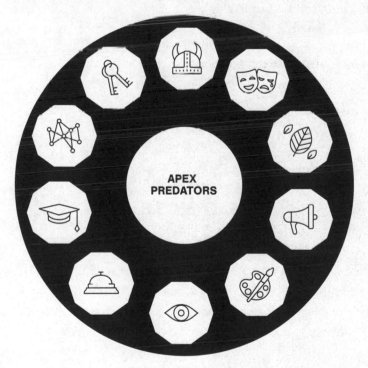

The Ten Retail Archetypes

THE 10 RETAIL ARCHETYPES

To assist you in your thinking, my belief is that there will be at least ten key evergreen questions that customers will be seeking answers to well beyond the pandemic. Questions that the apex predators and mini-marketplaces are likely *not* going to be the answer to. Becoming the clear answer to one of these questions will not only allow a brand to distinguish itself in its category but also, if the brand is smart, offer lucrative opportunities for outsized revenue and margins.

Rather than considering these questions in the abstract, I've built them into what I see as ten corresponding and distinct retail archetypes. Not only does each archetype represent a clear and easily understood market position, but it also directly responds to a legitimate and frequently asked customer question. Finally, each archetype provides directional guidance on the operational focus required to embody and animate it.

As you peruse them, ask yourself which of these (if any) sounds most like your brand.

THE STORYTELLER

THE QUESTION: WHICH BRAND INSPIRES ME?

The scene opens to show a long, desolate strip of highway, stretched out toward the horizon against a vast expanse of sky. Only the white noise of grasshoppers and the faint, rhythmic sound of feet striking the pavement can be heard. In the distance, heat rises off the pavement and a person slowly but steadily makes their way into the frame. A narrator's voice is heard saying, "Greatness. It's just something we made up. Somehow, we've come to believe that greatness is a gift. Reserved for a chosen few. For prodigies. For superstars. And the rest of us can only stand by watching. You can forget that."

Now coming fully into view, this person is revealed to be a young boy, clearly overweight, struggling heroically to confront his challenge—the challenge to keep going. The scene concludes with the narrator saying, "Greatness is not some rare DNA strand. It's not some precious thing. Greatness is no more unique to us than breathing. We're all capable of it. All of us." The piece concludes with a simple graphic reading "Nike" and "Find Your Greatness."[2]

The spot, the first in Nike's Find Your Greatness campaign, featured Nathan Sorrell, a young man from London, Ohio, and debuted on July 27, 2012, during the Olympic Games in London.

If you're even remotely human, you can't watch this piece without emotions welling up. You feel this kid's pain, and you sense the sort of strength and determination it takes to do what he's doing. We've all had a moment in our lives where we had to summon the courage to overcome. A moment where through sheer determination and tenacity, we triumphed.

Most brands engage in marketing to move merchandise. But a rare few engage us in stories to move our hearts and minds. To inspire us. And those that do, do so through the intense power of storytelling.

Storyteller Retailers are those that have become so intrinsic and iconic within their category that they supersede its boundaries. Storytellers become more closely associated with an ideal, a movement, or a human aspiration that connects deeply with their customer and provides fertile ground for rich and varied content and experiences across channels.

Nike is one such brand.

"Just Do It" is not just a tagline. It's an idea through which stories about human performance can be told with consistency. It's a battle cry. More recently, Nike's ode to former NFL quarterback Colin Kaepernick's silent take-a-knee protest has become another cultural lightning rod, causing controversy, debate, and ultimately an even greater level of allegiance to the Nike brand.

In fact, Nike is a case study in brand storytelling.

When dissected, the brand's stories tend to follow a very classical model, using a construct found in Greek mythology. First, there's always a protagonist, one who sets out to achieve a goal or conquest. Along the way, seemingly insurmountable obstacles present

A Nike store in Shanghai exemplifying the brand's focus on spaces that become key storytelling and customer acquisition points in the market

themselves. When giving up and accepting defeat might have been easier, the protagonist digs deep for the ethereal courage and strength to overcome the obstacle. It doesn't matter if the protagonist is a star athlete or a regular person just like you or me; the story is one of triumph over adversity, strength of character, and the sheer human will to cross the finish line, be it metaphorical or otherwise. The morals conveyed in each story, whether the now iconic "Just Do It" or the more recent "Believe in something. Even if it means sacrificing everything," are universally relatable ideas. All of it derives from classic Greek mythology. And it works.

Nike consistently creates rich and compelling story lines that anchor deeply with its customers. Once the story is written, the company recruits participants to bring it to life—for example, Michael Jordan's motivational story of Failure, in which he recounts the many performance missteps and shortcomings that he conquered on the way to success. The story then manifests itself across all touchpoints and invites customers to become characters in it, at every brand touchpoint both on- and offline.

The point is that Nike, as a brand and retailer, isn't in the business of selling shoes. It's far bigger than that. It's in the business of human performance, perseverance, and achievement. That's a very different idea, and one that is far more difficult for its competitors to reverse engineer than is a pair of running shoes.

This is not to suggest that the quality and performance of a Storyteller's products don't matter. They absolutely do. The difference is that for storytelling brands, products are an occupation. They are not a preoccupation. What matters most is that the story the brand is telling in the market is always being refreshed, rewritten, and recast to maintain connection to customers. It's the story the customer is buying. The product is just the material artifact.

For Storytellers, their physical stores become stages and studios through which those compelling stories can be told. Stores, whether online or off, aim at drawing the customer into those stories and, in doing so, galvanizing a long and enduring relationship that can play out across all channels and formats.

THE ACTIVIST

THE QUESTION: WHICH BRAND ALIGNS WITH MY VALUES?
In 2011, the U.S. retail market was still reeling from the collateral damage of the Great Recession. Retail sales, although steadily recovering, had still not reached pre-meltdown levels, and most retailers were still feeling the heat. By Black Friday—the high holy day of retail—the stakes were tremendously high, with retailers of all categories elbowing one another out of the way across media channels as they vied for customer attention and, above all, sales.

Yet on that same day—in the midst of all the market clamor and hand wringing—another company took out a full-page ad in *The New*

DON'T BUY THIS JACKET

Patagonia's Don't Buy This Jacket advertisement shows the commitment of the brand to its own values of environmental protection

York Times. The layout was simple, spartan, and to the point: one image, centrally framed. A jacket. Emblazoned in bold print above it sat the words "Don't Buy This Jacket." If that weren't crazy enough, the ad included two columns of copy laying out in detailed terms the environmental impact of the products the brand sold, and it discouraged customers from buying more; it even mentioned a branded resale marketplace it had established to offer customers alternatives to buying any new products at all.

The advertisement, which has now become an iconic piece of retail folklore, had been placed by outdoor clothing brand Patagonia as a means of calling attention to its Common Threads initiative. The initiative is aimed at educating the public on the environmental impact of human consumption, and makes the point that even given Patagonia's high standards for low-impact materials and manufacturing, the company's products still produce waste, still off-gas CO_2 into the environment, and still eventually become landfill. The only way to truly reverse the impacts of climate change, the ad declared, is to reduce consumption. To buy less, to repair more, and to wear longer. Finally, the company directed customers to a Patagonia storefront on eBay that offered nothing but used Patagonia items for resale.

Having the clarity of conviction and, let's face it, the sheer balls to do things like this has cemented Patagonia's position as an Activist Retailer.

Founded in 1973 by rock-climbing guide Yvon Chouinard, Patagonia has grown into a global business that by 2018 was selling approximately $1 billion in merchandise annually and had locked itself into the top spot among global outdoor apparel brands, a position won through baking social responsibility into every action and reaction the company takes.

Since 1985, the company has given 1 percent of its annual sales (whether it was profitable or not) directly to environmental organizations. To date, Patagonia has raised more than a quarter of a billion dollars through this commitment.

In 2017, the company—in coalition with the Hopi Tribe, Navajo Nation, Ute Indian Tribe, Ute Mountain Ute Tribe, and Pueblo of Zuni—sued the Trump administration over its reduction in size of two iconic national monuments, Bears Ears and Grand Staircase-Escalante, claiming the reduction was for no other reason than to appease the desires of coal, oil, gas, and uranium producers.[3]

In 2019, ahead of the pandemic, Patagonia debuted its Worn Wear store, a pop-up concept in Boulder, Colorado, featuring resale Patagonia merchandise.

In the same year, the company opened what it called the Action Works Café in central London. An extension of the company's Action Works digital platform, an online community connecting customers with local environmental action groups, the café is billed as a community training point and event space to foster climate activism.

But to paraphrase the late basketball coach John Wooden, the true test of your character is what you do when no one is watching. To that end, Patagonia is every bit as committed to its cause behind the scenes as it is in public. The company has committed to being carbon neutral by 2025—meaning it will either capture, mitigate, or eliminate the carbon dioxide produced through its supply chain. It has further committed to use only sustainable or recycled materials in its garments in the same time frame. These are only a couple of initiatives on a long list of actions the company has undertaken.

Most incredible perhaps is the fact that Patagonia not only hires activist employees who share the brand's ideals and love of the natural world, but it will also bail those same employees (and their partners) out of jail should they be arrested during peaceful protests. It will also cover the employees' legal fees and wages while the employees are going through the court process.

Like Patagonia, Activist Retailers not only champion a cause, but they bake it directly into their products, supply chain, value chain, and profit model. They align every communication and experiential touchpoint back to the North Star of their cause, affirming themselves to customers as not just leaders in their category but leaders of a social or environmental movement. Customers and employees alike select Activist Retailers based on their own sense of moral alignment with the cause.

That Patagonia is an Activist Retailer may not surprise you. What may be surprising however, is the degree to which such levels of corporate social responsibility translate into profitability. In 2018, consulting firm IO Sustainability and Babson College reviewed over two hundred studies on corporate social responsibility and determined that the financial outcomes of those businesses employing an integrated approach to social responsibility far outperformed those without such a commitment.

The benefits include sales gains as high as 20 percent over market, dramatically reduced employee turnover (Patagonia has only 4 percent turnover), an increase in company share price of up to 6 percent, and a brand equity dividend of up to 11 percent of market capitalization.[4]

It's important to raise a distinction, however. There are two very different approaches to corporate social responsibility: extrinsic and intrinsic. The extrinsic approach is one where the company engages in corporate social responsibility purely for financial gain, for brand perception, or to avoid public scorn. Intrinsic, on the other hand, is where dedication to a cause or mission is core to the company's being, born out of a genuine desire to effect positive change, and designed into every aspect of the operation. Patagonia and retailers like it embody the latter.

Other legitimate Activist brands include The Body Shop with its vocal stance against animal cruelty, Ben and Jerry and its courageous position on racial injustice, and Levi's and its high ground on issues like gun violence and climate change. In fact, Levi's, whose pre-pandemic performance was remarkably strong, credits much of its recent success to its emphasis on activism.

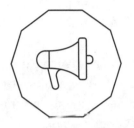

THE TASTEMAKER

THE QUESTION: WHERE CAN I DISCOVER
WHAT'S NEW AND COOL?

The first Neighborhood Goods store—a start-up retail concept calling itself the department store of the future—was established in Texas. The irony in that is that Texas is also home to JCPenney.

Once one of America's largest department chains, in its heyday JCPenney had over two thousand stores across the country. It offered shoppers a wide showcase of products and became a fixture in the lives of middle-class consumers. Customers looked to department stores to guide their tastes and sense of style. But in today's world, where the customer has unfettered access to just about everything imaginable, this advantage simply no longer exists—with no better proof being JCPenney's ultimate collapse and declaration of bankruptcy on May 15, 2020.

Yet, in 2017, deep in the heart of Texas, Neighborhood Goods founder Matt Alexander set about working to reinvent the channel that JCPenney and others once defined.

I first spoke to Alexander in 2018 when he was about to launch his first store in Plano, a city located about twenty-five minutes by car from Dallas. Sporting a hipster beard and streetwear, Alexander looks like someone who would be more at home in a recording studio than a retail boardroom. But early into the conversation, it became apparent that this young, British-born serial entrepreneur is all business.

I wondered, with news headlines at the time dominated by the death of physical retail and the dominance of companies like Amazon and Alibaba, what would inspire a young entrepreneur to make such a big bet on brick and mortar.

> We came together around the conversation of what it was going to take to help more digitally native customer brands get into physical retail and how to lower the barriers to entry and how to sort of create a whole new type of retail experience around it. The core thesis of it was creating ostensibly a new kind of department store, but rather than having that fixed landscape of racks and seasonal products, instead it would feature this ever-changing landscape of different brands and brand activations, from all sorts of different companies, not just the direct-to-customer crowd.[5]

Alexander realized that attitudes to physical retail space were changing. Brands, especially digitally native and direct-to-consumer brands, were beginning to regard physical presence not as cost of sales but rather as an effective marketing expense. According to Alexander, "Through that lens, it's led a lot of people to start thinking differently about what can be done with physical space."

As Alexander describes the project, it seems to me that Neighborhood Goods is a unique convergence of a number of concepts that have emerged over the past decade. Start-ups like Storefront, which as early as 2013 began disrupting commercial leasing by offering pop-up space to emerging brands. Story, a single-store experiential retail store in New York City, founded by Rachel Shechtman, who was an early innovator in the idea that retail was less about sales per square foot and more about becoming a media channel for brands. And a variety of other start-ups that developed the idea that retail is really a capture point for valuable customer data and the monetization

Neighborhood Goods' New York City store offers a variety of emerging and direct-to-consumer brands for shoppers to discover

of consumer/product interactions—all complemented by offering physical retail as a platform, so brands can tell their story without the worry or expense that comes with running a retail operation. Neighborhood Goods combines aspects of each concept.

At just under fourteen thousand square feet, Neighborhood Goods features forty or so brand activations and installations across categories at any given time. The store also offers a restaurant serving light meals and coffee during the day and cocktails in the evening. Just about everything in the space is shoppable, from the cutlery in the restaurant to the cookware used to make your meal.

Above all, Alexander says, Neighborhood Goods is designed to be a welcoming social space, where people can feel comfortable spending time. This has as much to do with the people he hires as it does with the design aesthetic of his stores: "We provide all the staff, and we have pretty strong aesthetic guidelines and parameters. So it feels very consistent and cohesive. The staff are very much trained and oriented around hospitality, so they're very informed and talkative about the brands they're representing."

Alexander describes the revenue model as somewhat flexible depending on the brand partner. In some cases, he says, brands pay a fixed monthly fee. Staffing, data access, and any required merchandising are covered by this fee. Neighborhood Goods handles all the technologies and transactions. Brands may take space for thirty days to twelve months.

The other model, Alexander points out, is more popular with some younger brands that the company is bringing in to pilot and test. While providing the same general level of experiential support, Neighborhood Goods simply takes a lesser fee, in addition to a percentage of sales. A percentage that, according to Alexander, is "still a lot less than they would give up at wholesale if they were trying to do a pop-in with a department store, but still a positive revenue stream for us."[6] In addition, says Alexander, the company has other revenue streams through its e-commerce platform and restaurant offering.

"For us, it proves to be quite a responsible model," he says. "If you look at it from a traditional retail real estate perspective, it has a really aggressive payback period and really strong sales per square foot, all these sorts of core metrics, and it turns into quite a profitable model."

Almost exactly two years after my initial conversation with Matt Alexander, he opened his second store in New York City's iconic Chelsea Market. Barely more than a month later, New York entered a state of lockdown. I caught up with Alexander in June of 2020, expecting to find him, like so many retailers, devastated by the turn of events, but instead, he told me the company's ongoing digital sales were actually beating expectations. His is a rare voice of optimism in an otherwise reeling retail world.

Beyond its economic merits, Neighborhood Goods' business model has, by definition, made it a Tastemaker Retailer. Tastemaker Retailers sift through the universe of new, unique, or emerging brands and curate them, creating points for customer discovery. As Benedict Evans, a partner at venture capital firm Andreessen

Horowitz, puts it, "The Internet lets you buy anything you could buy in New York. It doesn't let you shop the way you can shop in New York."[7] This joy of discovery through carefully curated and merchandised assortments offers value to the more discerning shopper.

The Tastemaker business model can operate in any number of ways, from conventional wholesale to retail models such as Williams Sonoma's to a more capital-light, retail-as-a-service or retail-as-media model such as that of Neighborhood Goods.

In essence, Tastemakers boil the ocean of choice down to a distinct and highly edited point of view that customers learn to trust.

THE ARTIST

THE QUESTION: WHERE CAN I ENJOY THE BEST EXPERIENCE?
"We don't even sell that many toys," Ben Kaufman, founder of New York City's most unique toy store, Camp, tells me.[8] In fact, according to Kaufman, only about a quarter of the company's revenue is derived from the sale of toys. Yet despite his eschewing the toy store label, you can't help but think that Camp is precisely the sort of toy store that Toys"R"Us should have and could have been—something Kaufman is quick to clarify. "Toys"R"Us," he says, "answered the question, Where do we go to buy a toy? [Instead,] The question we answer is, What are we going to do today? And when that's the question, the solution is pretty open ended."

It was the summer of 2018. Kaufman (a former marketing chief for Buzzfeed) and his wife were living in New York City with their eighteen-month-old son. Only two months earlier, Toys"R"Us had declared bankruptcy, prompting a realization on Kaufman's part. "I realized that there really wasn't anywhere left in the city to buy toys," he says. Moreover, he realized, there wasn't really anywhere that parents could go in the city to have fun with their children on a regular basis.

The inspiration for Camp, he tells me, came from the question "How can you create a ritualistic experience, that captured the hearts and minds of families, together as a unit? Not just kids, but together as a family, how do you create a fun and interactive environment?" A Starbucks for play, as it were.

With that, he embarked on setting up Camp, so to speak, on New York's Fifth Avenue.

A visit to the store confirms Kaufman's assertion that it is hardly a toy store in the conventional sense. In fact, only about 20 percent of the space is dedicated to conventional retail. The back 80 percent is what Kaufman and team refer to as a black-box theater of experiences for kids and their families. "We build everything behind what we call our Magic Door, as a rotating themed experience that changes about quarterly, and those themes are often sponsored by brands."

In addition to toys, the store sells apparel, gifts, and food, as well as products for parents and grandparents. "The actual toy that your kid's going to walk out with is such a fraction of our focus," he says. Beyond products, Camp has two other key revenue streams. The company holds events in-store for which it sells tickets and, as mentioned above, also creates elaborate themed experiences for which brands can buy sponsorships.

What is perhaps most intriguing about Camp is the team that Kaufman has put together to bring these themed experiences to life. "Our team comes out of theater," Kaufman says. Experience designers, he points out, come to Camp with a Broadway background, with some having worked on sets for productions like *Hamilton*. And it shows. When I checked out the store in January of 2020, I have to confess that stepping beyond the secret door and into the fantastical "stage," as Kaufman calls it, is a bit of a rush—even for a near-adult like myself.

As someone who spent years of my own life working in the theater, I can't help noticing, through my conversation with Kaufman, that

Camp's Fifth Avenue location in New York City includes a 1,200-square-foot toy store and an 8,500-square-foot black box theater of experiences for children and families

the creative process that he and his team employ closely mirrors that of a theatrical production team:

> We write a story. That's the way we design these experiences. We have a linear path through our store. You open the Magic Door, and we've set the stage. For cooking camp, you walk through a set of fridges, and then you wind up in the farm, and you follow the evolution of food from the farm.

It's only once the story is written that the Camp team begins considering the sorts of products that could be positioned at each point of activity. Every story, Kaufman points out, has play moments where children can engage contextually with various products.

What Kaufman has done, knowingly or unknowingly, is create what I call an Artist brand.

Artist Retailers very often sell products that are similar or even identical to those of other retailers, but through sheer creativity and capacity for design and stagecraft, they create experiences around those products that are so highly unique, engaging, and entertaining, the retailers win distinct positioning in the minds of consumers. They are retailers that differentiate based almost entirely on customer experience both on- and offline. In many cases, as with Camp, Artist Retailers then monetize not only their product sales but also the experience itself, either through admission fees or brand sponsorships. The Artist Retailer mindset is fundamentally different because it begins not by focusing on selling products but rather by designing experiences. Indeed, very often the experience *is* the product. The product becomes a souvenir of sorts and something to mark the experience.

As Kaufman puts it,

> our largest asset is that we have an audience that comes on a regular basis to hear the messages that we share. If I think back to my Buzzfeed days, we have an audience that comes on a repeatable basis that wants to hear the stories that we share and that's a media business.

This is not to suggest that selling things doesn't matter. It surely does, but it's not a preoccupation. "Sure, we conduct transactions as well and that's valuable," Kaufman says, "but the fact that our brand is standing behind another brand should actually have more value than the fact that we can sell a thingamajig for a fifty-point margin."

Only roughly a month after I visited the Camp store, New York City went into a state of lockdown—a nightmare scenario for a new, high-touch, experiential retailer. But Kaufman and the Camp team made an almost immediate pivot to translating their proposition to digital. "Someone on our team said, 'What about virtual birthdays?' We looked into our database and realized that there are sixty to seventy kids a day that celebrate their birthday. So we started hosting virtual birthdays. In the last three months, we've celebrated thousands of kids' birthdays. Then, we started selling sponsorships into digital birthdays and doing what we do, which is you build an audience then you sell brand partnerships into it." It was a move that caught the interest of another company, Walmart, and in July, Camp by Walmart was launched.

"Almost everyone has a digital summer camp, but they all amounted to the same sort of thing—a downloadable PDF of things you could do with your family," Kaufman says. "But that didn't feel engaging enough for us as a brand. So we partnered with an interactive video company called Echo and Walmart to create a virtual summer camp with interactive video-based activities. Every activity has product against it that you can buy with one click."

Again, by focusing primarily on delivering experiences as opposed to physical products, Camp was vastly more able to quickly translate its value proposition into something that could be conveyed and monetized online.

I ask Kaufman whether he believes that incumbent retailers can make the transition over to experiential retail. After a moment of thought, he replies that it's difficult for legacy retailers to change their thinking on design, largely because measures for success are outdated:

> You've seen this so many times in the past. Retailers start Skunk Works and stores of the future and innovation labs, but when push comes to shove, those initiatives are going to be measured on the same metrics that the core business is measured on, and when you do that, it'll never be apples to apples. Because they can't quantify the cool thing, the cool thing can't ever live there.

When I ask Kaufman what he sees for the future of retail, his view is at once dire and hopeful: "I don't think there will be many incumbents, outside of the Walmarts of the world and those providing essential services, that will survive," he says. "With lots of open real estate and not much competition, what you end up with is an opportunity." Then, with his tone turning more optimistic, Kaufman says, "At the highest level, retail is going to go from a utility to something that's more entertainment-based and be much more based on discovery than the transaction. And I can't wait for that."

What Kaufman and a handful of other true Artist brands recognize is that access to product is no longer the central issue for customers. It's access to wonderful, beautifully designed, and memorable experiences that they truly crave, and they will reward those companies with the creativity and skill to provide those experiences. And reward them handsomely.

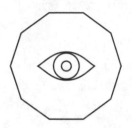

THE CLAIRVOYANT

THE QUESTION: WHO UNDERSTANDS ME BEST?
"When I opened the Stitch Fix box and pulled the jeans on, I felt that modern amalgam of elation and disquiet when totally nailed by an algorithm, like when Spotify pushes a perfectly pleasing new blues tune into my curated mix."[9] *Fast Company* journalist Lauren Smiley was describing her first experience ordering a Fix box from digital apparel retailer Stitch Fix.

Founded in 2011 by Harvard Business School grad Katrina Lake, Stitch Fix is one of the most profitable and high-profile digitally native businesses in the world. In fact, the company has been profitable since 2014, with net income for 2019 hitting $36.9 million.[10]

The concept is simple. As a customer, you begin by completing an extensive survey so that Stitch Fix can gauge your size and style preferences. From there, the company uses a unique mash-up of data science, machine learning, and 3,900 human stylists to begin sending you boxes of apparel, or "fixes" as they call them. Keep what you like, return what you don't, and the company uses that keep/return

Clairvoyant brands like Stitch Fix hone their understanding of the consumer in order to anticipate their needs

data to refine its ability to predict items for your next fix. Each successive fix becomes more aligned to your personal style.

The company now boasts over 3 million active customers and offers more than seven hundred brands on the platform.[11]

At its core, though, Stitch Fix isn't a retailer—at least not in a conventional sense. It's a data company. Data powers everything at Stitch Fix, from the descriptions and physical attributes of each garment right through to customer recommendations. Even the company's own open-to-buy process and rebuying triggers are informed by algorithms, enabling Stitch Fix to consistently achieve inventory turns that are significantly higher than industry average. According to Lake, "Data science isn't woven into our culture; it *is* our culture. We started with it at the heart of the business, rather than adding it to a traditional organizational structure, and built the company's algorithms around our clients and their needs."[12]

Everything is algorithmic, and the more data those algos get fed each day, the more accurate they become over time. Hence, feedback loops, like Style Shuffle, a micro-survey built into the company's app that allows customers to quickly rate a few images of apparel items each day, give the company tremendous predictive insight into customer preferences.

While many retailers are still musing about the need to hire even one data scientist, Stitch Fix employs eighty of them, many holding PhDs in fields such as neuroscience, mathematics, statistics, and astrophysics. This intrinsic use of data at the core of its business makes Stitch Fix the patron saint of Clairvoyant Retailers.

The Clairvoyant Retailer is one that uses technology and/or human intuition to predict the needs, preferences, and desires of its customers. Unlike brands that provide largely latent recommendations based narrowly on what customers have already bought, Clairvoyant Retailers build an open relationship with customers on the premise of data sharing, thus enabling them to achieve accurate precognition of customer needs. The more information customers provide, the more accurate the recommendations become, in turn prompting customers to provide more information. The result is an upward spiral of value for customers and increasing revenues and loyalty for the brand.

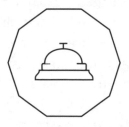

THE CONCIERGE

*THE QUESTION: WHERE CAN I GET THE
HIGHEST LEVEL OF SERVICE?*

There is a perception in the retail industry that truly legendary service is the realm of luxury or at least higher-end retail brands. Analysts typically point to the robust margins afforded by luxury sales as being the fuel necessary to support both the pay levels and training requirements to deliver an epic service experience. And yes, it is true that Nordstrom, Gucci, Ritz-Carlton, and other brands of similar ilk have become emblematic in discussions around customer service excellence.

There is also a perception that great customer service is, by definition, high touch and highly engaged. That too can be true. Apple stores, for example, maintain a 1:5 staff-to-shopper ratio to ensure someone is always nearby for personal assistance. Similarly, Gucci divides labor in such a way that your salesperson will never depart to the stock room to retrieve merchandise. That's work left to *store runners*, who do nothing but fetch goods and bring them to salespeople.

When we think of great service, therefore, these are the kinds of brands that are top of mind. But a different form of customer service defies both of these axioms. A form of customer service that is largely invisible, and one that has made Costco the sustained success it is today.

If you've ever shopped at Costco, you might be thinking, "Hang on, Costco is a warehouse retailer that doesn't really offer *any* customer service." And that's precisely the point. Costco's customer service is so good you're not even consciously aware of it. Its model defies the idea that great service must be either high touch or fueled by high-margin sales.

In fact, unlike Nordstrom and many other retailers, Costco makes very little on the products that it sells. Estimates vary, but most analysts agree that Costco's gross margin on product sales sits somewhere between 8 and 12 percent,[13] a drop in the bucket compared with the 30–50 percent margins of most other retailers. The company makes most of its revenue from the sale and more importantly *the renewal* of its at least 97 million customer memberships worldwide.[14]

It's a model that bakes in the need for exceptional customer service. Why? First, in order to function profitably, Costco must ensure the highest possible level of throughput in the store. Customer flow

The Nordstrom name has become synonymous with legendary service

must be completely unimpeded and optimal at all times. Therefore, you will never have to step around a forklift, pallet truck, or staff member merchandising a display. Never. That's because all merchandising for the day is done prior to opening the store.

You will never have to ask for a price on a product, because all merchandise is clearly signed, usually with just enough information to make a cogent buying decision but not so much as to be complex or confusing. If a product requires demonstration or trial, Costco will most often tap the vendor to support the product in-store with demonstrations, merchandisers, or taste testing.

Consistent store layouts and systems make it easy to shop in any Costco store in the world. My wife and I never hesitate to shop in a Costco anywhere we travel because we always know exactly what to expect. We'll be greeted at the door and have our membership card validated. The store entry typically spills into the electronics department and leads us passed key item specials. Fresh groceries are at the back of the store while packaged items line one side of the space.

Pharmacy is near the checkout and apparel in the mid-court. We could navigate a Costco blindfolded.

Despite the insane levels of volume, checkout is a finely tuned machine. The highly systematic two-person approach to checkout gets you out quickly and efficiently. If your membership is up for renewal, you can pay for that at the same time.

But here's the punchline. If you're not completely satisfied with anything you buy at Costco, you can return it for a full refund anytime within a year of purchase. A year! And if you forget your receipt, don't sweat it. Costco has got your entire purchase history at its fingertips.

There is nothing in a Costco that feels elaborate, complex, or non-intuitive. The company does not fill its stores with unnecessary merchandising, displays, or technology. No gratuitous staff with tablets patrolling the aisles. Nope. Costco merely executes the simple things to a level of mastery. And in the rare exception that you really do need the help of a staff person, staffers tend to be extremely helpful and friendly. That could have something to do with the fact that the average Costco store employee is paid substantially more than one employed by competitors such as Walmart.

As a consequence of reliably solid brand experience, over 90 percent of Costco's North American customers renew their memberships each year. In Europe, the figure is just under 90 percent.[15] These are outstanding renewal rates.

I've often said that Costco is the only store I frequent where I will go to buy pork chops and leave with pork chops and a kayak. Costco's invisible yet masterful application of customer service promotes that level of sometimes irrational spending.

Both Nordstrom and Costco, therefore, are what I term Concierge Retailers—retailers that take very different approaches to meet the same end. Excellent service. Service that isn't merely a series of learned steps but a product of systematic execution and exceptional experiential design.

THE ORACLE

THE QUESTION: WHERE CAN I GET THE BEST ADVICE?
Several years ago, on a trip to California, my wife bought me a DSLR
camera. It was my first *real* camera, so to speak. As I tend to be somewhat obsessive about learning how to use new things, I found myself
going down the photography rabbit hole that, as any photog will
attest to, is a really deep and expensive hole. I began reading articles
and blogs and watching videos and even enrolled in a local photography class. I was a sponge for all things photography.

Along my journey, the name of one retailer kept coming up in
online articles and discussions. The retailer was B&H Photo Video.

In 1973, Blimie and Herman Schreiber opened a small camera
shop at 17 Warren Street in New York City. Today, the relocated store
is on Ninth Avenue, occupying three stories and housing more than
400,000 products.[16] Hailed as a destination for professional photographers, the store has become an iconic institution in New York City
but also serves an international clientele through its digital channels.

As you enter, you're immediately aware of the whir of roller-style
conveyor belts overhead. B&H uses the Willy Wonka–esque system to
move customer orders from a massive fulfillment area at the back of
the store to waiting cashiers at the front. Inside the store is usually a
crush of people from curious tourists to professional photographers,
with a healthy dose of aspirational novices like me thrown into the mix.

It is, simply put, shutterbug Shangri-La. What is perhaps most
remarkable about B&H, however, is that very little under its roof cannot be found, perhaps more affordably, elsewhere. The vast majority

The warehouse that powers B&H's tremendous sales volumes

of what it sells could be ordered from your sofa—that is, with the exception of one product: B&H's expertise.

Notice I didn't use the term "product knowledge." A visit to B&H's website will illuminate my choice of words. Unlike many retailers, who treat their employees as an amorphous "team" often represented by what looks like a piece of stock photography, B&H posts actual photos and bios of their experts. A quick scan of those bios marks another significant difference. The employees are legitimate experts!

Unlike some electronics chains, B&H does not look for people happy to work retail and willing to learn about photography. No. They hire professional photographers who are willing to work retail. The difference is that the first kind of employee develops product knowledge by taking a course. The B&H employee brings expertise from years of professional work, passion, and enthusiasm. It's that difference which creates a fundamental competitive advantage. The former is simply a retailer. The second is what I call an Oracle Retailer.

Oracle Retailers go beyond simply offering product knowledge, instead rising to become the default choice for true expertise in their category. The difference is critical. Knowledge is something that can be gained without experience. I can gain knowledge about the Greek islands without ever visiting. Expertise, on the other hand, simply cannot be honed without personal experience. It's a difference that matters more today than at any time in history. Why? Because knowledge has, like so many things, become a commodity in a post-digital world. In fact, a 2017 study of consumers found that 83 percent feel that when shopping for a particular item, they are more knowledgeable than retail sales associates.

Expertise, however, can be gained only through real-life experience, and it's this deeper level of expertise that Oracle brands offer.

Skeptics will point to the fact that B&H is a one-store independent. "That may work for B&H," they'll say, "but it would be impossible for a large chain to achieve."

I'll admit that scale can be the enemy of Oracle Retailers, as they rely on a very thin and premium slice of the talent pool to support their archetypal position. That said, large national retailers like Recreational Equipment Inc. and Sephora also hire and nurture category enthusiasts and do so at scale, proving that it can indeed be done.

Anyone can buy a camera on Amazon. What they won't find there is the expertise and guidance B&H provides.

THE ENGINEER

THE QUESTION: WHERE CAN I GET
THE BEST-DESIGNED PRODUCT?

In 1983, after 5,127 prototypes, James Dyson had done it. He'd finally completed work on a product that would, in the end, revolutionize an entire consumer category.

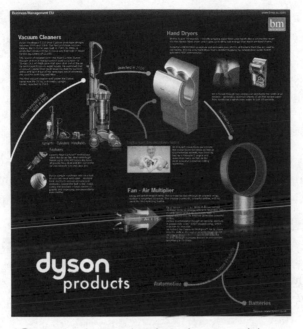

A Dyson advertisement that shows the company's heavy focus on product engineering

Five years earlier, Dyson, a design engineer and inventor, had become frustrated that his household vacuum lost suction and collected dust over time. With that, he did what any self-respecting engineer would do. He took the damn thing apart. It was while he was disassembling his vacuum cleaner that a fundamental design flaw revealed itself. He discovered that the design of his vacuum—like all vacuums manufactured since their invention in 1901—employed a bag system that lent itself to clogging. This, in turn, led to a steady reduction in suction over time. But how, he wondered, could the bag be eliminated?

Coincidentally, Dyson had just installed a cyclonic tower in his own factory that was used to separate out and capture airborne paint particles. He realized that using the same sort of cyclone technology could reinvent the physics of a vacuum cleaner.

In 2002, Dyson entered the U.S. market with its first product, the Dyson DC07, a strikingly unique-looking vacuum, different from others in the market. Best Buy was the first retailer to gamble on introducing the brand to Americans. Initially, competitors in the industry weren't overly concerned. Dyson's vacuums cost up to three times more than those of rival brands like Hoover. And most competitors viewed vacuums as the poor cousin of the appliance family: the outcast that spent most of its dirty, dusty life in a closet. They viewed Dyson's value proposition as outlandish. What few knew at the time, however, was that Dyson had already been successful in a court battle with Hoover, in which England's highest court supported Dyson's accusation that Hoover had infringed on a patent for Dyson's "triple vortex" design. Two years later, just as Dyson was entering the U.S. market, and after an unsuccessful appeal of the ruling, Hoover was forced to pay Dyson approximately £4 million.[17]

By October of that same year, Best Buy had sold ten times more DC07s than initially expected, and soon after, Target began selling DC07s as well.[18] He understood something that the vacuum cleaner industry didn't. Dyson saw that customers appreciated appliances that were not only highly functional but also beautiful to look at. And they were willing to pay more—much more than usual—to obtain them.

Worldwide, Dyson now employs almost six thousand engineers across a range of disciplines[19] and sells almost $6 billion in household gadgets each year in sixty-five countries. From vacuum cleaners and fans to hair dryers to industrial hand dryers, the company's engineering-led approach has created new and lucrative market space. With all of the company's products carrying a reassuringly pricey premium, Dyson's market position has also proven to be lucrative.

To call Dyson's physical spaces stores does them a disservice. They are better described as galleries, where Dyson products are displayed like pieces of art. Dubbed Demo Stores, the spaces are just that—an opportunity for customers to actually use Dyson products and discover, firsthand, their design and performance differences. Demo Stores are experiential playgrounds that pay homage to the brand's engineering and design prowess.

Engineer Retailers, like Dyson, figure shit out. They use superior technology and design thinking to solve customer problems, problems that elude not only competitive brands but very often customers themselves. In the same way no one ever asked for a bagless vacuum, few saw the need for an iPhone—that is, until we used one for the first time and felt the benefits of its superior engineering and design. Soon, we were camping out in lineups overnight, in cities around the world, for a chance to be the first to pay 50 percent more for an iPhone than it cost at the time to own a Blackberry.

Engineer Retailers apply this thinking not only to what they sell, but also to how they sell it, often taking an innovative and design-led approach to customer experience across channels. All organizational focus and energy goes into maintaining, displaying, and communicating the unique benefits of their products' savvy engineering and design.

THE GATEKEEPER

*THE QUESTION: WHERE CAN I GET ACCESS
TO THE PRODUCT I NEED?*

You're in the mall, and you realize you need new frames for your eyeglasses. You look at the mall directory, and you see three retailers who offer lenses and frames. In the interest of being a smart shopper, you decide to visit all three. By the third, however, you begin to notice something. The selection, product, and even pricing seem to be largely uniform across all three retailers. With that, you ultimately make your purchase and chalk the whole thing up to coincidence.

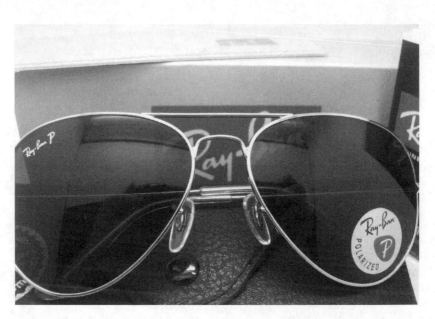
By 2019, Sunglass Hut had amassed a retail network of 3,429 stores

But it's very likely no coincidence at all. That's because two companies control the vast percentage of the $100 billion global eyewear industry. Essilor, a French maker of lenses, and Luxottica, an Italian frame manufacturer, control 45 and 25 percent of their markets respectively, with more than 1.4 billion users of their products globally.[20]

In March of 2018, these two dominant forces received approval in both the United States and the European Union to become one, and while not deemed to create a monopoly in the strictest sense, the merger sent a shudder through the industry. It wasn't the first shudder either.

In 2014, I was asked to speak at a meeting of optometrists in the Canadian market, who were still reeling from the news that Essilor, one of their primary suppliers, had that same year purchased Clearly Contacts—a Canadian company that sells contact lenses strictly online. Clearly (as it's now known) was a direct competitor to eyecare specialists. Optometrists were feeling that they too could be squeezed out of the value chain, because Clearly allows the customer to enter their own prescription information, entirely avoiding the need to get an eye exam. The optometrists' association was looking for help in trying to orient its members around the changing retail landscape, the threat online companies posed to the status quo across categories, and the changes that optometrists ought to be considering relative to their own customer experience, changes that would be required to fight back. It's a battle that continues today.

More recently, EssilorLuxottica entered negotiations to acquire the number two global player, Grandvision, for a proposed $8.3 billion, which, if approved, would potentially add up to seven thousand points of distribution to EssilorLuxottica's kingdom.

Can other companies in the optical market compete against the leviathan that EssilorLuxottica has become? Perhaps. Will it be easy? Absolutely not.

Gatekeeper Retailers like EssilorLuxottica are those that maintain position through a number of means, including regulatory or financial barriers to entry. They often dominate a market individually or as part of a small oligopoly of companies. The Gatekeepers' energy and work is, for obvious reasons, dedicated to maintaining the competitive moat around their brands. They do so through a variety of actions including pursuing mergers and acquisitions, buying up licensing agreements, and, of course, government lobbying. Given their outsized share of the market, Gatekeepers trade largely on powerful combinations of top-of-mind awareness and convenient access to distribution.

But being the Gatekeeper in any category comes with a curse. Dominance can breed complacency, and Gatekeepers often suffer from what can be charitably characterized as indifferent customer service experiences. Moreover, the lack of competition in their categories often leads them to distort the price/value equation with what are often absurdly high retail prices and markups. Thus, while the competitive barriers they construct may protect them in the short term, Gatekeepers are also constantly vulnerable to attack from the final archetype: the Renegade.

THE RENEGADE

*THE QUESTION: WHO OFFERS A BETTER WAY
FOR ME TO BUY THIS PRODUCT?*

In 2012, Ernie Garcia III was attending a wholesale car auction in Phoenix when a remarkably simple idea hit him—an idea that would change an entire industry. Garcia came from a family with deep experience in the auto industry. His father, Ernest Garcia II, had, among other things, made a living in the used car market and the finance market.

As he sat watching the used car auction that day, the younger Garcia realized that the dealers, using only a comprehensive spec sheet, were making go-no-go decisions about which cars to buy in a matter of seconds and confidently plunking down their cash in exchange for keys. Meanwhile, Garcia thought, customers could take days, even weeks, to find the right vehicle, sometimes having to visit multiple dealerships to find a vehicle they liked. It struck him then that the only significant difference was that the dealers at the auction were covered by a guarantee. Buyers knew that if any hidden problems existed with the vehicle, they'd have seven days to return it for a full refund. That single, yet profound, difference gave them the confidence to purchase a vehicle without ever turning the key.

Why couldn't the same conditions apply to consumer auto purchases? he wondered. Why couldn't used car buyers make buying decisions based on photos and a vehicle report and then take seven days to ensure that they're satisfied? And if the entire process could be not only painless but maybe even fun, thought Garcia, it could revolutionize the way automobiles are purchased. With that, Carvana was born.

A mere five years later, in April of 2017, Carvana launched an initial public offering. By December of the same year, the stock had gained 46 percent in value. Today, Carvana is valued at more than $30 billion with annual revenues of $3.94 billion, representing an increase of more than 100 percent year on year.

Carvana, a Renegade in its category, had changed the course of automobile sales forever.

Renegade brands challenge incumbents in a market, and even entire industries, by identifying game-changing innovations that radically alter the price/value equation and/or customer experiences in their market. They leverage technology, people, supply chain efficiency, and systems thinking to redefine customer experience in their chosen categories. In doing so, they often redefine the industry status quo, with a bias toward vastly upgrading the customer experience while delivering a product that is close to or as good as the incumbent offering.

The Renegade Retailer dedicates all its energy, resources, and communication assets to its battle against the status quo, highlighting inherent shortcomings in the current in-category customer experience and trumpeting its uniquely better method. Renegade brands differentiate on the basis of product and/or experience and reinforce their simplified or enhanced approach at every touchpoint.

Carvana vehicle pickup towers add to the unique customer experience while saving the company delivery expenses

CHOOSE YOUR DOMINANT ARCHETYPE

If you found an archetype that resembles your business or that you believe your business could aspire to become, congratulations. If, on the other hand, you found no archetype that resonates with your brand, you'll have to fix that—fast.

No single archetype is necessarily better or more sustainable than another, and that's the point; they are entirely different, each with its own distinct value to customers. Each provides an answer to a clear and relevant customer question. Each offers a solid and sustainable market position to which you can anchor your brand.

What is essential, though, is that businesses make a clear choice of one archetype and work to become the dominant version of that archetype in their category. Every element of the marketing and operational plan must serve to reinforce that one all-important archetypal position.

THE FOUR DIMENSIONS OF VALUE

This model can be further understood by breaking it into four distinct operational quadrants.

Culture: For some retailers, their primary source of dominance will come from their ability to communicate and indoctrinate customers into their unique and powerful brand *culture*. Culture is really nothing more than an accepted system of beliefs, customs, and artifacts. What we believe, the customs and rituals we observe, and the articles and symbols we use to represent those beliefs and customs are the essence of any culture. The role of retailers dominating in this quadrant is to distil and embed that culture and its values into every brand touchpoint. Culture-based brands don't just acquire customers. They recruit followers, believers, and disciples.

Entertainment: For other brands, dominance may be found in the realm of *entertainment*, engaging the shopper both physically and

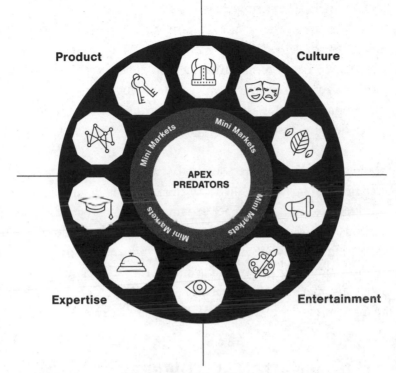

Product

Culture

Mini Markets

Mini Markets

APEX
PREDATORS

Mini Markets

Mini Markets

Expertise

Entertainment

The Four Quadrants of Value

emotionally across the shopping journey, incorporating sensory elements into the experience, whether on- or offline. Entertainment-dominant retailers will routinely agonize over the most nuanced aspects of the customer journey to deliver experiences that are truly unique and engaging at every turn. Brands centered on entertainment will over-invest in creative and design resources to power the continuous reimagining of their customer experience. For such brands, the product itself is secondary. The experiential production they mount around the product is primary.

Expertise: Others still will lay claim to the mantle of *expertise* in their category. Expert retailers will build out every experiential and communication touchpoint as a portal to their superlative level of category knowledge and a concierge level of customer service.

Benchmark training programs, certifications, seminars, classes, workshops, and other elements provide a constant feed of information to knowledge-hungry customers. Expertise brands will over-invest in staff hiring, training, and tools that are required to share that expertise with the public. Technology is used not to subjugate human staff but rather to empower and enhance their skills, knowledge, and abilities.

Products: Finally, some retailers will dominate through a laser focus on creating and selling aesthetically and functionally superior *products* and doing so with a customer experience that reflects their design ingenuity. Product brands will over-invest in research, development, and testing of new and superior product platforms. Also in this realm are those brands that, through acquisition or monopolization, dominate consumer access to a specific product. Their enormous stake in the market renders them the top-of-mind choice.

DOMINATION AND DIFFERENTIATION

If you've identified an archetype you believe aligns to your company's DNA, that's a great first step. By becoming a dominant archetype in your category, you'll not only become a bright beacon for shoppers; you'll also establish a clear compass heading for your executive team. That said, becoming a dominant archetype is no easy feat. What I mean by "dominant" is becoming so exemplary, iconic, and outstanding that you assume the default position in the consumer's mind within your category or market.

However, the simple choice of an archetype alone is not enough to sustain your brand over the long term—especially in a post-pandemic crush of evolving competition. While providing valuable strategic organizational focus, the archetype offers only one leg of support under your brand. What we want to create, though, is a solid three-legged structure.

Therefore, the next step in your brand's evolution requires that you bolster that position by further differentiating in two more quadrants. Not to be mistaken for dominating, differentiating simply means what it implies: providing something that is unique or different.

For example, as noted earlier, Patagonia clearly dominates as an Activist brand by weaving environmental causes directly into all aspects of its business model. As a result, Patagonia *dominates* in the culture quadrant, relative to others in its category.

However, the company further strengthens that position by *differentiating* in the product quadrant by sourcing unique, high-quality, and more sustainable assortments of goods. Second, Patagonia focuses on delivering a differentiated level of expertise in its stores. As stated on its website,

> We also seek [...] core Patagonia product users, people who love to spend as much time as possible in the mountains or the wild. We are, after all, an outdoor company. We would not staff our trade show booth with a bunch of out-of-shape guys wearing white shirts, ties, and suspenders any more than a doctor would let his receptionist smoke in the office.[21]

By dominating as an Activist archetype in the culture quadrant, and then differentiating in two other operational quadrants, Patagonia becomes a competitive Rubik's Cube and very difficult to compete against. The unique alchemy of culture, product, and expertise makes reverse engineering by competitors difficult. And while some of what Patagonia sells may be found within the ecosystems of apex predators like Amazon, it's unlikely that Amazon will ever go deep enough into the category to pose a meaningful challenge.

Brands that are able to carve out a dominant archetypal position, further supported with two points of strong differentiation, will not only survive in the post-pandemic era; they'll operate happily amongst the apex predators.

THE ART OF RETAIL

A beautiful body perishes, but a work of art dies not.
Leonardo da Vinci

S o how does your brand archetype come to life? How do you build a proposition so powerful, meaningful, and valuable to consumers that it pierces the domed ecosystems of the apex predators, freeing consumers to experience your unadulterated awesomeness?

It's a journey that begins with a few key acknowledgements. The first of which is…

EVERY COMPANY IS AN EXPERIENCE COMPANY

We've all heard the impassioned platitudes that are perennially shared in books and at business conferences. In the future, we're told, "Every company will have to become a data company." Or "Every company will have to consider itself a media company." And my personal favorite, "Every company must become a technology company."

While these familiar tropes all sound beguiling, and make for great conference platitudes, in reality they're complete and utter bullshit. Don't delude or distract yourself by listening to them. Don't take this personally, but there's an exceptionally good chance that your brand will never be the data company that Amazon is, the media company that Alibaba is, or the logistics companies that JD.com and Walmart are. It just won't happen.

Yet there is one thing that every company is. Whether you know it or not, acknowledge it or not, or like it or not, every company is an experience company. It doesn't matter what you sell or who you sell it to, if you have a customer and that customer has an experience, whether by accident or design, you're in the experience business.

Experiences aren't just pixie dust either. Companies that excel at delivering empirically better customer experiences also happen to outperform from a revenue standpoint by as much as 4 to 8 percent on average. Companies that outperform on experience also tend to have significantly more engaged employees.[1] Still not convinced? Consider that a 2018 report from Salesforce found that 80 percent "of customers say the experience a company provides is as important as its products and services" and 76 percent "say it's easier than ever to take their business elsewhere."[2]

How's that for motivation?

So the first and most important acknowledgement is that all retailers today are, by default, experiential retailers. The only thing left for debate is the nature of the experience you deliver.

DEFINING EXPERIENCE

But what *are* experiences? It may seem like a silly question, but given the wide range of interpretations of experiential retail that we've seen in the market, it's worth coming to some consensus. Some see service as synonymous with experience. Others equate experience with the aesthetics of a store while others feel experience is more closely linked to entertainment value. I think I can propose a simpler definition.

EXPERIENCES ARE CONTENT

At their essence, retail experiences are the sum of the physical, emotional, and cognitive stimuli we are exposed to in any given situation. What we see, touch, taste, hear, and smell, as well as how those elements make us feel, combine to form an experience. Each of those stimuli are simply elements of content—be it physical or digital.

Exposure to that content, like anything we experience, leaves us, as shoppers, with an impression. The more relevant, deliberate, powerful, sensorily engaging, and well-crafted that content is, the deeper into our long-term memory that experience will penetrate and the more likely we'll be to recall the experience and the brand that provided it. The more moving, entertaining, or unique the content, the more likely we are to want to share it with others.

Therefore, great experiences are simply great content.

So when I say every company is an experience company, what I'm really saying is that every company is a content company—and if you're not presently, you must become one, and there's no time to waste. In a post-pandemic world, purpose is your positioning, and content is your most effective means of animating it.

THE ALCHEMY OF EXPERIENCE

Speaking of content, imagine, if you will, that you have produced for your company a TV ad that was scheduled to air during the Superbowl. There's only one catch. No one in your company can be entirely certain what the ad will look like. The reason is that you never bothered to develop a script. What's more, the actors were hastily cast without much thought given to their ability to represent the brand. Add to this that the set was haphazardly thrown together for the shoot and the production crew was never properly briefed. Nonetheless, your commercial is going to play at the halftime gun to millions of viewers. Are your palms getting sweaty yet?

Of course, no one reading this would ever risk such a debacle. After all, it's your brand that's on the line, right? Who wouldn't carefully construct and execute such an important brand impression set to be seen by millions of people?

Yet every day, around the world, brands open their stores and leave the experiences customers will have within them largely to chance. They throw open their doors with only a vague understanding of the show they're about to present. Each day, for hours on end, companies—whether they accept it or not—are running live commercials for their brands. Commercials that will ultimately influence brand perception, sales, and profitability. And no one really knows what the commercial ought to look like.

Like any good piece of content, the experiences your brand offers customers must be intentional, meticulously planned, and created according to a design. In the same way that Shakespeare's *Hamlet* is not simply a series of unrelated words thrown on a page, great experiences are not a random series of inputs and actions. The experiences your brand delivers must be treated like carefully staged pieces of performance art.

Having spent decades researching and building customer experiences from Asia to North America and Australia to Iceland, I've been able to distil the alchemy of a great customer experience into some key principles. The first and perhaps most fundamental of these is that great customer experiences are completely intentional. Nothing is left to chance or interpretation.

Second, great experiences are the result of sweating the small stuff. Every moment and micro-moment along the customer's journey with the brand is mapped. Every aspect of the experience is clearly defined and designed. Brands that create great experiences don't merely train their staff the mechanical steps involved in the guest experience. They practise, rehearse, and perfect the execution of each step to reach a level of mastery.

Most importantly, I've determined that remarkable experiences have five key attributes. It doesn't matter whether we're talking about a great experience in a hotel, a shoe store, or a bank. I have found that truly memorable experiences include most or all of the following elements.

Great experiences are...

SURPRISING

Any great experience contains an element of surprise: something happens during the course of it that is pleasantly unexpected.

In Alibaba's Freshippo stores, for example, there are a number of things you certainly won't find in the average grocery store. First, every item in store is scannable, allowing shoppers to gather information about the item's freshness, provenance, or ingredients on their mobile device. Or if they prefer, they can scan and add items to their online order for delivery. While guests shop, online orders are being picked all around them by a team of in-store shoppers. Orders then whir around in the ceiling of the store, as they're transported to the back of the store for shipping. Shoppers can also select fresh items in-store and have them prepared for eat-in dining in the in-store café, which, as it turns out, is staffed by robots! If that all isn't surprising enough, when you're done you can simply leave and have your entire order delivered to your home in thirty minutes or less. The ability to pleasantly surprise your customer and to introduce delightfully unexpected value is key to delivering a great experience.

UNIQUE

Brands create unique experiences by changing the script in their category. By "script," I mean the typical experience that competitors in a given category tend to deliver. Competitors in any given industry tend to visit the same trade shows, read the same industry publications, and even hire the same consultants. The result? Most shoe stores sell shoes the same way. Most banks operate in the same way. Most grocery stores simply replicate the same standard grocery shopping experience over and over and over again.

But remarkable things can happen when a business has the courage to break that script. For example, in a world where bookstores are steadily becoming a rarity, one Tokyo bookstore decided to break all the rules. Bunkitsu is a collective made up of one creative agency and two booksellers and is as much a gallery experience as it is a typical bookstore. First, there's the admission fee. Yes, an admission fee. Guests are required to pay 1500 yen (about $13) just to enter the store. However, that admission includes a bottomless cup of coffee or tea and all-day access to the store's more than thirty thousand titles. The uniqueness doesn't end there, though. Most bookstores merchandise books according to category and title. Not Bunkitsu, or at least not always. Sometimes, the store may simply put all the red books in a single section. Some books are even purposely hidden, inviting guests to go on a treasure hunt to find them. In addition, a small café caters to those that want to take advantage of the all-day admission privilege!

It's these unique, trademarked elements of the customer experience that set Bunkitsu apart from all other bookstores.

PERSONALIZED

Great experiences make customers feel like the experience that day was just for them. This can be achieved in numerous ways across the journey with your brand. Studies indicate that when shoppers feel a high degree of personalization in their shopping experience, they're 110 percent more likely to add additional items to their basket, 40 percent more likely to spend a greater amount than intended, and 20 percent more likely to rate the retailer highly in terms of net promoter score.[3] Furthermore, studies indicate that best-in-class companies not only spend more on personalization capabilities, but they also intend to spend significantly more in the future.

Personalization may be as simple as customizable products or as complex as acquiring and deciphering granular, real-time customer data. For example, beauty retailer Sephora emails its clients with product suggestions based entirely on each individual recipient's past purchases. Nordstrom remembers customers' sizes. Nike allows customers to design their own runners, and NET-A-PORTER actually sends physical gifts to its best customers based on items they've purchased in the past.

ENGAGING

The brain has a region called the hippocampus. The hippocampus's primary role is to transport information from your short-term memory over to your long-term memory. Hence, something becomes truly memorable once this process takes place. The retailer's job is to aid that process by making the experiential information the brain is receiving as powerful as possible. Therefore, establishing a path of engagement that involves as many senses as possible is key.

For example, outdoor apparel brand Canada Goose opened what it calls its Journey store in Toronto. But when you enter the store, you're not greeted by the company's trademark parkas or accessories. Instead, you enter by walking across a floor resembling an ice field that seemingly begins to crack under your weight. Once across, you enter a 360-degree theater, and you're greeted by your Journey Teller, who is there to guide you through the space. Then, you receive a multimedia experience that speaks to the brand's heritage as a clothing company built for extreme conditions. The film I saw was narrated by four-time Iditarod champion dog sledder Lance Mackey, who is one of the company's brand ambassadors. From there, you head into the in-store cold room, replete with several inches of snow on the ground, to try on Canada Goose parkas and experience the feel of the garments under cold conditions. While trying out the clothing, you're treated to yet another media experience inside the cold room. When you're done, your Journey Teller can assist in sizing and ordering your coat, which can then be shipped to your home in a few hours.

Every aspect of what Canada Goose has developed is engaging. What you see, hear, and feel excites the senses and drives the experience into your long-term memory.

The same principles of engagement apply to digital experiences. If all you're offering customers is a grid-based web catalog or an app that looks and acts like every other brand's app, you're leaving the door wide open for apex predators and mini-markets. Instead, you'll have to compete on the memorability of your digital experience. The more sensory inputs you can build into that experience, the more likely it will be moved into your customer's long-term neural filing cabinet. Music, sound, video, imagery, human faces, and voices—these all build retention and recall.

REPEATABLE

Finally, remarkable experiences are repeatable in design and execution. Truly great retailers don't simply train their people; they rehearse them. Some might call this contrived. And to those people I would ask, Is it any more contrived than a sold-out Broadway performance of *Hamilton*? Any more contrived than an outstanding meal you had at a Michelin-starred restaurant? Any more contrived than the luxury car in your driveway? What some call contrived, I regard as finely engineered: deliberate and designed. Why would any business want anything less?

You can remember the five key attributes of experience easily with the acronym S.U.P.E.R. S.U.P.E.R. experiences break through. S.U.P.E.R. experiences get noticed. And ultimately, S.U.P.E.R. experiences win.

EMBRACE YOUR SPECIALTY

Another important acknowledgement is that if your brand doesn't happen to be an apex predator or an emerging mini-marketplace, you're now a specialty business. It doesn't matter if you sell groceries, cosmetics, snow tires, or even all of the above; the unprecedented scale and expansion of these massive competitors will render most other retailers specialty brands by comparison—at least in the eyes of shoppers. As such, you have to be prepared to delve to new depths into your category, deeper than any of your larger competitors can or would care to do, in order to meet heightened customer expectations.

This doesn't mean you have to carry more products necessarily. It does mean that you have to tell a deeper, more engaged, and more powerful story. You have to become the emotionally and experientially electrified alternative to the mechanistic and cognitively centered experience provided by your competitors.

THE NEW MEDIA

But how can you compete with the apex predators' New Retail approach? An approach they're all systematically adopting in an effort to surround their customers with an ecosystem of entertainment, buying formats, payment platforms, and logistics systems. From banking, education, and finance to transportation and healthcare, they are commandeering a growing array of categories, making themselves indispensable in the lives of their customers.

The vast majority of brands and businesses, of course, will never achieve such an all-encompassing position in any customer's life. But while you cannot compete on the basis of the New Retail, your brand can dominate in the realm of what I'll call the "New Media." To do so requires your understanding of a monumental transition in the market.

MEDIA IS THE STORE

Traditionally, we've used media as a tool to drive consumers down "the marketing funnel" to a point of distribution, be it a physical or digital storefront. Brands have agonized over building new and improved tools to intercept customers and then speed the customer down the funnel.

In a post-pandemic world, however, media, at least in the consumer's mind, is no longer simply a callout to visit a store, be it online or digital. Media *is* the store. TikTok, Instagram, a text message, or a Facebook post—all have become "the store." But to be clear, I'm not suggesting you create more advertising. In fact, please, on behalf of humanity, don't! We don't need more ads. Instead, I'm imploring you to embark on creating content that people actually care about. Content that people want and enjoy. Content that gets shared.

In reflecting on the magazine industry's reliance on advertising models for revenue, Andrew Essex wrote the book *The End of*

Advertising: Why It Had to Die and the Creative Resurrection to Come. He puts it this way: "I am bullish on any media that produces a product worth paying for, or that has an authentic and engaged audience who can't live without it."[4]

I can't help believing that retail must adopt the same point of view. Retailers must move away from building ads designed to serve their own selfish needs and begin building creative content that serves their customers—and especially their most engaged customers. Content that customers would miss if they no longer received it. Content that, if push came to shove, customers would pay for.

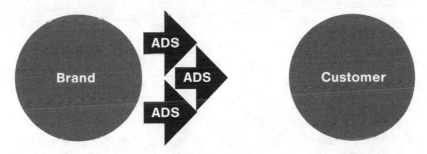

Conventional Marketing Communication Model Powered by Advertising

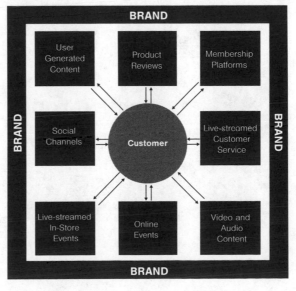

The Media Ecosystem Model, Powered by Dynamic, Live, and Personalized Content

This means transitioning away from the idea of pushing promotional messages at customers and instead creating content, experiences, and events online that offer value and encourage engagement. Content that entertains, informs, and inspires.

The point is simply that every one-way monologue you push in the faces of customers is another reason for them to seek a divorce. And no number of cookies on their browsers, retargeting ads, or pop-up ads are going to reconcile the relationship.

Instead, brands must put the customer at the center of a genuinely creative media universe and shower them with content that is relevant and, above all, interactive.

Creating this stream of content—one that is specific to your brand's archetype and categories—should be of paramount importance. Every message, every touchpoint, every interaction with customers should articulate, animate, and bolster your chosen archetypal position.

The result is a continuous content loop whereby the insights gained from customer interactions are poured back into the creative process and new, powerful media created.

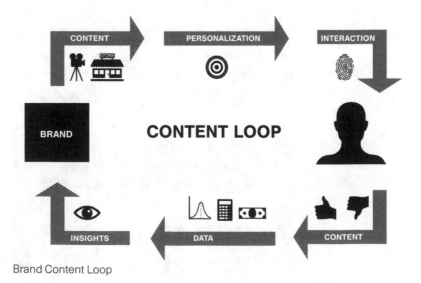

Brand Content Loop

But here's where it gets really crazy. Imagine if each of your stores also contained a creator studio. Imagine if in-store events, product drops, demonstrations, influencer appearances, and more could be developed into content and those assets then added to the media ecosystem. All of a sudden, content production, exposure, and interaction with customers grows exponentially—not because you just spit up more ads at customers, but because they actually want to engage with the unique and interesting content you share with them.

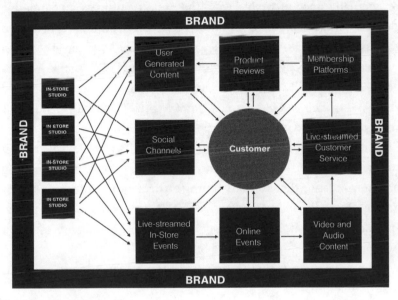

The New Media Ecosystem

If this sounds like common sense, then it's worth asking why it doesn't happen more. Why are brands still largely relying on interruptive, scattershot ads? Worse, why are they investing in more and more tools to follow us without our consent? Why don't they just create awesome media that we actually want to engage with?

All these are worthy questions that can be summed up in one sentence. You see, most corporate leaders would rather use a tactic they know won't work than a tactic they don't understand. That sounds harsh, but we've all seen it play out. The entire retail industry resisted the lure of the Internet for years, not because e-commerce was implausible but because most retail leaders just didn't understand the Internet or its potential. We fear what we don't understand.

Also, it's easier to plug an ad in a new or different media mousetrap and tell the boss you innovated than to actually accept the risk of creating something truly unique.

Building great interactive content, on the other hand, requires creativity, and a surprisingly high percentage of business leaders are actually uncomfortable with the creative process and creative people. I know that sounds counterintuitive, but studies have shown that upwards of 50 percent of executives surveyed say they feel unprepared to recognize or embrace creativity![5] For many leaders, creativity is actually seen as a source of discomfort, uncertainty, and risk. And while most companies claim to prize creativity as an asset, most don't reward it to any meaningful extent.

The subtext here is that if your marketing isn't super creative, it might not be your agency's fault. The agency could be delivering amazing creative that's simply falling on deaf ears inside your organization. Regardless, if you're not giving your customer engaging and interactive content, if you're just sticking to retargeting ads and banner buys, you're fighting a losing battle.

The good news is that there's no time like a pandemic to immunize your approach.

SHOPPABLE MEDIA IS NOT THE NEW ADVERTISING

Once you've made the decision to ween off ad buys and to create more compelling content, the next step is to ensure it's all 100 percent shoppable. Customers increasingly expect every media message to act as a direct portal to purchase.

Studies have shown that as many as a third of Instagram users have purchased directly from a promoted post on the platform.[6] What's more, 60 percent of users say they've discovered new products on

Instagram. In fact, in March of 2019 the company launched Checkout on Instagram, allowing its 130 million plus users to buy from branded posts without exiting Instagram.

We also know that 72 percent of people would rather view video to learn about a new product or service.[7] Companies like droppTV are capitalizing by enabling easy conversion of video into a shoppable format that exists directly within the viewing experience. Viewers simply click a drop button when an item in the video catches their eye and are able to buy the item from directly within the experience.

Similarly, TikTok recently partnered with NTWRK—a start-up that could be described as the Home Shopping Network for Gen Z—to sell a limited line of apparel by artist Joshua Vides. The live-streamed videos included opportunities to buy directly while watching the live stream, without ever leaving the app.

So the clear desire on the part of consumers is not to be advertised to. It's to engage with media that offers entertainment value, information, inspiration, and a direct path to purchase. This can take many forms:

- ➤ Shoppable video
- ➤ Visual stories
- ➤ Images
- ➤ Product reviews
- ➤ User-generated content

Media is the new store, and that new store needs to be shoppable.

But now you may wonder what this portends for brick-and-mortar stores. I mean, if media is the store, does it mean we don't need physical stores anymore?

Not a chance. Physical stores are more important than ever before. But not for the distribution of products.

YOUR STORES ARE MEDIA

Anyone who knows me knows that since at least 2015 I've been howling like a mad dog at a full moon about a coming transition in the retail industry. Well, I may stop howling now because the transition is complete. I'll explain.

COVID-19 has finally awakened the retail industry to the impracticality of physical stores as a reliable means of distributing products, given their vulnerability to disruption. Increasingly frequent interruptions brought on by social unrest, climate change, weather events, and, of course, pandemics all foreshadow trouble for physical stores in the future. And the inherently limited availability and access offered by brick-and-mortar stores renders them increasingly inconvenient in a digital society.

But if we're totally honest, even in their heyday, such stores were a problematic means of putting products in the hands of customers. The inherent restrictions on operating hours, together with high working capital and payroll costs, ate into profitability. Minimum merchandising thresholds often meant that stores, in order to fill racks and shelves, had to carry too much inventory. This led to markdowns and drains on margins, which were then further softened by damaged goods, write-offs, and of course theft.

None of this, however, negates the tremendous value of physical retail spaces. I repeat. This does not negate the value of physical space. On the contrary, it alters and enhances it.

Stores are transforming from a product distribution channel to a media channel, and in a post-pandemic world, their role as a media channel will be even more vital than it is today.

For one thing, the cost of digital media has escalated to the point of becoming an impractical means of customer acquisition for many brands. For example, in 2019, retailer Outdoor Voices warned that the cost of each incremental customer acquired through digital media channels now outweighed the revenue opportunity that each new customer brought with them. To this point, according to a 2018 U.S. research study, digital ad spending increased 21 percent year on year, prompting a 17 percent year-on-year increase in the average cost per click. Actual clicks increased by a disappointing 7 percent. What CFO would knowingly continue to increase ad spending by 21 percent for a 7 percent lift in clicks? Meanwhile, the cost of a Facebook ad increased by more than 100 percent between 2017 and 2018.[8] So by as early as 2018, retailers were already experiencing diminishing returns on increased digital ad spend, because customers found themselves swimming in a never-ending river of digital ads.

While the cost of advertising has moderated somewhat as a consequence of the pandemic, it's a fair assumption that once light appears at the end of the tunnel, brands will be flooding back into the market with ad spending. In the longer term, digital advertising as a means of acquiring new customers is clearly becoming a prohibitively expensive and marginally effective tool.

Yet in pre-pandemic New York, it wasn't unusual to see lineups at Glossier, Supreme, and Kith. As far away as Melbourne, hundreds of shoppers lined up, sometimes hours before opening, to get into streetwear emporium Culture Kings. On a 2019 trip to Tokyo, I witnessed throngs of young shoppers waiting eagerly outside chic retail stores in Harajuku and Shibuya.

Physical retail stores are not only a powerful media channel; I'd go so far as to argue that they're now the most manageable, tangible, and measurable media channel available to a brand. Unlike digital media, where the consumer's true level of interest or engagement can be debatable, a physical store can validate the consumer's actual presence and participation in the experience.

We can connect directly and intimately with them.

This may change in the short term, given the uncertainties around COVID-19. But it will almost certainly hold true in the long term. The pandemic will not kill the value of physical retail experiences. In all likelihood, we'll crave physical and social interaction more than ever, and retail stores can help to satisfy that need. That said, the pandemic will profoundly raise the customer's expectations for the quality of those experiences. Having adapted over what will be two or more years of accelerated digital commerce, customers will undoubtedly be far more discerning when it comes to making the effort to engage in real-life experiences.

And that means we have to find new uses for the spaces formerly known as stores.

STORES AS STAGES

Before the pandemic, I was in Melbourne, Australia, for some client work. I got up early the first morning and headed out to check out the retail scene. At about 8:00 AM, I came across a lineup of young people stretching halfway down the block. Some had brought camp chairs and blankets, indicating that they'd been there some time already. They were waiting for the opening of the store mentioned above, Culture Kings. Culture Kings is an Australian streetwear retailer with eight stores across the country. I decided to come back a couple of hours later and check it out.

When you enter, any illusions that Culture Kings is "just another store" evaporate. First, you feel the bass from the sound system crawl up your legs and into your chest. Then, you're struck by the sheer size of the multi-level space, which looks more like a nightclub in Rio than a retail store. Next, you notice the DJ elevated twenty feet above a basketball half-court below. On that half-court, staff are entertaining customers by holding a free-throw competition. Upstairs, you can grab a snack and a haircut. And despite the company's diminutive size, compared with, say, the Foot Locker chain, it's not at all unusual to find international celebrities from the world of music, film, and sports roaming Culture Kings' aisles with you.

Above all, you feel a distinct theatricality. The space, the sounds, the lighting, the staff engagement levels—all of it reinforces the feeling that you haven't just slipped into a regular store. You've entered a different world entirely. Within the walls of that space, Culture Kings has created a physical stage where its branded productions can be delivered to an adoring audience.

I didn't buy anything that day. Frankly, I'm not Culture Kings' intended customer. What I did leave with, however, was the most important product: a highly positive brand impression. Positive enough that I'm sharing it with you here.

But if brands are creating amazing content like this in their stores, why should it be experienced by only those within the store? Why not let the world experience it too?

STORES AS STUDIOS

Nema Causey has a sweet business. Literally. Candy Me Up is a San Diego–based, family-owned confectionary business, specializing in selling to retail clients for special occasions.

Shortly before the pandemic, Causey—along with her brother Jonny, who heads up the distribution side of the business—noticed a slight decline in orders. When COVID-19 hit, the problem only became worse. "I was 99 percent sure we were going to shut down," she said.[9]

In a moment of desperation, she opened a TikTok account and with Jonny, began making videos from inside the store. The store, colorful and bright, with loads of candy, provided the perfect backdrop for their antics. The pair also jumped on trends like the Jelly Fruit Challenge—an online challenge in which participants film themselves biting into jelly-filled candies, which, as you quickly learn, can explode when bitten into, sending jelly, at great speed, onto cameras, clothing, and the faces of nearby friends.

It wasn't long before Causey and her brother began attracting a following on TikTok. Thanks to a shout-out from a YouTube celebrity, the company almost immediately landed another 40,000 followers.

Soon, followers turned into orders, and Nema Causey rapidly built the company's first online store. She quickly ran headlong into the enviable problem of selling out of items featured in her videos—in one case, selling ten times more than expected.

In case you're wondering, the content Causey and her brother Jonny create isn't high production value. It's just fun and creative. In addition to viewing behind-the-scenes glimpses into store life, the audience can live vicariously through the pair as they show, explain, and yes, gorge on the array of exotic candies the company carries.

Today, Candy Me Up has close to 450,000 followers on TikTok and is now in the process of growing its Instagram following as well. As for the Causeys, their biggest problem now is keeping up with demand.

What Causey and her brother have discovered is that their store is in fact the perfect film studio from which to promote their business, and that they are the essential characters in the story. From that studio, the Causeys have developed not only an audience but an entirely new and expanded market.

MORPHE-ING INTO MEDIA

Cosmetics brand Morphe (pronounced Mōr-fee) is growing. Once an online pure play in the beauty space, Morphe drew up plans in 2019 to expand its physical presence in the United Kingdom, United States, and Canada. But these are hardly the sort of spaces you think of when imagining a typical cosmetics store—in part because the retailer is building full-fledged production studios into its locations to drive brand awareness through customer-generated content. Budding content creators in the beauty space can book studio time, and with the support of staff, access a full array of cameras and lighting equipment. Each studio also doubles as a makeover space where customers can receive free twenty-minute makeovers or learn new techniques.

The result is over one hundred video tutorials which now appear on the brand's website, with hundreds more being distributed through the channels of engaged and influential content creators. Factor in the network effect of all those contributors engaging their audiences with content created at Morphe, and it becomes a branding campaign that would rival that of the largest beauty companies on Earth. In all, the company aims to have over fifty of these spaces across North America and the United Kingdom.[10]

Again, this underscores the point that stores can be powerful stages or places for live commercial theater. They also make wonderful studios for content creation. In fact, even in the pre-pandemic world, I was so committed to this idea that I had already created a new division of Retail Prophet, focusing on in-store, live-stream production services for retailers—assisting them in building their stores into sets and stages for weekly live-streamed productions. What seemed somewhat innovative only a year ago is a no-brainer today. In a post-pandemic world, leveraging stores as physical backdrops for the creation of remarkable physical and digital content is an idea that has clearly come to the mainstream.

The point here is that every day around the world in retail spaces large and small, magic happens. But those experiences need not be contained to the four walls of a store when they could be used to reach massive global audiences. Every archetype has a story, and every story, an audience.

RENT IS THE NEW COST OF CUSTOMER ACQUISITION

Given the massive shift in the market to online, and the corresponding shift to using stores less as a distribution channel and more as a media channel, we must completely rethink the way we measure the productivity and contribution of physical stores. In a world where online retail is now growing furiously by double digits—while offline languishes in the low single digits—it's logical to assume that the four-wall revenue of many retail spaces will decline. But does that mean the store is less important? Absolutely not. But it does demand that we measure its value differently.

My friend Rachel Shechtman is the founder of Story, an early pioneer in the realm of experiential retail. I was speaking with Rachel recently about how retail is measured. She said, "Media has always been effective wherever people gather in numbers. All you need is a message and an audience and voila! You have a media channel." And she's absolutely right. A thousand years ago, that gathering place was the market bazaar, where people socialized, gathered news and information, and, of course, discovered merchants and must-have products. Then, the printing press became the more efficient means of media distribution, and newsprint then dominated. The advent of radio allowed for new levels of both immediacy and reach. Soon after, television became the primary hub from which customers received their information. Today, digital media has largely displaced all others as the primary social campfire we gather round to know what's happening, what's new, and what's next.

But with the cost of that media now soaring and its effectiveness becoming marginalized, retailers that intend to survive the next decade will have to begin not only treating their physical assets as media but also measuring them as such.

MEASURING THE RETAIL SPACE OF THE FUTURE

The key to effectively measuring the true productivity of a store is found by focusing on a metric we're already familiar with from the marketing side of the industry—but that, until now, we've never applied to physical stores. The key metric is establishing a value per media impression. In other words, determining the value of a positive brand impression delivered via a physical experience.

By illustration, I was speaking a while back with the chief marketer for a major beauty company that operates more than two dozen brands. I asked how many customers per year he estimated came to the company's various branded physical retail locations. He estimated roughly 100 million. Out of curiosity, I asked how much he felt it would cost his brand to engage with a Madison Avenue advertising agency, with the objective of targeting 100 million customers per year. By "engage," I meant to have customers consume not a thirty-second pre-roll ad on YouTube or a series of sponsored posts on Instagram, but rather a prolonged (say twenty-to-thirty-minute) immersive media experience—one that would allow a customer to truly internalize the brand story, learn about the products, and begin to feel a part of the brand's community and culture. In other words, to have a truly remarkable and memorable human media experience.

"The cost would be incalculable. It would be astronomical!" he said. He was absolutely right. The cost of such a campaign would be beyond the budgetary dreams of even the largest companies.

But here's the thing: by his own admission, the brand was already engaging an audience of that size with precisely such a media experience. The problem was that the company was not accounting for that value anywhere in its financials. They weren't even measuring it!

In other words, if my beauty client is coming into contact with 100 million customers per year in its stores, then the stores delivering those brand impressions should be credited with at least an approximation of the market value of those same impressions. The point is that physical retail is no longer simply a product distribution strategy — it's a customer acquisition strategy with an inherent and attributable return of value. We must somehow account for that value, or we're not capturing the full value of physical retail.

VALUING EXPERIENCE

The question is, What is the appropriate value to attribute to physical stores? It's a great question and one that requires two components: first, an internally agreed-upon *value* per customer impression; and second, and more importantly, a gauge of the *quality* of the average impression.

VALUING IMPRESSIONS

The first of these components requires some educated assumptions to arrive at an internally-agreed-upon value per impression. This is not a number that will appear in any quarterly shareholder report, so what's important is only that it's internally accepted as an appropriate and realistic figure. For the sake of argument, let's assume that you agree internally that the value of one positive in-store customer experience is, from the standpoint of effectiveness, worth five times the value of a fleeting advertising impression on Facebook. If your Facebook cost per impression is ¢80, then the value per impression garnered in a store would be $4. In the case of my beauty client and its 100,000 in-store impressions per year, that's

$400 million dollars in value per year. But because the brand is measuring only sales and profits, no one is accounting for the value of this in-store media.

QUALIFYING IMPRESSIONS

Once you've established a value per impression, the next step is to qualify the degree to which the impressions are positive or negative. In my experience, the best and simplest possible gauge to achieve a level playing field is by measuring net promoter score (NPS). Put simply, NPS simply gauges what percentage of your customers would rate the experience of shopping with you as positive, neutral, or negative. If a store's NPS is highly positive, that value should then be added, for internal purposes, to the store's performance metrics. The point is that a store may be generating $1 million in topline revenue, but it may also be delivering an additional $100,000 in media value.

If the NPS is positive, we can assume that the media value is similarly positive. If the NPS is neutral, we can assume that shoppers are largely split on the experience and that the value of impressions may be nil. If the NPS is negative, we can assume that the store is likewise contributing a negative media value and that every minute that it's open to the public, it may be doing grave reputational damage to the brand.

All this matters because we are moving at the speed of light toward a reality in which a majority of the things we buy will be purchased digitally. I've estimated that will be case by as early as 2033. So if the only means on which you judge a store's worth are sales and profit, you're likely going to want to close all your stores eventually. That would be a huge mistake precisely because those stores have a media value. And if you're not measuring that value, you could end up closing not only the wrong stores but so many stores that you end up throwing away millions of dollars in media value.

Consider this example. Store A sells $5 million worth of merchandise in a year, but also generates $2 million worth of positive impressions for the brand, meaning that the store's true contribution—at least from an internal perspective—is $7 million in value. Conversely,

Store B generates $8 million in sales but $3 million in negative brand impressions, giving it a true net value of $5 million.

Which store would you close if you had to choose? If the decision was based solely on sales, the answer would be simple but completely erroneous. However, by including an internally-agreed-upon media value per customer, we get to a result that more accurately reflects each store's true contribution.

Put differently, I've been to small stores that generate awesome customer experiences and contribute greatly to a positive brand impression. I've also been to elaborate, expensive flagship stores that are absolutely horrible and do nothing but devalue the brand. If you evaluate stores on the basis of sales alone, you'll never know the difference, and even worse, you'll probably end up closing exactly the wrong locations.

BUILD CLICKABLE STORES

Experiential roadblocks that might have been considered annoyances before the pandemic will become increasingly unbearable to customers in a post-pandemic reality. The online convenience we all became highly accustomed to during lockdowns will be contrasted against the friction often found in physical retail spaces. Waiting for information about products, waiting for service, or waiting to pay—frankly, waiting for anything—these all have to become things of the past.

In the consumer's mind, any remaining separation between the digital and physical worlds that may have existed pre-2020 was demolished by the wrecking ball that is COVID-19. The ability to use your mobile device to gather information, instruction, or even ordering capabilities while in-store will rapidly become a base expectation that we as customers have of retailers. This will be particularly true for retailers that aren't service intensive in their models. The ability to add items to an online cart on your app, then visit a store and add more to the order from that physical space, and later have it all delivered to your home—this is the sort of flexibility we will demand.

By connecting the customer to the store and across the entire experience through technology, you're not only adding value to that experience but also opening up a potential data and communication channel with them at different junctions within it. The real-time insights you can gain on customer navigation, product appeal, merchandising effectiveness, and dwell times should be incentive enough—never mind the access to insights about O2O (online-offline/offline-online) behaviors.

To be clear, though, I'm not promoting mindless proliferation of screens and technology into retail spaces. I'm suggesting that you provide an interface upon which both customers and staff can access the information they want and need at exactly the time and place they need it.

SINK THE FLAGSHIPS

Okay, sort of a dramatic subheading there I admit, but there's a reason. I don't want to leave any room to conflate the concept of customer experiences with the notion of "flagship" stores.

I say this for a few reasons. First, it's been my experience that flagship stores often become orphaned children in retail companies. Store operations teams often view them as marketing's unwanted offspring. They are frequently regarded as frivolous and expensive baubles and not a "real store" from an operational point of view. Marketing, conversely, sees flagships as the purview of store operations, relying on their ability to bring all the beautiful and expensive working components of the experience to life. If the flagship's performance fails to meet expectations, finger pointing often ensues. Everyone is to blame, and therefore, no one is to blame.

The second problem is that despite their uniqueness, flagships often get measured by the same conventional standards for financial performance that regular stores do. The problem of course is that flagships usually run with an expenses-to-sales ratio much higher than their conventional store counterparts.

Finally, in a purely practical sense, why would any brand want to establish an experience that makes all its other locations seem inferior by comparison? Customer experience should not be a novelty item, available in only certain locations or cities. It should be democratized across every customer touchpoint. In essence, every store should be considered a flagship.

MAKE EVERY STORE A CONCEPT SPACE

That's why I've always preferred that brands think in terms of concept stores instead of flagship stores. A concept implies iteration, invention, and ongoing development. Concept stores also tend to produce more valuable and scalable innovations that can be migrated to all locations, and concepts can be jointly owned and executed by both marketing and operations teams. Flagships say, "This is the best we can do." Concept stores, on the other hand, say, "We never stop innovating."

Flagships make the assumption that bigger experiences are better. Yet very often in life, it's the small experiences that bring the most satisfaction. Consider haute cuisine. When great chefs prepare remarkable dishes, the portion sizes are often small. While the cynic in us might assume that doing so is merely a means of the restaurant making more money, there are legitimate physiological reasons why small portions are better.

First, small portions are more aesthetically pleasing. A small portion looks better on the plate and can be more artistically presented, thus immediately increasing the diner's desire for it. More importantly, however, science also tells us that our tastebuds are disproportionately activated by the first three to four bites of any food item. After that, it's all just more of the same. Also, smaller portions offer the ability to experience a greater variety of dishes within the same meal.

What we can take from that is that bigger experiences do not imply better experiences. Indeed, some of the most elegant, enjoyable, and memorable experiences I've ever had while shopping have been in some of the smallest retail spaces.

DON'T BEG FOR LOYALTY.
CHARGE FOR MEMBERSHIP

The loyalty industry has a dirty little secret: loyalty programs don't make customers fundamentally more loyal. In fact, studies have shown that the material difference in loyalty behaviors between a retailer's loyalty program members and non-members is negligible. In fact, what many loyalty programs foster is not brand loyalty at all, but merely what experts call *deal loyalty*, where shoppers become responsive only to discounts or giveaways. But my real issue with loyalty programs is that they're a really narrow, one-way conversation between a brand and its customer. It's a conversation made up of not much more than offers, points, and purchases.

Imagine if your relationship with your spouse was structured that way. "Hey, honey! You've collected one hundred fidelity points this month and bonus points for taking the garbage out. Care to redeem now for dinner and a movie?" Perhaps this is why free loyalty programs tend to perform best in categories where competitors are largely undifferentiated, such as the grocery, airline, hotel, credit card, and fuel industries. I mean, what's the difference really between a Hilton or a Sheraton hotel apart from which of the two chains might give you more reward points? That's the problem. Retailers mistake inertia for loyalty. Customers don't remain because they're particularly loyal. They remain because there's no real difference in the experience they'll receive by defecting to your competitor.

The other downfall of most loyalty programs is that they are extrinsic to the experience itself. What I mean is that the rewards for loyalty aren't built into the shopper's experience but rather sit outside of it. I get a reward only after the experience. I've always found it perplexing, for example, that Starbucks asks me what I want, asks me for my name, and then scans my loyalty app only after I place my order. Why wouldn't they scan my app first and ask me, by name, if I'm having the usual? They might even notice that I'm a freak for oatmeal cookies and offer me one with my coffee.

The point is that my loyalty shouldn't be extraneous to the experience. It should shape it. This is why I much prefer paid membership programs.

Paid membership programs are superior to loyalty programs in numerous ways. First and foremost, paid membership is a means of surfacing your most truly engaged customers. Amazon Prime members, for example, spend 250 percent more each year than non-Prime members. But Amazon is hardly the only brand leveraging the power of membership. In 2016, home furnishings retailer Restoration Hardware revamped its entire strategy to eliminate all promotional discounting in favor of establishing a paid membership program that provides consistent, everyday member pricing across every item, as well as a host of other tangible benefits including annual in-home design consultations. As the company detoxed itself from discounting, its sales results suffered, causing many to question the move to membership. By 2018, however, Restoration Hardware had silenced critics by posting strong results and declaring that a full 95 percent of its volume was now being purchased by paying members.

Membership also implies a far more meaningful exchange. Members are willing to provide a greater level of transparency into their activity in return for more personalized, prioritized, and relevant interactions with the brand. As the brand gains more insight into the customer, the experience becomes richer, and the customer is inclined to share more data, feeding what becomes a virtuous circle of trust.

Finally, paid membership programs offer a recurring revenue stream whereas most loyalty programs sit as a liability on the balance sheet. This essential difference is what prompts companies to seek ways of limiting, conditioning, and even decreasing the value of their loyalty programs. Retailers who offer paid membership, however, tend to look for ongoing ways to enhance and add value to their programs.

Regardless of what you sell or to whom you sell it, I strongly recommend that you devise a compelling paid membership strategy and an even more engaged experience for your most engaged customers.

While the apex predators will excel at *big data*, membership programs will provide you with *best data*.

NEVER EVER DISCOUNT. EVER

This may sound overly purist of me, I know, but I firmly believe that discounting is like heroin, in that no one was ever better off for having done it. In fact, it usually just leads to a feeling of needing more. This year's one-day sale becomes next year's two-day sale. As sales targets and shareholder expectations weigh heavy, this month's two-for-one becomes next month's three-for-one. I know. I've been under that gun too. But I'm going to say it again: never discount.

First, the discounts you offer almost never deliver the incremental sales required to justify them. A 10 percent discount, for example, requires that you sell 20 percent more product only to arrive at the same place on the bottom line. Not only is such a lift unlikely, but in the process of pursuing it, you've now trained customers to expect future discounts.

Even if you wish to reward or recognize your best customers, never do so through a discount. The subtext of a discount is that you overcharge most of the time and that your relationship with the customer is merely transactional. Discounting also cheapens your craft as a merchant and your product as a brand.

Instead, think of your relationship with customers like they're a beloved life partner. Find new ways to add value to their lives. Push the boundaries of the price/value equation. Find the means to delight them while charging more for what you sell. Your competitors may run their businesses into the ground attempting to be surprisingly cheap. To invoke a now-famous tagline used by Stella Artois beer many years ago, you want your brand to be perceived as "reassuringly expensive."

CHOOSE YOUR ADVENTURE

In a post-pandemic retail landscape filled with insatiable apex predators and fast-growing mini-marketplaces, only two other classes of retailer will remain: the average and the artful. Which are you?

An Average Retailer	An Artful Retailer
Positions itself in the market	Fulfills a defined purpose for consumers
Sells products	Sells big, human-centric ideas
Attempts to be all things to all people	Works to be loved by its chosen customers
Thinks in sales per square foot and cost per click	Thinks in experiences per square foot and sales per click
Sees its stores as distribution	Animates its stores as media
Believes media is advertising	Believes media is the store
Trades on product and price	Trades on experiences and value

Average Versus Artful Retailers

If most of your affirmation fell in the left-hand column, you're going to want to fix that. If you ended up in the right-hand column, welcome to the future. We've been waiting for you!

7

REINCARNATION OF THE MALL

America is a great disappointment to me.
As I said in one of my books, other societies create
civilizations; we build shopping malls.
Bill Bryson

"I expect to see a third of the malls go a lot sooner than we thought," said Jan Kniffen, in a recent interview with CNBC.[1]

How much sooner? A full ten years sooner than anticipated, according to Kniffen, who is not some doomsday pundit with a bad attitude; he's a former department store executive with decades of experience in the industry. He's also not alone in his dire assessment of the shopping center landscape.

Indeed, as far back as 2017, Credit Suisse suggested that as many as 25 percent of American shopping centers would close by as early as 2022. That was pre-pandemic. Post-pandemic prognosticators doubled down, suggesting that the carnage could be twice as much.

Today, the industry finds itself in wholly uncharted territory. With the effects of the pandemic still battering it, the shopping center industry sits on the cusp of a potential implosion that may have devastating effects, afflicting financial markets through 2021.

THE NEXT BIG SHORT

In May of 2020, *The Wall Street Journal* reported that during the first week of May, foot traffic fell an average of 83 percent compared with the year before at a sampling of reopened malls in seven states, including Georgia and Texas. By July, surveys of U.S. customers suggested that 32 percent felt "unsafe" or "very unsafe" visiting shopping malls.[2]

Even Nordstrom, a fixture in many higher-end malls, is calling it quits. According to its CEO, Erik Nordstrom, the company is shifting away from being a mall-dependent company. Its mall stores, according to the company, now represent 36 percent of sales.

The likelihood of anything even approximating a full return to normal in malls is simply impossible until such time as consumers feel safe. And even with the advent of effective vaccines, the complexity of their distribution suggests that such a sense of safety may take some time to restore.

COMMERCIAL REAL ESTATE CRISIS

Exacerbating the problem for shopping centers is that fact that about 60 percent of malls today are anchored by department stores—50 percent of which will likely close within a year, according to a report by Green Street Advisors.[3]

Unpaid rent will, of course, fall to landlords, putting massive strain on shopping centers, many of which were already struggling. In September of 2020, for example, *The Wall Street Journal* reported that Starwood Capital Group, a real estate investor, had "lost control of seven malls after a recent debt default, surrendering properties the firm acquired for $1.6 billion seven years ago."[4]

Defaults and losses like this will not be unusual as the sector deals with tenant defaults and wildly volatile credit markets.

Some landlords have gone to the extent of taking ownership stakes in failing retailers; Simon Properties, a major owner of U.S.-based malls, took a stake in Forever 21 and department store chain

JCPenney. In an earnings call, CEO David Simon claimed that Simon Properties was making such investments because, in his words, "we think there's a return on investment."[5] What was less clear was how. Beyond rent continuance, how would buying up zombie brands like JCPenney make money? Many in the industry, including me, saw the acquisition of JCPenney as only forestalling the inevitable. If anything, it indicated more the degree to which shopping center owners had painted themselves into a corner, relying too heavily on particular anchor tenants.

As landlords begin to feel the pain, they will quite likely stop making mortgage payments on their properties—many of which are no longer worth the loans drawn on them. In fact, a recent *Wall Street Journal* investigation revealed an industry already on the brink before the pandemic. A study of $650 billion in mortgages that originated from 2013 to 2019 found that "even during normal economic times, the mortgaged properties' net income often falls short of the amount underwritten by lenders."[6]

That would suggest that the mortgages studied were subprime, something that was actually known and warned against as far back as June of 2019, when the Bank for International Settlements pointed to the United States and United Kingdom as leaders in a disturbing trend. A "rise in borrowing in recent years by businesses with low credit scores meant the market for corporate debt was becoming increasingly unstable."[7] And that's "unstable" in pre-pandemic times. But it gets even scarier.

The report went on to say this:

> The study shows risks in the $1.4 trillion market for commercial mortgage-backed securities, or CMBS, where loans on malls, apartment buildings, hotels and the like get packaged into bonds bought by investors, often with guarantees from the government. The findings suggest that loans sold to investors before the pandemic frequently featured overstated income and could have more trouble staying current in case of a downturn.[8]

That's Latin for "your pension fund just got obliterated." Just as in the run-up to the financial crisis of 2008-9, Wall Street has developed a penchant for bundling up subprime mortgages into shiny, new investment products. When the residential mortgage house of cards came tumbling down, they moved on to commercial mortgages and started a new house of cards.

CREDIT CRISIS

That, my friends, is how you create a global credit crisis. Lenders holding a significant amount of commercial debt in the retail sector now own subprime (read junk) mortgages on properties that aren't generating enough income to service their loans. In the meantime, many of those same loans have been bundled up into securities that were sold to investors as high-quality, collateral-backed investments—which we now know they are not. That means that we could be on the brink of a collapse, and not only of the global commercial real estate industry. Banks and institutional investors have a scary level of exposure to the collapse, because the assets they hold no longer line up to their ratings.

Could this underlying condition add up to a 2008-like financial crisis? It's difficult to know for sure. But the moral of the story is that even if this doomsday scenario is averted and even when customer activity rises to pre-pandemic levels, it will return shopping centers to where they began: losing ground in a world that is increasingly finding other things to do.

HOW'D WE GET HERE?

Why are malls, and Western malls particularly, in such a calamitous position? For starters, almost 50 percent of the more than one thousand shopping centers in America are anchored by legacy department stores like JCPenney and Sears—the dead men walking of the retail industry. Furthermore, over 60 percent depend on mid-tier brands like Victoria's Secret for traffic[9]—brands that have been particularly devastated by the pandemic but that were also losing ground with customers before it. But the decline of shopping centers is in no way a problem exclusive to the United States.

In late 2018, the BBC reported that over two hundred U.K. shopping centers were on the brink of crisis.[10] According to the report, many of these ailing centers are owned by American private equity firms. In other places like Canada, shopping center giants like Cadillac Fairview are slashing operating hours by as much as 30 percent in an effort to stave off disaster.

But the truth is we don't need to delve deep into the data to understand why we are about to witness the demise of so many shopping centers. The numbers and statistics serve only to enumerate what most of us already know. Shopping centers, as we have known them, are an industrial-age business model rotting away in a world that no longer needs them. And that's because the modern shopping center industry was, at its inception, built on a foundation of three fundamental conditions.

ACCESS

When I was a teenager in the late 1970s and early '80s, shopping centers were essentially our analog version of the Internet. The mall was Facebook, a gathering place to meet up with friends and family. The mall was Tinder, where more than a few relationships were begun…and ended. It was Netflix, often housing the local movie theater, perhaps the only one in town. It was Uber Eats, a place with lots of food options in the food court. It was Ticketmaster, often the only local point to buy tickets to live events—that is, if you were willing to line up for hours in advance just to get a wristband. Finally, the mall was Amazon, the place where most shopping journeys began and ended, amidst what seemed at the time like a dazzling array of categories, brands, and products.

Unlike malls today, which are a sea of apparel brands, at the local mall of the past, you could buy everything from sandals to snow tires and lawnmowers to lipstick. Maybe you could even get a checkup with your doctor at the same time. The local mall was the epicenter of middle-class life, a cornerstone of commercial activity, and the stomping grounds of middle-class kids and their families. Malls offered access, and in some cases, the only access customers had to brands, products, social circles, and entertainment.

In the post-digital era, however, the mall has ceased to fill any of these functions. Just as the smartphone eventually replaced about forty other electronic devices that were purchased and used independently, the Internet simply replaced almost everything the shopping mall once offered. In fact, it could be said that the largest mall in the world resides comfortably in the palm of your hand. And the selection of goods and services makes the average shopping center look like a weekend yard sale by comparison.

Moreover, if the industry ever does produce a capable technology for virtually trying on clothes, shoes, and other items—enabling a more confident online purchase of apparel—malls may find themselves confronted by another, perhaps fatal, exodus of merchants.

ECONOMICS

The growth of shopping centers in North America followed the growth of the post-WWII middle class. Today, middle-class consumers are about as plentiful as snow leopards, but there was a time when the middle was precisely where the majority of consumers happily resided.

In the post-WWII developed world, the middle class was a politically bipartisan passion project that aimed to provide returning GIs with educations, financing for homes, and the protection of organized labor. Since the early 1980s, the middle class in many countries has been disappearing. By the late 1980s and '90s, despite often having two income earners, the average family was treading water—barely keeping up with inflation.

The disassembling of union power, suppressing of wages, and offshoring of work, not to mention the implementing of disruptive technologies like robotics and computers, has had two results: record-high profits and stock values for corporations and worryingly stagnant wages for middle-class earners both in the United States and abroad. To put a point on it, between 1978 and today, worker pay in the United States increased by 12 percent. CEOs did better by comparison. How much better, you ask? Try 928 percent better. You read that correctly. According to the Economic Policy Institute, today's CEOs make 940 percent more than they did in 1978. So the next time the voice coming out of the speaker at the drive-thru sounds a little disheartened, you'll appreciate why.

Meanwhile, expenses such as housing, healthcare, and education have gone through the roof. Between 1979 and 2005, for example, mortgage payments increased by 76 percent, health insurance premiums by 74 percent, automobile expenses by 52 percent (many families needed two cars), childcare costs by 100 percent, and the tax rate for a two-income family by a whopping 25 percent.[11]

The gap between haves and have-nots has only increased.

Today, upwards of 80 percent of U.S. stocks are held by the wealthiest 10 percent of society.[12]

In 2018, the median level of pay for Amazon employees was $35,000. Yet on January 30, 2020, in a single day of trading, Amazon CEO Jeff Bezos increased his wealth by $13 billion as the company's stock soared.

The savings rate in the United States in 2020 reached a fifty-year high. But for the bottom 90 percent of us, that meant savings of slightly above 1 percent of total income. That followed a long period prior where the savings rate was actually below zero. For the top 10 percent, however, savings reached beyond 10 percent, and for the top 1 percent, the figure soared to 40 percent.

The last minimum wage hike in the United States, for example, came in 2009, at the height of the Great Recession, when the federal minimum wage was set at $7.25 per hour. Meanwhile, since that time, the cost of living in the United States has increased by 20 percent on average.[13] Certain specific costs, like housing and education, have increased at an even steeper rate.

The pandemic will only exacerbate the income gap.

This leads us to where we are today, with high-end luxury malls on one side and outlet malls on the other and millions upon millions of square feet of bad news between the two. Shopping centers that were designed for a middle-class consumer who increasingly no longer exists.

SUBURBANIZATION

The growth of Western department stores also coincided with the post-war exodus to the suburbs, and the availability of millions of acres of cheap asphalt, loads of eager mall workers, and a resident population of car-driving customers looking to spend their freshly minted, middle-class bucks. Between the 1950s and 1990s, they couldn't build malls fast enough to meet demand. When the tide shifted in the 2000s, and jobs, wealth, and income headed back to major cities, some suburban shopping centers spent heavily on reinvention and repositioning to become luxury malls, but most didn't and simply never recovered. Beginning in 2007, no new enclosed malls were constructed in the United States until very recently when new megamalls like New York City's Hudson Yards and American Dream in East Rutherford, New Jersey, were built. Now, with the effects of the pandemic, even their future hangs in the balance.

WE DON'T SELL TENTS

In the short term, we'll see a repurposing of suburban shopping centers. Since 2017, a growing number of malls have undergone conversion to become industrial spaces. Shopping centers within proximity to populations of customers are being converted to last-mile fulfillment centers and warehousing facilities. By July of 2020, fifty-nine such projects were ongoing in the United States alone.[14]

By August of 2020, Amazon was already reportedly in negotiations with Simon Properties to assume closed Sears stores. The plan, according to reports, is for Amazon to convert the spaces to mini–logistics hubs. Such a move, if successful, would potentially enable Amazon to not only further speed delivery but to do so at dramatically lower cost.

Others, like Ingka Group, the owner of almost all of IKEA's stores worldwide, are betting on a pandemic discount on real estate in or near major cities. It's part of a broader move. In 2015, my company engaged in a strategic project with IKEA in which we determined that if IKEA is to continue to flourish, it will have to better penetrate urban centers. With that, we developed an urban design store concept that would enable the company to take its kitchen, bath, and storage planning business into major cities, reaching younger, affluent customers. The concept has since rolled out several spaces, with plans for more. Select suburban shopping centers would give IKEA yet another chess piece on the board.

As with any food chain, the remains of one creature become food for another.

Some, including non-profit advocacy groups, have even called on governments to step in to convert dying shopping centers to low-income housing. But as others point out, the cost of renovating a shopping center to accommodate permanent residences could potentially outweigh the cost of starting fresh.

All of this leads us back to the same inescapable conclusion: the shopping center is an industrial concept groping for relevance in a post-digital world. Malls that exist purely for consumption purposes can succeed but will be relegated to the perceived extremes of value: discount versus luxury. Eventually, even those concepts will prove invisible, as both luxury and off-price become more widely available online.

However, a more critical truth underpins all of these more pragmatic reasons for the mall's downfall. Shopping centers are dying because the companies that own and operate them still believe they're in the commercial real estate industry.

Some, however, like Mark Toro, see the situation very differently.

Toro is the chairman of North American Properties, an Atlanta-based company that designs and builds mixed-use commercial spaces. The company's most recent projects include a unique mixed-use development called Avalon, in Alpharetta, Georgia. When I first met Mark, I asked him how long he'd been in the commercial real estate business. He replied, "I'm not in the commercial real estate business. I'm in the hospitality and entertainment business."

"Wait…what?" I thought. "Haven't heard that one before."

As I've come to know Mark and learn about his company, I've also come to understand clearly what he meant by that comment. At Avalon, for example, the company stages roughly 260 events per year. That's roughly 5 events per week! It's not unusual for some of these events to gather crowds of thousands from the surrounding area. Concerts, outdoor movie nights, fireworks—hell, people get married at Avalon! Furthermore, Mark's team also attends hospitality courses provided by Ritz-Carlton. They don't call themselves mall management but rather "experience makers." They don't just keep a finger on the pulse of the industry; they study it intently. When asked what precisely it is that they deliver, Toro proudly declares: "We trade in human energy."[15] It's an energy he sees as both infectious and fundamental to success in the industry.

This highlights precisely the problem with the majority of shopping center development and management companies. They believe they're in the shopping center business. A business that builds commercial boxes, negotiates long leases, keeps places in good repair, and collects rent, often based on a percentage of sales, from retailers and other businesses.

What they don't realize is that that industry died two decades ago. In fact, it's worth asking whether the term "shopping center" is even relevant in a world where online retail was growing at a pre-pandemic rate almost four times greater than brick and mortar? As a model, the shopping center is already over. Recently, debate has ensued around aesthetics. Should malls be bigger, smaller? Should they have more retail, less retail, ski hills, or roller coasters? Should there be more or fewer of them?

The answer to all of the above depends on one all-important question: What's the story?

Think of it this way. When Cirque du Soleil is planning a new show, its team doesn't first gather to debate the size or color of the tent they'll perform in. Cirque du Soleil is not in the business of selling tents. It's in the business of creating remarkable stories.

Instead, the team at Cirque begins by writing that unique and compelling story. What is it? Who are the characters? How can the story come to life through circus skills? What is the journey on which they intend to bring the audience? Until all of these questions are answered, it's impossible to know how big the show will be. Without knowing how big the show will be, it's impossible to decide how big the tent should be or what it should look like.

Thus, the core problem in the commercial real estate industry is that it still believes it's in the tent business. It's failed to understand that while the tent is important, the show is what people are coming for.

So what is the shopping center of the future? How will it depart from its industrial-era ancestors? I'll leave the design to the architects. But from my experience, here are the essential operating imperatives.

AN ACTUAL PLACE

On a visit to the United Kingdom in late 2018, I visited the new mixed-use development called Coal Drops Yard in Kings Cross, London. Set among the freight rail yards of the Victorian era, the avant-garde project was designed by renowned architect Thomas Heatherwick. As beauty is always subjective, some lauded the design, and others were less enamored with it.

What is indisputable, however, is the distinct sense of place that the development captures. The long, authentic, and somewhat checkered past of Kings Cross is beautifully articulated throughout. The design provides a well-defined central square, nestled within with a mix of housing, almost Dickensian-looking retail spaces, and integrated office space, as well as hospitality and food options in and around the site.

To say that a shopping center should be "a real place" sounds obvious, but the truth is that many of today's shopping centers are monolithic concrete boxes surrounded by a sea of asphalt. They offer nothing at all unique, inspiring, or distinct. Nothing, save, in some cases, the name of the center, even alludes to the community they're located in. They could be anywhere or nowhere. It wouldn't matter.

Now, not every development can be a Coal Drops Yard, nor does it need to be. But whatever place you choose to build a center, think of it as the stage on which a wholly unique story will unfold. The more authentic and organic that stage is, the more people will be drawn to it. The stronger the sense of place it embodies, the more inclined people will be to gather there.

A FUNCTIONING COMMUNITY

American architect Victor Gruen, the man widely regarded as the father of the modern shopping mall, never set out to create what we see in our communities today. In fact, prior to his death in 1978, Gruen was quoted as saying, "I am often called the father of the shopping mall [...] I would like to take this opportunity to disclaim paternity once and for all. I refuse to pay alimony to those bastard developments. They destroyed our cities."[16]

In fact, as legend now has it, Gruen's original intent was to build places more akin to Roman marketplaces or the Greek agora, spaces where people could gather and participate in community life.

Walk through any European city, and I'll wager that you will find your way to the public square or central gathering place. A place that embodies Gruen's original vision. In fact, many cities were designed specifically to lead you into those central malls, and so has been the case for several millennia. We are social creatures who crave belonging. Our taste in yoga pants might change, but our need for community will endure. Therefore, shopping centers should be designed first and foremost around the premise of becoming a community gathering point. Without that as the linchpin, little else will fall into place.

The other wonderful thing about the city squares and piazzas of Europe is that people live, work, eat, sleep, and play there. They are the centers of real, functioning communities. This organic human activity and the energy it creates draws us in.

Whether your shopping center is in the suburbs or the city, the inherent energy of a genuine mixed-use community and its resident population will be essential to creating that all-important sense of place.

A MEDIA NETWORK

As brick-and-mortar sales volumes naturally decline and a greater percentage of sales are cleaved off into digital platforms, an increasing number of retailers will begin to do one of two things: either close their stores or, as discussed in chapter 6, begin to regard their physical stores less as a distribution channel and more as a media channel. Shopping center operators will have to evolve their thinking in lockstep, acting as a media network, similar to more literal networks like HBO. Just as HBO's role is to promote the quality and uniqueness of its television and movie lineups, the role of the shopping center as a media network is to create unique programming, special events, and community gatherings that bring audiences to each retailer's individual show. In doing so, the center now begins to take a more active role in driving favorable brand impressions for its tenants. In other words, it's no longer on retailers to drive traffic to the center. It's the center that must drive traffic to the retailers.

In this sense, I believe that the typical shopping center marketing team will have to evolve to become more akin to a television production team. The center will have to become a 365-day-a-year variety show executed by a team that not only plans well in advance but that also has the ability to think on their feet, flexing those plans based on local happenings in each community. The goal should be to bring audiences to the center—even those who have no intention of buying anything. Audiences that drive media value for the retailers in the center.

A NEW REVENUE MODEL

This migration to physical retail as a media channel puts a new elephant in the room. At some juncture in the near future, someone in the shopping center industry is going to reinvent the model for revenue. Not because they want to but because they have to. In a world soon to be dominated by online retail, we can no longer base rental agreements solely on any of the traditional sales metrics and lease clauses we use today. If retailers increasingly maintain brick-and-mortar spaces as a media play aimed at customer acquisition, then the center has to develop its understanding of the value of each of those consumer impressions to a brand. Ultimately, consumer impressions are the most valuable asset a center owner has, and yet very few are even attempting to assess their monetary value.

So a new formula is going to be required, and it will have to be based on a retailer's access, within the center, to those consumer impressions. Just as NBC or CBS understand the volume and demographic makeup of their audiences, as well as which shows to position in which timeslots, retail centers will have to begin to understand their guest populations in a granular way to ensure just the right lineup of retail programming to provide to them. More importantly, centers will have to become skilled at giving that population new reasons to visit the center again and again.

A FOMO MACHINE

No marketing tool or tactic in the history of humankind is as powerful as the fear of missing out (FOMO). FOMO is far and away the most powerful and predictable customer incentive. One study among Millennials found that just shy of 70 percent claim to experience anxiety about missing out on experiences.[17] That shouldn't come as a surprise to any of us. In a world where almost everything seems unlimited, on demand, time shifted, and mass produced, the feeling of actually missing out on something completely is jarring.

The role of the shopping center is to create such moments, events, appearances, and spectacles, with the objective of deliberately building disappointment into the model. By delivering one-of-a-kind, get-it-while-you-can entertainment and excitement, you'll create legions of fans. By limiting access to those events, you'll throw even more fuel on the FOMO fire.

Bottom line: the center's role is to create things that can't be experienced anywhere else, and that's going to require enormous creative horsepower.

A KALEIDOSCOPE OF VARIETY

We live in a swipe-left world. The Internet has trained our brains to expect and even crave a never-ending stream of variety and newness. We fly through our limitless Instagram accounts, "liking" hundreds of pictures along the way. We scroll quickly through our inexhaustible Facebook feeds to see what new things are happening in our world. We find a boundless list of new movies on Netflix to watch.

Then, we go to the mall, and our souls are crushed as we slog past the same two hundred retail tenants again. All of them selling mostly the same stuff. In much the same way. Since forever.

The challenge, frankly, for anything that exists in the physical world is to rival the newness and variety that the Internet has conditioned us to expect. Therefore, shopping centers have to be designed to offer a more diverse and ever-revolving array of merchants, entertainment venues, food options, and experiences.

Similarly, the physical space should be designed to be flexible and reconfigurable to accommodate shorter leases, pop-up activations, events, and marketplace concepts. On a four- to six-week time frame, the center should look, feel, sound, smell, and act entirely different— giving the local community never-ending reasons to visit.

You'll never have a problem securing a lululemon or a Levi's, but they also will not make your shopping center a go-to destination. That's not a disparagement of either brand; they're both very good names. It's just reality. The creative capacity of the center operator themselves is what will ultimately determine the center's success or failure.

A PLATFORM, NOT A MALL

Rather than thinking of shopping centers as hard assets with gross leasable area, the center of the future will see itself more as a boundless, connected platform that exists simultaneously in both the digital and physical worlds. A platform accessible to tenants, shoppers, maintenance service providers, and the resident community.

A platform that offers shoppers
- A two-way communication channel between customers and the center for any needs
- Commerce across multiple channels (online to offline or vice versa)
- Membership programs offering premium services, experiences, and access to special events
- Personal shopper services across categories
- A hub for live events and streamed entertainment
- A completely searchable space (retailer, brand, product, etc.) via mobile
- An experiential backdrop for memorable moments in customers' lives

A platform that offers the community
- Support and a venue for local initiatives and causes
- Real-time information on center sustainability and social responsibility initiatives

A platform that offers tenants
- Real-time market intelligence and a data source for tenants
- Testing ground for retail, entertainment, food and beverage, or unconventional tenancy concepts
- A plug-and-play platform for fast and easy merchant setup, both online and off
- A financing and incubation platform for start-up retail
- A logistics platform to support ship to home, click and collect, or international delivery
- A production space for creating engaging live or recorded media

When the center is viewed not merely as a monolithic physical structure but rather as a technologically infused and flexible platform, all of this becomes possible.

AN ARCHETYPAL PARADISE

Finally, the best shopping centers will employ the same approach to their tenant mix that I'm advocating retailers take in addressing their positioning. They will ensure that every tenant on site has a clear purpose and value. Instead of the usual amorphous lineup of boring brands, imagine a center filled with archetypal retailers, where every single retail space is occupied by a living, breathing answer to a customer question. Where tenants are selected because they appeal on the basis of culture, entertainment, expertise, or product, and because they fully animate their unique in-store experiences.

In the end, the world doesn't need another shopping center. It needs unique and authentic gathering places; places charged, as Mark Toro puts it, with human energy. In a world where a universe of products sits at the tip of our fingers, and anything we want is two taps away, the "shopping center" of the industrial era will have no choice but to carve out its new role as community center in a post-digital and post-pandemic age.

8

RESURRECTING
RETAIL

From the ashes, a fire shall be woken,
a light from the shadows shall spring.
J. R. R. Tolkien

round the time I was completing this book, I happened to be
rearranging some things in my basement when I came across
another book that I'd completely forgotten I owned. It's an
original printing of a work called *The Romance of Commerce*, written
by H. Gordon Selfridge, founder of the eponymous British department store and regarded, to this day, as one of the greatest merchant
entertainers of all time. The book was graciously given to me by a
wonderful client. With its thick, roughly cut and bound pages and
beautiful block-printed illustrations, it is considered to be one of the
most comprehensive and important works on the history of retail.
What is perhaps even more coincidental, bordering on spooky, is that
the first date of publishing was 1918. Ring a bell?

What, I wondered, was going through Selfridge's mind as he
penned his thoughts on the industry over a hundred years ago, in the
midst of the Spanish flu outbreak? Could he have conceived that little
more than one hundred years later, retailers and industry scribes like

me would find ourselves in his very same position? What might he offer us in the way of advice, were he here today? What wisdom might he impart to fill our sails?

As I sat, thumbing through its pages, one paragraph immediately jumped off the page at me:

> The world is ripe for a new philosophy; perhaps for a new religion, as understood in its broadest meaning. We are hungry for higher ideals, higher inspirations, standards beyond those which man has thus far conceived. Our minds are finite. We can and do improve our physical condition. Our lives are made continually easier. We have many clever devices which aid us to live. We can and do better our methods, our systems. This is easy because there is so much left to accomplish in that direction before perfection is reached, but our mental development is limited indeed.[1]

These words from more than a century ago seemed to me just as relevant and poignant today. While the retail industry has indeed progressed over time, it's hardly become *progressive*. We too have many "clever devices," things Selfridge could never have conceived, yet none of them have made the retail industry great. Not yet at least. And our minds, while becoming smarter, have lacked the vision and creativity to think bigger.

In pursuit of efficiency and ever-increasing profit, we've siphoned the artfulness and theater out of our industry. How disappointed would Selfridge be if he went shopping today, only to find the cold concrete cathedrals of consumption we call big box stores, hypermarkets, and malls, devoid of much of the energy, theatrics, and thrills retail can and should provide.

The supply chains we operate today may be more elaborate but are really just extrapolations of the cotton trade. While we talk a lot more today about fair trade, we turn a blind eye to rampant inequality and modern-day slavery so long as it provides cheap labor. While we have an ever-keener awareness of the environmental damage our industry causes, it has not slowed our reckless behavior to any material extent.

Today, we live in a world where a portion of the population, in order to feed its lust for more and more material wealth and possessions, travel from country to country, robbing the other portion of civilization of their resources, rights, and labor. When they've tapped all the value a particular country can provide, they move on to exploit another. It's been that way for hundreds, if not thousands, of years.

It would be easy to conclude from this that we are lost and without hope. But there's another way to view our current predicament. Perhaps COVID-19 is really the Universe tapping us on the shoulder and saying, "What the hell are you doing?" Perhaps the pandemic is exactly the incentive we as a global neighborhood need to understand our interconnectedness. And maybe it's the moment when we, in this industry, change everything.

I mean, who among us with a conscience would design a system like the retail industry we know today?

And the more important question is, Who will fix it?

The sad truth is that it likely will not be our political leaders.

BRANDS ARE THE NEW CHURCH AND STATE

In fact, as a global community, we are losing faith in our governments at a precipitous rate. A 2019 Pew Research study indicates that only 17 percent of Americans believe they can trust the government to "do what is right."[2] In 1964, that figure was 77 percent. Likewise, a poll of over thirty-three thousand residents of the United Kingdom found that more than two-thirds do not feel adequately represented by any of the main political parties.

Adding to our anxiety is the fact that the institutions we've traditionally relied on to maintain our sense of civility and community—government organizations—have themselves become so divided, polarized, and partisan that they often end up widening the ideological chasms they seek to bridge. One recent study suggested that "72% of U.S. consumers cite government and political leaders as playing a significant role in dividing society."[3] The pandemic is likely to only exacerbate this belief.

In many parts of the world, the appeal of organized religion is also faltering. According to a 2018 pan-European study by Saint Mary's University, London, the proportion of young Europeans purporting to have "no religious affiliation" is on a sharp incline, with 75 percent of Swedes aged sixteen to twenty-nine, for example, claiming to have absolutely no religious affiliation at all.[4] According to the same study, the majority of Spanish, Dutch, British, and Belgians in the same age group claim never to attend any form of religious service. North America is registering a similar decline in those identifying as Christian and a corresponding uptick in those identifying as atheist, agnostic, or "nothing in particular."

The problem is that declining trust in institutions like the state and the church doesn't suppress our fundamentally human desire for belonging, purpose, and meaning in our lives. The need to be a part of a community that aligns to our moral compass lies so deep in our makeup as human beings that no amount of social or political disaffection can drain it out of us. We must believe in something or someone.

The result is a societal vacuum for courageous brands to fill. A 2018 global study by Edelman—of eight thousand consumers across eight markets—suggests that almost two-thirds of us make buying decisions based on a brand's positioning on social or political issues. More importantly, 53 percent of us believe that brands can do more to solve social problems than governments.[5] Let that thought marinate for a moment. A majority of us now place more faith in brands to change the world than in traditional social institutions.

So brands find themselves with a unique and historic opportunity: the potential to move beyond merely offering running clubs or yoga classes and become global "brand-nations," filling the void in values, in meaning, in belonging that has been left by government and religion.

But if this is meant to be our moment as an industry to redeem ourselves, it means building a new business from back to front.

BUILD FOR UNCERTAINTY, NOT COST

In the pandemic's earliest stages, one of the first elements of global retail structure to implode was supply chains. Some retailers found themselves on the receiving end of orders they couldn't sell. Others cancelled orders with their manufacturers or simply refused the invoices. In other cases, retailers couldn't even access items they desperately needed to maintain revenues. All of these problems were not bugs, but rather features of the system the global industry had collectively built to serve one selfish need: lowest cost.

John Thorbeck, for one, believes this is about to change. Thorbeck is the chairman of Chainge Capital, a company that specializes in helping brands create more resilient and sustainable supply chain systems.

The way he sees it, we've spent the last several hundred years building supply chains with the aim of lowering costs. This has meant an escalating dependence on long-term demand planning, protracted order cycles, massive order quantities, and the never-ending need to access ever-cheaper labor from all corners of the Earth. This all means that retailers are now required to put more and more capital at risk on the front end to support their low-cost competitiveness.

The problem with this thinking, however, says Thorbeck, is that it creates inherent risks on the back end—the kind of risks that bit the industry directly in the ass when the pandemic hit.

Given that the world is an increasingly uncertain place as a result of natural disasters, political and civil unrest, and yes, the threat of pandemics, Thorbeck's remark means that brands are actually increasing the level of risk to which they are subjecting their capital. Couple this with ever-more-fickle consumers who have access to an exploding universe of influences and information, and it makes triangulating consumer preferences increasingly difficult. The result is massive levels of markdowns and in many cases, destruction of unsold garments and other products.

Even prior to COVID-19, fashion supply chains in particular were a risky bet. Enormous orders, placed months in advance, aimed at predicting fashion trends in the future created a high risk of interrupted supply, customer returns, and ultimately markdowns and hits to margin.

According to Thorbeck, some retailers, however, like Zara, have rethought the equation: "They've taken risk out of a high-risk business. They have a cycle for speed which allows them to bring fashion into stores more frequently, and flow those goods more often, therefore getting more store visits. And of course, that leads to higher margins, and fewer markdowns."[6]

In a practical sense, says Thorbeck, a few things must be done to build a resilient supply chain that reduces the risk to capital:

> Revisit current supply chain goals to determine what goals and metrics are driving the current system
> Work with partners to wean off behaviors aimed only at lowest cost and move toward behaviors that promise more speed, flexibility, and resilience among all supply chain partners
> Leverage technology along the supply chain to allow for real-time data flow, communication, and insight by all supply partners

The days of long lead times, labor arbitrage, and ludicrous waste must come to an end.

STOP BEING LESS BAD

I had the pleasure recently of interviewing William McDonough, co-author of the ground-breaking 2002 treatise on sustainability in design, *Cradle to Cradle: Remaking the Way We Make Things*. While discussing sustainability in retail, McDonough says something that I find provocative. He says, as an industry, we have to stop framing progress by the goal of doing *less harm*. Reducing harm is not the same thing, he says, as doing good:

> If you lived in Flint, Michigan and you told me that you're going to reduce the lead in my children's brains by 2025, you know, a little bit at a time, I would look at you like, "Have *you* been drinking too much lead?" This doesn't work, this is a toxin. You stop, you just stop.[7]

In other words, doing *less* harm is still doing harm, and that's not good. Why should we accept less harm as an outcome? Whether it's dumping less plastic in the ocean, pumping less carbon in the atmosphere, or tolerating a little less inequality, our goals are falling short as an industry. Instead, McDonough says, we should aim to do good. And good, according to him, comes when we cease running our businesses in a linear fashion and adopt circularity as an ethos.

THE CIRCULAR BUSINESS

Circularity, as a concept, has long been associated with environmental sustainability specifically, but it can be applied broadly to entire economies. The Ellen MacArthur Foundation defines circularity as follows: "A circular economy is based on the principles of designing out waste and pollution, keeping products and materials in use, and regenerating natural systems."

The idea is that in a circular economy, what is taken in—energy, resources, materials—is all eventually reused, recycled, or returned to the environment in a renewable fashion, available for use by generations to come. Instead of viewing the production and sale of goods as being linear, where what is produced eventually becomes useless waste, the circular model assumes that what is produced eventually gets reused. A system where inputs equal outputs.

But I believe that the concept of circularity is one that can and should be applied more broadly beyond the environmental lens. The challenge is to build a circular business in every respect, beginning with economic and social inequality. In fact, I would argue that until we solve the issue of inequality, for example, the notion of tackling climate change will remain a fantasy. Why? According to a 2019 report by *The Guardian*, the legal minimum wage for Bangladeshi garment workers was 8,000 taka or about $95 a month.[8] Not $95 an hour, a day, or even a week, but $95 per month. Now tell me how we can go about convincing a woman supporting a family on $95 per month that her overriding concern ought to be the cleanliness of the world's oceans or the amount of carbon in the atmosphere. The simple response is that those will never prevail as concerns, because we've made the daily struggle for survival her primary preoccupation.

But we certainly don't have to travel as far as Bangladesh to find inequality. Our industry is rife with it. Frontline retail workers earn subsistence wages while CEOs who, in some cases, helped to bankrupt their own companies are paid millions to leave. Meanwhile, U.S. retail workers fight to earn $15 per hour or about $31,000 per year, which when adjusted for inflation, is considerably less than their 1970 counterpart earned. And as it turns out in retail, as it all too often does in other industries, women and minorities are the primary victims of such inequality.

These are all symptoms of a linear operating model that views all inputs, including labor, as commoditized and disposable.

The circular business takes a different view. In the circular economy, the outputs of one system feed another:

➤ Fair and equitable wages, which allow employees to lead productive, safe, fulfilling lives and ensure that they can contribute to and invest in their communities
➤ Manufacturing processes that produce a net economic and environmental benefit to the communities the business operates in

- Materials that are safe, natural, and non-toxic and can be reintroduced into the environment as a food or energy source for future use
- Products that can be reused, resold, repaired, or recycled, dramatically extending their utility

Doing all this, however, will require a new brand of leader.

H.E.R.O. WORSHIP

On May 15, 2020, a headline appeared in *The New York Times* that read "Why Are Women-Led Nations Doing Better with COVID-19?" At the time, New Zealand Prime Minister Jacinda Ardern, Germany's Angela Merkel, Finland's thirty-four-year-old Prime Minister Sanna Marin, not to mention Tsai Ing-wen, the president of Taiwan, were all leading their respective countries to far better health outcomes in the pandemic's early, chaotic stages. The obvious conclusion we might draw from this is that women may simply be more capable of leading through crisis than are their male counterparts. That may indeed be the case.

What's particularly intriguing about that to me, though, is that when we turn to examine exemplary leadership across genders in the business sector throughout the pandemic, we discover the same sorts of key behaviors and qualities these four female global leaders exemplified. And I believe it's these behaviors and qualities that will be the essential skills for the new era of business.

HUMILITY

The leader of tomorrow is humble and willing to admit uncertainty. They are also willing to accept the vulnerability that comes with that admission. They are inherently curious in their approach, and while never purporting to have all the answers, they are skilled at divining the questions that move the organization toward those answers. They celebrate success and failure equally, focusing in both cases on what the organization learns in the process.

EMPATHY

The leader of tomorrow is one who is sensitive to the social and economic conditions of others. They seek out experiences that allow them to relate to both staff and customers—spending time in their shoes, so to speak. They are active listeners who work to diffuse the anxiety of their partners, customers, and staff. They seek equity and fairness in balancing the interests and feelings of all stakeholders.

RESILIENCE

Intrinsically motivated, the leader of tomorrow is one who rebounds from obstacles and challenges. They are inherently willing to try new methods, systems, and processes. Where others see failed initiatives, they see only successful experiments. They view crises as opportunities and change as a positive force to be embraced.

OPENNESS

The leader of tomorrow defers to expert opinions and information while maintaining a broader view across the enterprise. They are inherently receptive to the views of others and willing to have their own opinions challenged and actions critiqued. They prize diversity as a core organizational strength, particularly in times of crisis, allowing them to benefit from a plurality of perspectives and experience.

Those who rise to achieve all of these qualities have achieved what I call H.E.R.O. leadership. And in this story, the hero could be you.

TOWARD A NEW AND BRIGHTER ERA

So with Selfridge's words in mind, it's up to us. We can squander the opportunities catalyzed by the pandemic, retreat from the future, and stick to the status quo, which many companies have clearly already determined to do. But the more courageous choice will be to embrace the once-in-a-century opportunity we are being given to reflect, rethink, and resurrect. Resurrect our businesses, our communities, and our industry—not simply returning to our old paradigms but forging new ones. Not a return to "normal" but a journey to something infinitely better and brighter.

I believe that, in the fullness of time, we'll look back to realize that the pandemic gave birth to a new generation of brilliant and creative retailers. Retailers that will take to their stages both on- and offline, imbued with a clear sense of purpose and value to consumers. Archetypes—all with their own remarkable stories to tell—that will pave the way to the future of retail. Extraordinary businesses that will trade on creating culture, staging entertainment, delivering expertise, and designing remarkable products, and power these propositions by creating consumer-centric ecosystems of outstanding digital and physical content.

The shopping center of yesterday will become the community center of tomorrow, constructing beautiful and authentic spaces woven into the fabric of our cities and suburbs. It will be a place with palpable energy and vibrance, offering time and money well-spent.

COVID-19 was an uncontrolled burn of the global retail forest. The deadwood has been turned to ashes. But from those ashes, a better, healthier, and more prosperous industry will emerge. Those with the vision, courage, and strength to not only see but embrace the opportunity with which this crisis presents us—they will be the masters of the new era of retail.

NOTES

INTRODUCTION: HANDSHAKES AND HUGS

1. C. Todd Lopez, "Corps of Engineers Converts NYC's Javits Center into Hospital," U.S. Department of Defense, April 1, 2020, https://www.defense.gov/Explore/News/Article/Article/2133514/corps-of-engineers-converts-nycs-javits-center-into-hospital/.
2. C. Todd Lopez, "Corps of Engineers Converts NYC's Javits Center into Hospital," U.S. Department of Defense, April 1, 2020, https://www.defense.gov/Explore/News/Article/Article/2133514/corps-of-engineers-converts-nycs-javits-center-into-hospital/.
3. Janet Freund, "Credit Suisse Warns That U.S. Store Closings May Worsen in 2020," *Bloomberg*, October 14, 2019, https://www.bloomberg.com/news/articles/2019-10-14/store-closures-may-be-even-worse-next-year-credit-suisse-says?sref=5zifHLEP.
4. Patricia Cohen, "We All Have a Stake in the Stock Market, Right? Guess Again," *The New York Times*, February 8, 2018, https://www.nytimes.com/2018/02/08/business/economy/stocks-economy.html#:~:text=A%20whopping%2084%20percent%20of,savings%20programs%20like%20529%20plans.
5. Josephine Ma, "Coronavirus: China's First Confirmed Covid-19 Case Traced Back to November 17," *South China Morning Post*, March 13, 2020, https://www.scmp.com/news/china/society/article/3074991/coronavirus-chinas-first-confirmed.
6. "Record Fall in G20 GDP in First Quarter of 2020," OECD, June 11, 2020, https://www.oecd.org/sdd/na/g20-gdp-growth-Q1-2020.pdf.
7. Noah Smith, "Why Coronavirus Is Punishing the Economy More Than Spanish Flu," *Bloomberg*, May 6, 2020, https://www.bloomberg.com/opinion/articles/2020-05-06/why-coronavirus-is-punishing-the-economy-more-than-spanish-flu?sref=5zifHLEP.
8. Drew Desilver, "10 facts about American workers," Pew Research Center, August 29, 2019, https://www.pewresearch.org/fact-tank/2019/08/29/facts-about-american-workers/.
9. Holly Briedis et al., "Adapting to the Next Normal in Retail: The Customer Experience Imperative," McKinsey & Company, March 14, 2020, https://www.mckinsey.com/industries/retail/our-insights/adapting-to-the-next-normal-in-retail-the-customer-experience-imperative#.
10. Rob Walker, "Why Most Post-Pandemic Predictions Will Be Totally Wrong," Marker, April 20, 2020, https://marker.medium.com/why-most-post-pandemic-predictions-will-be-totally-wrong-4e1bc1c71614.
11. Mary Mazzoni, "A Longstanding Pandemic Response Team Helped Intel Act Swiftly in the Wake of COVID-19," Triple Pundit, May 8, 2020, https://www.triplepundit.com/story/2020/intel-pandemic-response-team-covid-19/88991.

CHAPTER 1: PRE-EXISTING CONDITIONS

1. Rachel Siegel, "Hard-Hit Retailers Projected to Shutter As Many As 25,000 Stores This Year, Mostly in Malls," *The Washington Post*, June 9, 2020, https://www.washingtonpost.com/business/2020/06/09/retail-store-closure-mall/.

2. Nathan Bomey and Kelly Tyko, "Can Shopping Malls Survive the Coronavirus Pandemic and a New Slate of Permanent Store Closings?" *USA Today*, July 4, 2020, https://www.usatoday.com/story/money/2020/07/14/coronavirus-closings-retail-mall-closures-shopping-changes/5400200002/.

3. "Who's Gone Bust in Retail?" Center for Retail Research, 2020, https://www.retailresearch.org/whos-gone-bust-retail.html.

4. Chantel Fernandez, "The Contemporary Market Needs a Rebrand," *The Business of Fashion*, August 3, 2020, https://www.businessoffashion.com/articles/professional/contemporary-market-designers-department-stores-wholesale-retail.

5. Jeannine Usalcas, "Labour Market Review 2009," Statistics Canada, April 2010, https://www150.statcan.gc.ca/n1/pub/75-001-x/2010104/article/11148-eng.htm.

6. "Hard Times Forecast for Global Job Recovery in 2020, Warns UN Labour Agency Chief," UN News, June 30, 2020, https://news.un.org/en/story/2020/06/1067432.

7. Janet Adamy and Paul Overberg, "'Playing Catch-Up in the Game of Life.' Millennials Approach Middle Age in Crisis," *The Wall Street Journal*, May 19, 2019, https://www.wsj.com/articles/playing-catch-up-in-the-game-of-life-millennials-approach-middle-age-in-crisis-11558290908.

8. Janet Adamy, "Millennials Slammed by Second Financial Crisis Fall Even Further Behind," *The Wall Street Journal*, August 9, 2020, https://www.wsj.com/articles/millennials-covid-financial-crisis-fall-behind-jobless-11596811470.

9. Charlotte Swasey, Ethan Winter, and Ilya Sheyman, "The Staggering Economic Impact of the Coronavirus Pandemic," Data for Progress, April 9, 2020, https://filesforprogress.org/memos/the-staggering-economic-impact-coronavirus.pdf.

10. Ben Staverman, "Half of Older Americans Have Nothing in Retirement Savings," *Bloomberg*, March 26, 2019, https://www.bloomberg.com/news/articles/2019-03-26/almost-half-of-older-americans-have-zero-in-retirement-savings?sref=5zifHLEP.

11. Doug Stephens and BoF Studio, "Retail Reborn Episode 1: How Trauma Transforms the Consumer Psyche: Interview with Sheldon Solomon," *The Business of Fashion*, September 15, 2020, https://www.businessoffashion.com/articles/podcasts/retail-reborn-podcast-doug-stephens-consumer-psyche?source=bibblio.

12. Doug Stephens and BoF Studio, "Retail Reborn Episode 1: How Trauma Transforms the Consumer Psyche: Interview with Sheldon Solomon," *The Business of Fashion*, September 15, 2020, https://www.businessoffashion.com/articles/podcasts/retail-reborn-podcast-doug-stephens-consumer-psyche?source=bibblio.

13. Doug Stephens and BoF Studio, "Retail Reborn Episode 1: How Trauma Transforms the Consumer Psyche: Interview with Sheldon Solomon," *The Business of Fashion*, September 15, 2020, https://www.businessoffashion.com/articles/podcasts/retail-reborn-podcast-doug-stephens-consumer-psyche?source=bibblio.

14. Nidhi Arora et al., "Customer Sentiment and Behavior Continue to Reflect the Uncertainty of the COVID-19 Crisis," McKinsey & Company, July 8, 2020, https://www.mckinsey.com/business-functions/marketing-and-sales/our-insights/a-global-view-of-how-consumer-behavior-is-changing-amid-covid-19.

15. Cory Stieg, "Sports Fans Have Higher Self-Esteem and Are More Satisfied with Their Lives (Whether Their Teams Win or Lose)," CNBC Make It, July 23, 2020, https://www.cnbc.com/2020/07/23/why-being-a-sports-fan-and-rooting-for-a-team-is-good-for-you.html.

16. Utpal Dholakia, "How Terrorist Attacks Influence Customer Behaviors," *Psychology Today*, December 1, 2015, https://www.psychologytoday.com/us/blog/the-science -behind-behavior/201512/how-terrorist-attacks-influence-consumer-behaviors.

17. Quoted in Anand Damani, "Does It Really Take 21 Days to Form Habits?," Behavioural Design, June 28, 2016, http://www.behaviouraldesign.com/author/ananddamani/ page/8/#sthash.x6IH9ST3.dpbs.

18. Benjamin Gardner, Phillippa Lally, and Jane Wardle, "Making Health Habitual: The Psychology of 'Habit-Formation' and General Practice," *British Journal of General Practice*, vol. 62, issue 605, December 2012, pp. 664–66.

CHAPTER 2: THE WORMHOLE

1. "The Rise of the City," Lumen, no date, https://courses.lumenlearning.com/boundless -ushistory/chapter/the-rise-of-the-city/.

2. CitiesX, "The Rise of Suburbs: Edward L. Glaeser in Conversation with Lizabeth Cohen," YouTube, January 29, 2018, https://www.youtube.com/watch?v=WpO3qRYn52A.

3. Steven Pinker, *The Better Angels of Our Nature: Why Violence Has Declined* (New York: Penguin Books, 2012).

4. Parag Khanna, "How Much Economic Growth Comes from Our Cities?" World Economic Forum, April 13, 2016, https://www.weforum.org/agenda/2016/04/how-much-economic -growth-comes-from-our-cities/.

5. Robert D. Atkinson, Mark Muro, and Jacob Whiten, "The Case for Growth Centers: How to Spread Tech Innovation Across America," Brookings ITIF, December 2019, https://www.brookings.edu/wp-content/uploads/2019/12/Full-Report-Growth -Centers_PDF_BrookingsMetro-BassCenter-ITIF.pdf.

6. Saša Petricic, "Japan's Traditional Work Culture Takes Precedence over Physical Distancing in Tokyo," CBC, May 3, 2020, https://www.cbc.ca/news/world/japan -covid-19-coronavirus-1.5549504.

7. Casey Newton, "Facebook Says It Will Permanently Shift Tens of Thousands of Jobs to Remote Work," The Verge, May 21, 2020, https://www.theverge.com/facebook/ 2020/5/21/21265699/facebook-remote-work-shift-workforce-permanent-covid-19 -mark-zuckerberg-interview.

8. Candy Cheng, "Shopify Is Joining Twitter in Permanent Work-from-Home Shift," *Bloomberg*, May 21, 2020, https://www.bloomberg.com/news/articles/2020-05-21/ shopify-is-joining-twitter-in-permanent-work-from-home-shift?sref=5zifHLEP.

9. Rob Copeland and Peter Grant, "Google to Keep Employees Home until Summer 2021 amid Coronavirus Pandemic," *The Wall Street Journal*, July 27, 2020, https://www.wsj.com/ articles/google-to-keep-employees-home-until-summer-2021-amid-coronavirus-pandemic -11595854201?mod=e2tw.

10. Lawrence White, "Barclays CEO Says 'Putting 7,000 People in a Building May Be Thing of the Past,'" Reuters, April 29, 2020, https://uk.reuters.com/article/uk-barclays-results -offices-idUKKCN22B1O1.

11. Nicholas A. Bloom et al., "Does Working from Home Work? Evidence from a Chinese Experiment," *The Quarterly Journal of Economics*, vol. 130, issue 1, February 2015, pp. 165–218.

12. "The Benefits of Working from Home," Airtasker, March 31, 2020, https://www.airtasker .com/blog/the-benefits-of-working-from-home/.

13. Nicola Jones, "How Coronavirus Lockdowns Stopped Flu in its Tracks," *Nature*, May 21, 2020, https://www.nature.com/articles/d41586-020-01538-8.

14. Matt Clancy, "Remote Work Is Here to Stay," *The Economist*, May 27, 2020, https://eiuperspectives.economist.com/technology-innovation/remote-work-here-stay.

15. Matthew Haag, "Manhattan Faces a Reckoning if Working from Home Becomes the Norm," *The New York Times*, May 12, 2020, https://www.nytimes.com/2020/05/12/nyregion/coronavirus-work-from-home.html.

16. Clara Hendrickson, Mark Muro, and William A. Galston, "Countering the Geography of Discontent: Strategies for Left-Behind Places," Brookings Institute, November 2018, https://www.brookings.edu/research/countering-the-geography-of-discontent-strategies-for-left-behind-places/.

17. George Avalos, "Tech Employment in Bay Area Reaches Record Highs," *The Mercury News*, July 3, 2019, https://www.mercurynews.com/2019/06/14/tech-employment-bay-area-reaches-record-highs-google-apple-facebook-adobe/.

18. Andrew Chamings, "2 out of 3 Tech Workers Would Leave SF Permanently If They Could Work Remotely," *San Francisco Gate*, May 22, 2020, https://www.sfgate.com/living-in-sf/article/2-out-of-3-tech-workers-would-leave-SF-15289316.php.

19. Enrico Moretti, "Local Multipliers," *American Economic Review: Papers & Proceedings*, vol. 100, May 2010, http://click.nl.npr.org/?qs=02337b1a805597a01558212eb5e89755c4f6497f8c30f2eb6418641de8767ea65289307f9470c4f097646725a7df5d4f1e6edd9b18950abd.

20. "Activities US Adults Are Likely to Do Once the Coronavirus Pandemic Ends," eMarketer, April 2020, https://www.emarketer.com/chart/236000/activities-us-adults-likely-do-once-coronavirus-pandemic-ends-april-2020-of-respondents.

21. Simon Kuper, "How Coronavirus Will Change Paris Forever," *Financial Times*, May 7, 2020, https://www.ft.com/content/52ae6c52-8e75-11ea-a8ec-961a33ba80aa.

22. Derek Thompson, "The Pandemic Will Change American Retail Forever," *The Atlantic*, April 27, 2020, https://www.theatlantic.com/ideas/archive/2020/04/how-pandemic-will-change-face-retail/610738/.

23. Sarah Paynter, "There's a Record Number of Vacant Rental Apartments in Manhattan," Yahoo Finance, August 14, 2020, https://finance.yahoo.com/news/manhattan-rent-down-vacancy-up-193314128.html.

24. Matthew Haag, "Manhattan Vacancy Rate Climbs, and Rents Drop 10%," *The New York Times*, August 18, 2020, https://www.nytimes.com/2020/08/18/nyregion/nyc-vacant-apartments.html?smtyp=cur&smid=tw-nytimes.

25. Prashant Gopal and John Gittelsohn, "Urban Exiles Are Fueling a Suburban Housing Boom across the U.S.," *Bloomberg Businessweek*, August 20, 2020, https://www.bloomberg.com/news/articles/2020-08-20/covid-pandemic-fuels-u-s-housing-boom-as-urbanites-swarm-suburbs.

26. Sarah Butrymowicz, The Hechinger Report, and Pete D'Amato, The Hechinger Report, "A Crisis Is Looming for U.S. Colleges—And Not Just Because of the Pandemic," NBC News, August 4, 2020, https://www.nbcnews.com/news/education/crisis-looming-u-s-colleges-not-just-because-pandemic-n1235338.

27. Alexandra Witze, "Universities Will Never Be the Same after the Coronavirus Crisis," *Nature*, June 1, 2020, https://www.nature.com/articles/d41586-020-01518-y.

28. Lara Takenaga, "4 Years of College, $0 in Debt: How Some Countries Make Higher Education Affordable," *The New York Times*, May 28, 2019, https://www.nytimes.com/2019/05/28/reader-center/international-college-costs-financing.html.

29. James D. Walsh, "The Coming Disruption: Scott Galloway Predicts a Handful of Elite Cyborg Universities Will Soon Monopolize Higher Education," *New York Magazine*, May 11, 2020, https://nymag.com/intelligencer/2020/05/scott-galloway-future-of-college.html.

30. Doug Lederman, "Online Education Ascends," Inside Higher Ed, November 7, 2018, https://www.insidehighered.com/digital-learning/article/2018/11/07/new-data-online-enrollments-grow-and-share-overall-enrollment.

31. "Canadian Kids Bored and Missing Friends in Isolation, New Poll Suggests," CBC, May 11, 2020, https://www.cbc.ca/news/canada/toronto/canada-covid-children-poll-1.5564425.

32. Robert Puentes, "COVID's Differing Impact on Transit Ridership," ENO Center for Transportation, April 24, 2020, https://www.enotrans.org/article/covids-differing -impact-on-transit-ridership/.

33. Richard Florida et al., "How Life in Our Cities Will Look after the Coronavirus Pandemic," *Foreign Policy*, May 1, 2020, https://foreignpolicy.com/2020/05/01/future-of-cities -urban-life-after-coronavirus-pandemic/.

34. Laura Laker, "Milan Announces Ambitious Scheme to Reduce Car Use after Lockdown," *The Guardian*, April 21, 2020, https://www.theguardian.com/world/2020/apr/21/ milan-seeks-to-prevent-post-crisis-return-of-traffic-pollution.

35. David Folkenflik, "NPR Radio Ratings Collapse as Pandemic Ends Listeners' Commutes," NPR, July 15, 2020, https://www.npr.org/sections/coronavirus-live-updates/2020/07/ 15/891404076/npr-radio-ratings-collapse-as-pandemic-kills-listeners-commutes.

36. Randal O'Toole, "The Future of Driving," New Geography, August 10, 2020, https://www.newgeography.com/content/006738-the-future-driving.

37. Liam Lahey, "Survey: 28% of Canadians Will Work from Home after COVID-19 Lockdown Lifts," RATESDOTCA, June 22, 2020, https://rates.ca/resources/survey -28-canadians-will-work-home-after-covid-19-lockdown-lifts.

38. Cathy Buyck, "Novel Coronavirus Shakes Up Global Airline Industry," AIN Online, July 20, 2020, https://www.ainonline.com/aviation-news/air-transport/2020-07-20/ novel-coronavirus-shakes-global-airline-industry.

39. Eric Rosen, "How COVID-19 Will Change Business Travel," *Conde Nast Traveler*, May 28, 2020, https://www.cntraveler.com/story/how-covid-19-will-change-business-travel.

40. Eric Rosen, "How COVID-19 Will Change Business Travel," *Conde Nast Traveler*, May 28, 2020, https://www.cntraveler.com/story/how-covid-19-will-change-business-travel.

41. Hayley Skirka, "Are Flight Prices Set to Rise after the Pandemic?," The National News, May 18, 2020, https://www.thenationalnews.com/lifestyle/travel/are-flight-prices-set -to-rise-after-the-pandemic-1.1020897.

42. Chip Cutter, "Business Travel Won't Be Taking Off Soon amid Coronavirus," *The Wall Street Journal*, June 15, 2020, https://www.wsj.com/articles/business-travel-wont-be -taking-off-soon-amid-coronavirus-11592220844?mod=e2tw.

43. "Travel Retail Market by Product and Channel: Global Opportunity Analysis and Industry Forecast, 2018-2025," ReportLinker, October 2018, https://www.reportlinker .com/p05663919/Travel-Retail-Market-by-Product-and-Channel-Global-Opportunity -Analysis-and-Industry-Forecast.html?utm_source=GNW.

44. Jaewon Kang and Sharon Terlep, "Forget the Mall, Shoppers Are Buying Gucci at Airports," *The Wall Street Journal*, June 17, 2019, https://www.wsj.com/articles/forget-the-mall -shoppers-are-buying-gucci-at-airports-11560772801.

45. Dave Grohl, "The Day the Live Concert Returns," *The Atlantic*, May 11, 2020, https://www .theatlantic.com/culture/archive/2020/05/dave-grohl-irreplaceable-thrill-rock-show/ 611113/?utm_campaign=the-atlantic&utm_source=twitter&utm_medium=social&utm _term=2020-05-11T12%2525253A30%2525253A06&utm_content=edit-promo.

46. Taylor Mims, "Livestreams Are Moving to Hard Tickets to Replace Lost Touring Revenue," *Billboard*, April 2, 2020, https://www.billboard.com/articles/business/touring/9349897/ livestreams-tickets-replace-lost-touring-revenue.

47. Taylor Mims, "Livestreams Are Moving to Hard Tickets to Replace Lost Touring Revenue," *Billboard*, April 2, 2020, https://www.billboard.com/articles/business/touring/9349897/ livestreams-tickets-replace-lost-touring-revenue.

48. *Bloomberg* and Michelle Lhooq, "People Are Paying Real Money to Get into Virtual Zoom Nightclubs," *Fortune*, August 14, 2020, https://fortune.com/2020/04/14/zoom -nightclubs-virtual-bars-video-calls-coronavirus/.

49. Josh Ye, "Razer CEO Says Pandemic Will Change Sports and Entertainment Forever as Live-Streaming Comes to the Fore," *South China Morning Post*, March 27, 2020, https://www.scmp.com/tech/tech-leaders-and-founders/article/3077135/razer -ceo-says-pandemic-will-change-sports-and.

50. Josh Ye, "Razer CEO Says Pandemic Will Change Sports and Entertainment Forever as Live-Streaming Comes to the Fore," *South China Morning Post*, March 27, 2020, https://www.scmp.com/tech/tech-leaders-and-founders/article/3077135/razer -ceo-says-pandemic-will-change-sports-and.

CHAPTER 3: THE RISE OF RETAIL'S APEX PREDATORS

1. Jon Swartz, "Amazon Is Officially Worth $1 Trillion, Joining Other Tech Titans," MarketWatch, February 4, 2020, https://www.marketwatch.com/story/amazon-is -officially-worth-1-trillion-joining-other-tech-titans-2020-02-04#:~:text=Shares%20 of%20Amazon%20increased%202.3,last%20July%20and%20on%20Sept.

2. Wendy Liu, "Coronavirus Has Made Amazon a Public Utility—So We Should Treat It Like One," *The Guardian*, April 17, 2020, https://www.theguardian.com/commentisfree/2020/ apr/17/amazon-coronavirus-public-utility-workers.

3. Zoe Suen, "Amazon vs Alibaba: Which E-Commerce Giant Is Winning the Covid-19 Era?" *The Business of Fashion*, May 28, 2020, https://www.businessoffashion.com/ articles/professional/amazon-vs-alibaba-in-the-covid-19-era.

4. "Target Corporation Annual Report 2019," Target Corporation, no date, https://corporate.target.com/annual-reports/2019.

5. "Can Amazon Keep Growing Like a Youthful Startup?" *The Economist*, June 18, 2020, https://www.economist.com/briefing/2020/06/18/can-amazon-keep-growing-like -a-youthful-startup.

6. Ingrid London, "Amazon's Share of the US E-Commerce Market Is Now 49%, or 5 Percent of All Retail Spend," Tech Crunch, July 13, 2018, https://techcrunch.com/ 2018/07/13/amazons-share-of-the-us-e-commerce-market-is-now-49-or-5-of-all -retail-spend/.

7. Todd Spangler, "Amazon Prime Tops 150 Million Members," *Variety*, January 30, 2020, https://variety.com/2020/digital/news/amazon-150-million-prime-members-1203487355/.

8. Jay Greene, "10 Years Later, Amazon Celebrates Prime's Triumph," *The Seattle Times*, February 2, 2015, https://www.seattletimes.com/business/amazon/10-years-later-amazon -celebrates-primes-triumph/.

9. Kana Inagaki, "Amazon's Scale in Japan Challenges Rivals and Regulators," *Financial Times*, June 24, 2018, https://www.ft.com/content/f50c5f24-752f-11e8-aa31-31da427 9a601.

10. Tiffany C. Wright, "What Is the Profit Margin for a Supermarket?" *azcentral*, 2013, https://yourbusiness.azcentral.com/profit-margin-supermarket-17711.html.

11. "Amazon's $4 Billion Coronavirus Investment Will Shred Its Competitors," *New York Magazine*, May 5, 2020, https://nymag.com/intelligencer/2020/05/amazons-coronavirus -investments-will-shred-its-competitors.html.

12. Kiri Masters, "89 Percent of Customers Are More Likely to Buy Products from Amazon Than Other E-Commerce Sites: Study," *Forbes*, March 20, 2019, https://www.forbes.com/ sites/kirimasters/2019/03/20/study-89-of-customers-are-more-likely-to-buy-products -from-amazon-than-other-e-commerce-sites/#6ea572c84af1.

13. Zoe Suen, "Amazon vs Alibaba: Which E-Commerce Giant Is Winning the Covid-19 Era?" *The Business of Fashion*, May 28, 2020, https://www.businessoffashion.com/articles/professional/amazon-vs-alibaba-in-the-covid-19-era.

14. Caleb Silver, "The Top 20 Economies in the World," Investopedia, March 18, 2020, https://www.investopedia.com/insights/worlds-top-economies/.

15. "Alibaba Group Announces September Quarter 2019 Results," Business Wire, November 1, 2019, https://www.businesswire.com/news/home/20191101005278/en/Alibaba-Group-Announces-September-Quarter-2019-Results.

16. Matthieu Guinebault, "Tmall's Luxury Pavilion Reports $159,000 Average Spend per Customer since Site Launch," Fashion Network, April 17, 2018, https://www.fashionnetwork.com/news/tmall-s-luxury-pavilion-reports-159-000-average-spend-per-consumer-since-site-launch,968914.html.

17. Thomas Graziani, "How Alibaba Is Shaping the Chinese Entertainment Industry," Tech in Asia, July 30, 2018, https://www.techinasia.com/talk/alibaba-shaping-chinese-entertainment.

18. Adam Rogers, "A Look at JD.com's Revenue and Earnings Growth," Market Realist, June 21, 2019, https://marketrealist.com/2019/06/a-look-at-jd-coms-revenue-and-earnings-growth/#:~:text=JD.com%20has%20managed%20to,%2C%20and%2027.5%25%20in%202018.&text=Though%20decelerating%2C%20revenue%20growth%20remains%20impressive%20for%20JD.com.

19. "JD.com Statistics," Marketplace Pulse, 2019, https://www.marketplacepulse.com/stats/jd.

20. Jeremy Bowman, "Wal-Mart Shows It's Executing Its Turnaround Strategy Perfectly," The Motley Fool, October 14, 2017, https://www.fool.com/investing/2017/10/14/wal-mart-shows-its-executing-its-turnaround-strate.aspx.

21. Jason Del Rey, "Inside the Conflict at Walmart That's Threatening Its High-Stakes Race with Amazon," *Vox*, July 3, 2019, https://www.vox.com/recode/2019/7/3/18716431/walmart-jet-marc-lore-modcloth-amazon-ecommerce-losses-online-sales.

22. Jason Del Rey, "Inside the Conflict at Walmart That's Threatening Its High-Stakes Race with Amazon," *Vox*, July 3, 2019, https://www.vox.com/recode/2019/7/3/18716431/walmart-jet-marc-lore-modcloth-amazon-ecommerce-losses-online-sales.

23. Phil Wahba, "Walmart's Online Sales Surge during the Pandemic, Bolstering Its Place as a Strong No. 2 to Amazon," *Fortune*, March 19, 2020, https://fortune.com/2020/05/19/walmart-online-sales-amazon-ecommerce/.

24. Cindy Liu, "Walmart Is an Ecommerce Winner during Pandemic," eMarketer, May 25, 2020, https://www.emarketer.com/content/walmart-is-an-ecommerce-winner-during-pandemic.

CHAPTER 4: BIGGER PREY

1. Harry de Quetteville, "Amazon's $4bn Push to Vaccinate Its Supply Chain," *The Telegraph*, May 16, 2020, https://www.telegraph.co.uk/technology/2020/05/16/amazons-4bn-push-vaccinate-supply-chain/.

2. Doug Stephens, "On the Frontlines of Retail There Are No Heroes, Only Victims," *The Business of Fashion*, April 21, 2020, https://www.businessoffashion.com/articles/opinion/on-the-frontlines-of-retail-there-are-no-heroes-only-victims.

3. Verne Kopytoff, "How Amazon Crushed the Union Movement," *Time*, July 16, 2014, https://time.com/956/how-amazon-crushed-the-union-movement/.

4. Adele Peters, "Why This Clothing Company Is Making Its Factory Wages Public," *Fast Company*, August 8, 2018, https://www.fastcompany.com/90213069/why-this-clothing-company-is-making-its-factory-wages-public.

5. Jaewon Kang and Sharon Terlep, "Retailers Phase Out Coronavirus Hazard Pay for Essential Workers," *The Wall Street Journal*, May 19, 2020, https://www.wsj.com/livecoverage/coronavirus-2020-05-19/card/ioEmzIleJ8LFWee2cpPU.

6. Alyssa Meyers, "For Consumers, Brands' Care for Staff amid Pandemic as Important as Stocked Items," Morning Consult, April 15, 2020, https://morningconsult.com/2020/04/15/consumer-crisis-brand-communications-report/.

7. Aaron Smith and Monica Anderson, "2. Americans' Attitudes toward a Future in Which Robots and Computers Can Do Many Human Jobs," Pew Research, October 4, 2017, https://www.pewresearch.org/internet/2017/10/04/americans-attitudes-toward-a-future-in-which-robots-and-computers-can-do-many-human-jobs/.

8. Olivier de Panafieu et al., "Robots in Retail: What Does the Future Hold for People and Robots in the Stores of Tomorrow?" Roland Berger, 2016, https://www.rolandberger.com/publications/publication_pdf/roland_berger_tab_robots_retail_en_12.10.2016.pdf.

9. Drew Harwell, "As Walmart Turns to Robots, It's the Human Workers Who Feel Like Machines," *The Washington Post*, June 6, 2019, https://www.washingtonpost.com/technology/2019/06/06/walmart-turns-robots-its-human-workers-who-feel-like-machines/.

10. Sarah Nassauer, "Welcome to Walmart. The Robot Will Grab Your Groceries," *The Wall Street Journal*, January 8, 2020, https://www.wsj.com/articles/welcome-to-walmart-the-robot-will-grab-your-groceries-11578499200.

11. Drew Harwell, "As Walmart Turns to Robots, It's the Human Workers Who Feel Like Machines," *The Washington Post*, June 6, 2019, https://www.washingtonpost.com/technology/2019/06/06/walmart-turns-robots-its-human-workers-who-feel-like-machines/.

12. Brian Dumaine, "How Amazon's Bet on Autonomous Vehicles Can Help Protect Us from Viruses," *Newsweek*, May 18, 2020, https://www.newsweek.com/how-amazons-bet-autonomous-vehicles-can-help-protect-us-viruses-1504169.

13. Brian Dumaine, "How Amazon's Bet on Autonomous Vehicles Can Help Protect Us from Viruses," *Newsweek*, May 18, 2020, https://www.newsweek.com/how-amazons-bet-autonomous-vehicles-can-help-protect-us-viruses-1504169.

14. Reuters, "Amazon Sweetens $1.3 Billion Zoox Acquisition with $100 Million in Stock to Keep Workers," VentureBeat, July 9, 2020, https://venturebeat.com/2020/07/09/amazon-sweetens-1-3-billion-zoox-acquisition-with-100-million-in-stock-to-keep-workers/.

15. Prophecy Marketing Insights, "Global Autonomous Delivery Vehicle Market Is Estimated to Be US$ 196.2 Billion by 2029 with a CAGR of 11.2% during the Forecast Period—PMI," GlobeNewswire, June 12, 2020, https://www.globenewswire.com/news-release/2020/06/12/2047504/0/en/Global-Autonomous-Delivery-Vehicle-Market-is-estimated-to-be-US-196-2-Billion-by-2029-with-a-CAGR-of-11-2-during-the-Forecast-Period-PMI.html.

16. Lauren Thomas, "Most Shoppers Are Still Leery of Buying Their Groceries Online. But Delivery in the US Is Set to 'Explode'," CNBC, February 5, 2019, https://www.cnbc.com/2019/02/04/grocery-delivery-in-the-us-is-expected-to-explode.html.

17. Melissa Repko, "As Coronavirus Pandemic Pushes More Grocery Shoppers Online, Stores Struggle to Keep Up with Demand," CNBC, May 1, 2020, https://www.cnbc.com/2020/05/01/as-coronavirus-pushes-more-grocery-shoppers-online-stores-struggle-with-demand.html.

18. Jim Armitage, "Ocado Revenues Surge 27 Percent as Locked Down Shoppers Buy Food Online," *Evening Standard*, July 14, 2020, https://www.standard.co.uk/business/business-news/ocado-shopping-food-supermarkets-rose-a4497371.html.

19. Bernd Heid et al., "Technology Delivered: Implications for Cost, Customers, and Competition in the Last-Mile Ecosystem," McKinsey & Company, August 27, 2018, https://www.mckinsey.com/industries/travel-logistics-and-transport-infrastructure/

our-insights/technology-delivered-implications-for-cost-customers-and-competition
-in-the-last-mile-ecosystem#.

20. Doug Stephens and BoF, "Retail Reborn Podcast Episode 3," *The Business of Fashion*,
    September 29, 2020, https://www.businessoffashion.com/articles/podcasts/retail
    -reborn-podcast-doug-stephens-ecommerce-online.

21. Doug Stephens and BoF, "Retail Reborn Podcast Episode 3," *The Business of Fashion*,
    September 29, 2020, https://www.businessoffashion.com/articles/podcasts/retail
    -reborn-podcast-doug-stephens-ecommerce-online.

22. Liz Flora, "Brands Look to VR E-Commerce to Replace the In-Store Experience," Glossy,
    April 21, 2020, https://www.glossy.co/beauty/brands-look-to-vr-e-commerce-to-replace
    -the-in-store-experience.

23. Cecilia Li, "Alibaba Pictures Helps Drive China's Billion-Dollar Box Office in 2019,"
    Alizila, December 20, 2019, https://www.alizila.com/Alibaba-pictures-helps-drive
    -chinas-billion-dollar-box-office-in-2019/.

24. Todd Spangler, "Amazon's Prime Video Channels Biz to Generate $1.7 Billion in 2018
    (Analysts)," *Variety*, December 7, 2018, https://variety.com/2018/digital/news/
    amazon-prime-video-channels-tv-revenue-estimates-1203083998/.

25. Sarah Perez, "Twitch Continues to Dominate Live Streaming with Its Second-Biggest
    Quarter to Date," TechCrunch, July 12, 2019, https://techcrunch.com/2019/07/12/
    twitch-continues-to-dominate-live-streaming-with-its-second-biggest-quarter-to-date/.

26. Dieter Bohn, "Amazon Says 100 Million Alexa Devices Have Been Sold—What's Next?"
    The Verge, January 4, 2019, https://www.theverge.com/2019/1/4/18168565/
    amazon-alexa-devices-how-many-sold-number-100-million-dave-limp.

27. Dieter Bohn, "Amazon Says 100 Million Alexa Devices Have Been Sold—What's Next?"
    The Verge, January 4, 2019, https://www.theverge.com/2019/1/4/18168565/
    amazon-alexa-devices-how-many-sold-number-100-million-dave-limp.

28. Steve Cocheo, "Amazon Forges Financial Alliances as Bank Execs Brace for Full Invasion,"
    The Financial Brand, June 24, 2019, https://thefinancialbrand.com/84807/amazon
    -banking-checking-payments-small-business-lending-prime/.

29. Steve Cocheo, "Amazon Forges Financial Alliances as Bank Execs Brace for Full Invasion,"
    The Financial Brand, June 24, 2019, https://thefinancialbrand.com/84807/amazon
    -banking-checking-payments-small-business-lending-prime/.

30. Jacqueline Laurean Yates, "Century 21 Is Closing Its Doors after 60 Years," ABC News,
    September 11, 2020, https://abc13.com/century-21-is-closing-its-doors-after-60-years/
    6418840/#:~:text=%22While%20insurance%20money%20helped%20us,unforeseen
    %20circumstances%20like%20we%20are.

31. Alicia Adamczyk, "Health Insurance Premiums Increased More Than Wages This Year,"
    CNBC, September 26, 2019, https://www.cnbc.com/2019/09/26/health-insurance
    -premiums-increased-more-than-wages-this-year.html#:~:text=Premium%20increases
    %20have%20outpaced%20wage,%25%20and%20inflation%20by%202%25.

32. "Everything You Need to Know about What Amazon Is Doing in Financial Services,"
    CB Insights, 2019, https://www.cbinsights.com/research/report/amazon-across-financial
    -services-fintech/.

33. Bethan Moorcraft, "Amazon and Google 'the Next Generation' of Insurance Competition in
    Canada," *Insurance Business Canada*, November 3, 2018, https://www.insurancebusiness
    mag.com/ca/news/healthcare/amazon-and-google-the-next-generation-of-insurance
    -competition-in-canada-117644.aspx.

34. *Fortune* Magazine, "FedEx CEO Says Amazon Is Not a Problem," YouTube, April 19, 2017,
    https://www.youtube.com/watch?v=ODS1qlcZUqY.

35. "Amazon's Challenges in Delivery," Investopedia, April 13, 2020, https://www.investopedia.com/articles/investing/020515/why-amazon-needs-dump-ups-and-fedex-amzn-fdx-ups.asp#:~:text=Key%20Takeaways,FedEx%2C%20UPS%2C%20and%20USPS.

36. Marianne Wilson, "Amazon to Open 1,000 Neighborhood Delivery Hubs, Reports *Bloomberg*," Chain Store Age, September 16, 2020, https://chainstoreage.com/amazon-open-1000-neighborhood-delivery-hubs-reports-bloomberg.

37. Benjamin Mueller, "Telemedicine Arrives in the U.K.: '10 Years of Change in One Week,'" *The New York Times*, April 4, 2020, https://www.nytimes.com/2020/04/04/world/europe/telemedicine-uk-coronavirus.html.

38. "The $11.9 Trillion Global Healthcare Market: Key Opportunities & Strategies (2014–2022)—ResearchAndMarkets.com," Business Wire, June 25, 2019, https://www.businesswire.com/news/home/20190625005862/en/The-11.9-Trillion-Global-Healthcare-Market-Key-Opportunities-Strategies-2014-2022---ResearchAndMarkets.com.

39. John Tozzi, "U.S. Health Care Puts $4 Trillion in All the Wrong Places," *Bloomberg Businessweek*, June 11, 2020, https://www.bloomberg.com/news/articles/2020-06-11/u-s-health-care-system-was-totally-overwhelmed-by-coronavirus.

40. John Tozzi, "U.S. Health Care Puts $4 Trillion in All the Wrong Places," *Bloomberg Businessweek*, June 11, 2020, https://www.bloomberg.com/news/articles/2020-06-11/u-s-health-care-system-was-totally-overwhelmed-by-coronavirus.

41. "Amazon in Healthcare: The E-Commerce Giant's Strategy for a $3 Trillion Market," CB Insights, no date, https://www.cbinsights.com/research/report/amazon-transforming-healthcare/.

42. "Amazon Pilots Opening Health Care Centers Near Its Fulfillment Centers," Day One, July 14, 2020, https://blog.aboutamazon.com/operations/amazon-pilots-opening-health-care-centers-near-its-fulfillment-centers?utm_source=social&&utm_medium=tw&&utm_term=amznnews&&utm_content=Amazon_CrossoverHealth&&linkId=93844131.

43. Madhurima Nandy, "Amazon India Launches Online Pharmacy Service," Live Mint, August 13, 2020, https://www.livemint.com/companies/news/amazon-india-launches-online-pharmacy-service-11597331465887.html.

44. "Alibaba Raises $1.3B for Push into Online Pharmacy Business," PYMNTS.com, August 5, 2020, https://www.pymnts.com/healthcare/2020/alibaba-raises-1-3b-for-push-into-online-pharmacy-business/.

45. Christina Farr, "Walmart Buys Tech from Carezone to Help People Manage Their Prescriptions," CNBC, June 15, 2020, https://www.cnbc.com/2020/06/15/walmart-buys-tech-from-carezone-to-help-people-manage-prescriptions.html.

46. Bailey Lipschultz, "Walmart a 'Sleeping Giant' in Health Care, Morgan Stanley Warns," BNN Bloomberg, July 10, 2020, https://www.bnnbloomberg.ca/walmart-a-sleeping-giant-in-health-care-morgan-stanley-warns-1.1463512.

47. "Alibaba Launched the 'Help Help' App. Is It to Follow the Trend or Accelerate the Layout of the Online Education Field?" iiMedia, March 8, 2020, https://www.iimedia.cn/c460/69655.html.

48. "Smart Education," Tencent, no date, https://www.tencent.com/en-us/business/smart-education.html.

49. Aaron Holmes, "Allbirds Cofounder Calls Out Amazon for Its Knockoff Shoes That Cost Way Less, Calling Them 'Algorithmically Inspired,'" Business Insider, November 20, 2019, https://www.businessinsider.com/allbirds-cofounder-criticizes-amazon-for-knockoff-shoes-that-cost-less-2019-11.

50. Dana Mattioli, "Amazon Continues to Probe Employee Use of Third-Party Vendor Data, Jeff Bezos Says," *The Wall Street Journal*, July 29, 2020, https://www.wsj.com/articles/amazon-continues-to-probe-employee-use-of-third-party-vendor-data-jeff-bezos-says-11596063680.

51. Katharine Gemmel, "Amazon Announces 1,000 Jobs in Ireland, New Dublin Campus," *Bloomberg*, July 27, 2020, https://www.bloomberg.com/news/articles/2020-07-27/amazon-announces-1-000-jobs-in-ireland-new-dublin-campus?cmpid=socialflow-twitter-business&utm_campaign=socialflow-organic&utm_medium=social&utm_source=twitter&utm_content=business&sref=5zifHLEP.

52. Colin Leggett, "Amazon Is Hiring for Over 5,000 Positions across Canada," Narcity, June 2020, https://www.narcity.com/money/ca/amazon-canada-is-hiring-over-5000-new-employees-across-the-country.

53. Simon Goodley and Jillian Ambrose, "The Companies Still Hiring in the UK during Coronavirus Crisis," *The Guardian*, July 31, 2020, https://www.theguardian.com/world/2020/jul/31/how-covid-19-has-reshaped-the-jobs-landscape-in-the-uk.

54. Joe Kaziukėnas, "Target Marketplace One Year Later," Marketplace Pulse, February 25, 2020, https://www.marketplacepulse.com/articles/target-marketplace-one-year-later.

55. James Knowles, "Analysis: Why 44% of Retailers Are Launching Marketplaces," *Retail Week*, April 17, 2018, https://www.retail-week.com/analysis/analysis-why-44-of-retailers-are-launching-marketplaces/7028844.article?authent=1.

56. Kiri Masters, "The Company That's Saving Retailers during the Pandemic by Launching Their Online Marketplaces," *Forbes*, April 16, 2020, https://www.forbes.com/sites/kirimasters/2020/04/16/the-company-thats-saving-retailers-during-the-pandemic-by-launching-their-online-marketplaces/#50c1a95078de.

57. Jon Brodkin, "$100,000 in Bribes Helped Fraudulent Amazon Sellers Earn $100 Million, DOJ Says," Ars Technica, September 18, 2020, https://arstechnica.com/tech-policy/2020/09/doj-amazon-workers-took-bribes-to-reinstate-sellers-of-dangerous-products.

58. Mary Drummond, "Joe Pine—The Experience Economy is All about Time Well-Spent—S5E6," Worthix, April 27, 2020, https://blog.worthix.com/s5e6-joe-pine-the-experience-economy-is-all-about-time-well-spent/.

CHAPTER 5: THE ARCHETYPES OF THE NEW ERA

1. Trefis Team and Great Speculations, "How Much Does Walmart Spend on Selling, General and Administrative Expenses?" *Forbes*, December 17, 2019, https://www.forbes.com/sites/greatspeculations/2019/12/17/how-much-does-walmart-spend-on-selling-general-and-administrative-expenses/#7be8be6e15bc.

2. "Nike Launches 'Find Your Greatness' Campaign," Nike, July 25, 2012, https://news.nike.com/news/nike-launches-find-your-greatness-campaign-celebrating-inspiration-for-the-everyday-athlete.

3. "Hey, How's That Lawsuit Against the President Going?" Patagonia, April 2019, https://www.patagonia.ca/stories/hey-hows-that-lawsuit-against-the-president-going/story-72248.html.

4. Maureen Kline, "How to Drive Profits with Corporate Social Responsibility," *Inc.*, July 24, 2018, https://www.inc.com/maureen-kline/how-to-drive-profits-with-corporate-social-responsibility.html.

5. Doug Stephens, "Interview: Matt Alexander," Retail Prophet, December 2018, https://www.retailprophet.com/podcasts/.

6. Doug Stephens, "Interview: Matt Alexander," Retail Prophet, December 2018, https://www.retailprophet.com/podcasts/.

7. a16z, "The End of the Beginning: Benedict Evans," YouTube, November 16, 2018, https://www.youtube.com/watch?v=RF5VIwDYIJk&feature=emb_logo.

8. Doug Stephens and BoF Studio, "Retail Reborn Episode 4," *The Business of Fashion*, October 6, 2020, https://www.businessoffashion.com/podcasts/retail/retail-reborn-podcast-doug-stephens-experiential#comments.

9. Lauren Smiley, "Stitch Fix's Radical Data-Driven Way to Sell Clothes—$1.2 Billion Last Year—Is Reinventing Retail," *Fast Company*, February 19, 2019, https://www.fastcompany.com/90298900/stitch-fix-most-innovative-companies-2019.

10. "Stitch Fix Announces Fourth Quarter and Full Fiscal Year 2019 Financial Results," Stitch Fix, October 1, 2019, https://investors.stitchfix.com/news-releases/news-release-details/stitch-fix-announces-fourth-quarter-and-full-fiscal-year-2019.

11. Lauren Smiley, "Stitch Fix's Radical Data-Driven Way to Sell Clothes—$1.2 Billion Last Year—Is Reinventing Retail," *Fast Company*, February 19, 2019, https://www.fastcompany.com/90298900/stitch-fix-most-innovative-companies-2019.

12. Katrina Lake, "Stitch Fix's CEO on Selling Personal Style to the Mass Market," *Harvard Business Review*, May–June 2018, https://hbr.org/2018/05/stitch-fixs-ceo-on-selling-personal-style-to-the-mass-market.

13. Vanessa Page, "How Costco Makes Money," Investopedia, December 13, 2018, https://www.investopedia.com/articles/investing/070715/costcos-business-model-smarter-you-think.asp#:~:text=Costco%20doesn't%20publish%20its,is%20key%20to%20that%20definition.

14. Catherine Clifford, "How Costco Uses $5 Rotisserie Chickens and Free Samples to Turn Customers into Fanatics," CNBC Make It, May 23, 2019, https://www.cnbc.com/2019/05/22/hooked-how-costco-turns-customers-into-fanatics.html.

15. Trefis Team and Great Speculations, "An Overview of Costco's Q2 and Beyond," *Forbes*, March 8, 2019, https://www.forbes.com/sites/greatspeculations/2019/03/08/an-overview-of-costcos-q2-and-beyond/#181387b83905.

16. B&H Photo Video, "A Brief History of B&H," YouTube, December 24, 2018, https://www.youtube.com/watch?v=j6a3b9NBCvg.

17. Clare Dyer, "Hoover Taken to Cleaners in £4m Dyson Case," *The Guardian*, October 4, 2002, https://www.theguardian.com/uk/2002/oct/04/claredyer.

18. John Seabrook, "How to Make It," *The New Yorker*, September 13, 2010, https://www.newyorker.com/magazine/2010/09/20/how-to-make-it.

19. Aleesha Harris, "Dyson Engineer Talks New Vancouver Demo Shop," *Vancouver Sun*, February 20, 2020, https://vancouversun.com/life/fashion-beauty/dyson-engineer-talks-new-vancouver-demo-shop.

20. Sam Knight, "The Spectacular Power of Big Lens," *The Guardian*, May 10, 2018, https://www.theguardian.com/news/2018/may/10/the-invisible-power-of-big-glasses-eyewear-industry-essilor-luxottica.

21. "Culture/Life," Patagonia, no date, https://www.patagonia.com/culture.html.

CHAPTER 6: THE ART OF RETAIL

1. "Are You Experienced?" Bain & Co., April 8, 2015, https://www.bain.com/insights/are-you-experienced-infographic/.

2. "State of the Connected Consumer, Second Edition," Salesforce, 2018, https://c1.sfdcstatic.com/content/dam/web/en_us/www/documents/e-books/state-of-the-connected-customer-report-second-edition2018.pdf.

3. Mark Abraham et al., "The Next Level of Personalization in Retail," BCG, June 4, 2019, https://www.bcg.com/publications/2019/next-level-personalization-retail.

4. James Ledbetter, "Why an Advertising Pioneer Says Advertising Is Dead," *Inc.*, May 30, 2017, https://www.inc.com/james-ledbetter/why-an-advertising-pioneer-says-advertising-is-dead.html.

5. Jennifer Mueller, "Most People Are Secretly Threatened by Creativity," *Quartz*, March 13, 2017, https://qz.com/929328/most-people-are-secretly-threatened-by-creativity/.

6. Robert Williams, "⅓ of Instagram Users Have Bought Directly from an Ad, Study Finds," Mobile Marketer, September 19, 2019, https://www.mobilemarketer.com/news/13-of-instagram-users-have-bought-directly-from-an-ad-study-finds/563239/.

7. William Comcowich, "Follow These Best Practices to Create Superb Marketing Videos," Ragan's PR Daily, August 6, 2019, https://www.prdaily.com/follow-these-best-practices-to-create-superb-marketing-videos/.

8. Ginny Marvin, "Shopping Ads Are Eating Text Ads: Accounted for 60 Percent of Clicks on Google, 33 Percent on Bing in Q1," *Search Engine Land*, May 2, 2018, https://searchengineland.com/report-shopping-ads-are-eating-text-ads-accounted-for-60-of-clicks-on-google-33-on-bing-in-q1-297273.

9. Emily Bary, "Viral Videos Helped Candy Me Up Transition to the Online Age after the Pandemic Hurt Its Confectionery Catering Business," MarketWatch, September 14, 2020, https://www.marketwatch.com/story/tiktok-saved-my-business-candy-retailer-finds-internet-fame-as-covid-19-forces-a-pivot-11599847515.

10. Marissa DePino, "Morphe Beauty Is Tapping the Creative Customer with In-Store Studios," PSFK, April 17, 2020, https://www.psfk.com/2020/04/morphe-store-expansion-studios.html.

CHAPTER 7: REINCARNATION OF THE MALL

1. Lauren Thomas, "A Third of America's Malls Will Disappear by Next Year, Says Ex-Department Store Exec," CNBC, June 10, 2020, https://www.cnbc.com/2020/06/10/a-third-of-americas-malls-will-disappear-by-next-year-jan-kniffen.html.

2. Maurie Backman, "32 Percent of Customers Don't Feel Safe Shopping at Malls, and That Could Be Bad News for Investors," The Motley Fool, August 21, 2020, https://www.fool.com/millionacres/real-estate-market/articles/32-of-customers-dont-feel-safe-shopping-at-malls-and-that-could-be-bad-news-for-investors/#.

3. Lauren Thomas, "Over 50 Percent of Department Stores in Malls Predicted to Close by 2021, Real Estate Services Firm Says," CNBC, April 29, 2020, https://www.cnbc.com/2020/04/29/50percent-of-all-these-malls-forecast-to-close-by-2021-green-street-advisors-says.html.

4. Esther Fung, "Real-Estate Giant Starwood Capital Loses Mall Portfolio," *The Wall Street Journal*, September 9, 2020, https://www.wsj.com/articles/real-estate-giant-starwood-capital-loses-mall-portfolio-11599684081.

5. Esther Fung, "Property Owner Simon Sees Buying Tenants as a Way to Boost Malls," *The Wall Street Journal*, June 23, 2020, https://www.wsj.com/articles/property-owner-simon-sees-buying-tenants-as-a-way-to-boost-malls-11592913601#:~:text=In%20previous%20earnings%20calls%2C%20Simon,investment'%2C%E2%80%9D%20said%20Mr.

6. Cezary Podkul, "Commercial Properties' Ability to Repay Mortgages Was Overstated, Study Finds," *The Wall Street Journal*, August 11, 2020, https://www.wsj.com/articles/commercial-properties-ability-to-repay-mortgages-was-overstated-study-finds-11597152211.

7. Phillip Inman, "Corporate Debt Could Be the Next Sub-Prime Crisis, Warns Banking Body," *The Guardian*, June 30, 2019, https://www.theguardian.com/business/2019/jun/30/corporate-debt-could-be-the-next-subprime-crisis-warns-banking-body.

8. Cezary Podkul, "Commercial Properties' Ability to Repay Mortgages Was Overstated, Study Finds," *The Wall Street Journal*, August 11, 2020, https://www.wsj.com/articles/commercial-properties-ability-to-repay-mortgages-was-overstated-study-finds-11597152211.

9. Cathleen Chen, "Is This the End of the American Mall as We Know It?" *The Business of Fashion*, May 28, 2020, https://www.businessoffashion.com/articles/professional/american-retail-malls-middle-class-coronavirus.

10. Jennifer Harby, "More Than 200 UK Shopping Centres 'in Crisis,'" BBC, November 1, 2018, https://www.bbc.com/news/uk-england-45707529.

11. Doug Stephens, *The Retail Revival* (Hoboken, NJ: Wiley, 2013).

12. Jared Bernstein, "Yes, Stocks Are Up. But 80 Percent of the Value Is Held by the Richest 10 Percent," *The Washington Post*, March 2, 2017, https://www.washingtonpost.com/posteverything/wp/2017/03/02/perspective-on-the-stock-market-rally-80-of-stock-value-held-by-top-10/.

13. Aimee Picchi, "It's Been a Record 11 Years since the Last Increase in U.S. Minimum Wage," CBS, July 24, 2020, https://www.cbsnews.com/news/minimum-wage-no-increases-11-years/?ftag=CNM-00-10aab7e&linkId=94969144.

14. "U.S. MarketFlash: Retail-to-Industrial Property Conversions Accelerate," CBRE, July 23, 2020, https://www.cbre.us/research-and-reports/US-MarketFlash-Retail-to-Industrial-Property-Conversions-Accelerate.

15. Retail Prophet, "The Future of Shopping Centers in a Post-Pandemic World," YouTube, August 7, 2020, https://www.youtube.com/watch?v=iAN3Q7HaKf8.

16. Anne Quito, "The Father of the American Shopping Mall Hated What He Created," *Quartz*, July 17, 2015, https://qz.com/454214/the-father-of-the-american-shopping-mall-hated-cars-and-suburban-sprawl/.

17. "Millennials Fueling the Experience Economy," Eventbrite/Harris Poll, 2014, https://f.hubspotusercontent00.net/hubfs/8020908/DS01_Millenials%20Fueling%20the%20Experience%20Economy.pdf?_hstc=195498867.61f6a96c9f06737318752a85f54c44b4.1600225862133.1600225862133.1600225862133.1&_hssc=195498867.2.1600225862133&_hsfp=2460104009.

CHAPTER 8: RESURRECTING RETAIL

1. H. Gordon Selfridge, *The Romance of Commerce* (Plymouth, U.K.: William Brendon & Son, Ltd, 1918).

2. "Public Trust in Government: 1958–2019," Pew Research Center, April 11, 2019, https://www.pewresearch.org/politics/2019/04/11/public-trust-in-government-1958-2019/.

3. Dan Gingiss, "Study: Consumers Blame Government for Dividing the Nation but Look to Brands to Fix It," *Forbes*, February 11, 2019, https://www.forbes.com/sites/dangingiss/2019/02/11/study-consumers-blame-government-for-dividing-the-nation-but-look-to-brands-to-fix-it/#502716d26ac4.

4. Harriet Sherwood, "'Christianity as Default Is Gone': The Rise of a Non-Christian Europe," *The Guardian*, March 21, 2018, https://www.theguardian.com/world/2018/mar/21/christianity-non-christian-europe-young-people-survey-religion.

5. "Two-Thirds of Consumers Worldwide Now Buy on Beliefs," Edelman, October 2, 2018, https://www.edelman.com/news-awards/two-thirds-consumers-worldwide-now-buy-beliefs.

6. Doug Stephens and BoF Studio, "Retail Reborn Episode 2: Building Smarter, More Sustainable Supply Chains," *The Business of Fashion*, September 22, 2020, https://www.businessoffashion.com/articles/podcasts/retail-reborn-podcast-doug-stephens-supply-chains.

7. Doug Stephens and BoF Studio, "Retail Reborn Episode 2: Building Smarter, More Sustainable Supply Chains," *The Business of Fashion*, September 22, 2020, https://www.businessoffashion.com/articles/podcasts/retail-reborn-podcast-doug-stephens-supply-chains.

8. Sarah Butler, "Why Are Wages So Low for Garment Workers in Bangladesh?," *The Guardian*, January 21, 2019, https://www.theguardian.com/business/2019/jan/21/low-wages-garment-workers-bangladesh-analysis.

CREDITS AND PERMISSIONS

p. 3   "Operation COVID-19" by New York National Guard. CC BY-ND 2.0.

p. 7   (top) Chart created by Doug Stephens based on Hilary Brueck and Shayanne Gal, "How the Coronavirus Death Toll Compares to Other Pandemics, Including SARS, HIV, and the Black Death," Business Insider, May 22, 2020, https://www.businessinsider.com/coronavirus-deaths-how-pandemic-compares-to-other-deadly-outbreaks-2020-4; "Past Pandemics," Centers for Disease Control and Prevention, August 10, 2018, https://www.cdc.gov/flu/pandemic-resources/basics/past-pandemics.html; "SARS Basic Fact Sheet," Centers for Disease Control and Prevention, December 6, 2017, https://www.cdc.gov/sars/about/fs-sars.html; "Middle East Respiratory Syndrome Coronavirus (MERS-CoV)," World Health Organization, no date, https://www.who.int/emergencies/mers-cov/en/; "Ebola Virus Disease," World Health Organization, February 10, 2020, https://www.who.int/news-room/fact-sheets/detail/ebola-virus-disease.

p. 7   (bottom) Chart created by Doug Stephens based on Gita Gopinath, "The Great Lockdown: Worst Economic Downturn since the Great Depression," International Monetary Fund, April 14, 2020, https://blogs.imf.org/2020/04/14/the-great-lockdown-worst-economic-downturn-since-the-great-depression/.

p. 8   Chart created by Doug Stephens based on Elliot Smith, "UK Enters Recession after GDP Plunged by a Record 20.4 Percent in the Second Quarter," CNBC, August 12, 2020, https://www.cnbc.com/2020/08/12/uk-gdp-plunged-by-a-record-20point4percent-in-the-second-quarter.html; Saloni Sardana, "Eurozone GDP Shrinks at the Fastest Rate in History, Losing 12.1 Percent in the Second Quarter," Business Insider, July 31, 2020, https://markets.businessinsider.com/news/stocks/eurozone-gdp-contracts-12-in-q2-worst-rate-since-1995-2020-7-1029454734#; Julie Gordon and Kelsey Johnson, "Canada Second-Quarter GDP Likely to Fall Record 12 Percent on COVID-19 Shutdowns," Reuters, July 31, 2020, https://www.reuters.com/article/us-canada-economy-gdp/canada-second-quarter-gdp-likely-to-fall-record-12-on-covid-19-shutdowns-idUSKCN24W1Z3; Agence France-Presse, "Mexico GDP Slumps Record 17 Percent on Virus Impact," Rappler, July 30, 2020, https://rappler.com/business/gross-domestic-product-mexico-q2-2020; AFP, "COVID-19 Pushes World's Leading Economies into Record Slumps," *The New Indian Express*, August 17, 2020, https://www.newindianexpress.com/business/2020/aug/17/covid-19-pushes-worlds-leading-economies-into-record-slumps-2184613.html.

p. 19   Photo by Nick Bolton on Unsplash.

p. 27   Used with permission from Sheldon Solomon.

p. 29   Photo by Mick Haupt on Unsplash.

p. 33   Chart created by Doug Stephens with data from firsthand interview with Sheldon Solomon.

p. 43   Chart created by Doug Stephens based on Janine Berg, Florence Bonnet, Sergei Soares, "Working from Home: Estimating the Worldwide Potential," VoxEU CEPR, May 11, 2020, https://voxeu.org/article/working-home-estimating-worldwide-potential.

p. 48   Photo by Paulo Silva on Unsplash.

p. 55   Photo by Davyn Ben on Unsplash.

p. 58   Photo by Camila Perez on Unsplash.

p. 63   Art Gate VR.

p. 67   (top) Chart created by Doug Stephens based on Daniel Sparks, "Amazon's Record 2019 in 7 Metrics," The Motley Fool, February 6, 2020, https://www.fool.com/investing/2020/02/06/amazons-record-2019-in-7-metrics.aspx; Patrick Frater, "Alibaba Profits Rise to $19 Billion Despite Coronavirus Impact," *Variety*, May 22, 2020, https://variety.com/2020/biz/asia/alibaba-profits-rise-beat-expectations-coronavirus-1234614190/; "JD.com Announces Fourth Quarter and Full Year 2019 Results," JD.com, March 2, 2020, https://ir.jd.com/news-releases/news-release-details/jdcom-announces-fourth-quarter-and-full-year-2019-results#:~:text=For%20the%20full%20year%20of%202019%2C%20JD.com%20reported%20net,the%20full%20year%20of%202018; "JD Revenue 2013–2020 | JD," Macrotrends, 2020, https://www.macrotrends.net/stocks/charts/JD/jd/revenue; "Walmart Inc. 2020 Annual Report," Walmart, 2020, https://s2.q4cdn.com/056532643/files/doc_financials/2020/ar/Walmart_2020_Annual_Report.pdf.

p. 67   (bottom) Chart created by Doug Stephens based on Don Davis, "Amazon's Profits Nearly Triple in Q3 as North America Sales Surge 39%," Digital Commerce 360, April 30, 2020, https://www.digitalcommerce360.com/article/amazon-sales/; "Alibaba Group Announces March Quarter and Full Fiscal Year 2020 Results," Business Wire, May 22, 2020, https://www.businesswire.com/news/home/20200522005178/en/Alibaba-Group-Announces-March-Quarter-Full-Fiscal; Georgina Caldwell, "JD.Com Sees Revenue Climb 20.7 Percent as COVID-19 Sends Shoppers Online," Global Cosmetics News, May 19, 2020, https://www.globalcosmeticsnews.com/jd-com-sees-revenue-climb-20-7-percent-as-covid-19-sends-shoppers-online/; Shelley E. Kohan, "Walmart's Online Sales Have Surged 74 Percent during the Pandemic," *Forbes*, May 19, 2020, https://www.forbes.com/sites/shelleykohan/2020/05/19/walmart-revenue-up-86-e-commerce-up-74/#3103445166cc.

p. 68   Photo by Simon Bak on Unsplash.

p. 73   Bloomberg/Contributor.

p. 81   JD.com media kit.

p. 84   Walmart media kit.

p. 95   Used with permission from brand.

p. 102   Used with permission © 2020 Retail Prophet.

p. 118   Used with permission © 2020 Retail Prophet.

p. 127   Used with permission © 2020 Retail Prophet.

p. 128   Used with permission © Retail Prophet.

p. 130   Used with permission by Nike.

p. 131   Used with permission © Retail Prophet.

p. 132   Used with permission from brand.

INDEX

purpose and, 126–27; real estate and, 47–48, 195–97; specialities, 171–72; supply chains, 37, 79, 88, 215–16; trust in brands, 214–15; and working from home and transportation shifts, 45–46, 56. *See also* apex predators; e-commerce; experiences; media and entertainment; physical stores; retail archetypes; shopping centers; workforce